The Seventh Hero

The
Seventh
Hero

Thomas Carlyle
and the Theory
of Radical Activism

Philip Rosenberg

Harvard University Press

Cambridge, Massachusetts

1974

© Copyright 1974 by the President and Fellows of Harvard College
All rights reserved

Publication of this book has been aided by a grant from the
Andrew W. Mellon Foundation

Library of Congress Catalog Card Number 73-87659
SBN 674-80260-8
Printed in the United States of America

For Charlotte

Preface

For fifteen years Thomas Carlyle lived on the borderline that separates thought from action. From 1828 to 1843 he produced a body of works some of which are as close to being the tracts and pamphlets of an engaged political actor as they are to being the reflections of a detached intellectual, and all of which indicate in one way or another that their author was close to exchanging the role of the man of thought for that of the man of action. Carlyle was, I believe, the first English-speaking author to stake out this frontier for literature, and as such, he faced the problems inherent in this situation in a particularly acute form.

Today the role first established by Carlyle has become a familiar one on the literary scene, so that there is now a fairly substantial body of writers, with varying degrees of competence, producing works of social and political analysis which are too speculative to be genuinely tracts and too polemical to be purely literature. In Carlyle's day, however, such work was largely unprecedented. Anticipations of it are to be found, I believe, in the review essay, a genre which came to prominence in the British literary scene in the early years of the nineteenth century. Written for periodicals which had clearly established political identities, these essays purported to be disinterested criticisms of the books under review but tended inevitably to become more or less polemical in their own right. It was with the review essay that Carlyle began his career, in the course of which he elevated the reviewer's stance as a committed intellectual from minor to major literary status.

The tensions inherent in the role of the committed intellectual are easily recognizable, although our long familiarity with them has tended to diminish their salience and, what is more, historical and cultural changes over the last century and a half have considerably moved the cutting edge of the problem. Today an independent man of letters is not very likely to feel that his identity as an intellectual is compromised by the use of his talents for controversial writing; on the contrary, commitment is just now in such high repute that the gravitational pull may well be going the other way, making the detached intellectual as suspicious a character as the committed intellectual was in Carlyle's day.

Furthermore, it should be obvious that this problem is experienced by the writer as a problem of identity long before it is experienced by his audience as a problem to be dealt with in the evaluation of his works. That is to say, insofar as a writer is sensitive to this issue at all, he sees it primarily as a question of self-definition—as a question which for him takes the form: Why do I want to write? Is literature to be, for me, an approach to action or an approach to understanding? Ideally, the two are not incompatible, but this is not an ideal world. In a field like medical science, for example, it may be that understanding the pathology at hand and acting to cure it form a natural sequence; in the political world this is not the case, for here the amount of theory necessary for complete understanding may well take so much of a man's lifetime as to preclude the likelihood of his ever applying it, just as the amount of energy and time needed for engaging in meaningful political action can well preclude efforts at theoretical comprehension. For this reason, regardless of the ideal state of affairs, action and understanding are likely to appear as more or less mutually exclusive alternatives, forcing the potential committed intellectual to make a choice between them.

For many the choice is, I suppose, an easy one, insofar as the psychological attributes required for success in either of the two lines of endeavor do not often coexist in the same person. The sort of person who can enjoy the active engagement needed for organizing a political cause and can delight in the heated controversy of party polemics will rarely be the man capable of sitting month after month in the British Museum reading room. For someone equally capable of functioning at both these poles in such a way that one does not interfere with the other, no choice will be necessary between them; for those, by far the majority, who are strongly drawn by one and only residually if at all by the other, some choice will be necessary but making it will be a simple matter. But for those who feel strongly the pull of both, the choice will be difficult and may never in fact be made. In the role of the committed intellectual such men may find the possibility of reconciling the need for comprehension and the need for action.

Carlyle, as we shall see in the following pages, was a man simultaneously drawn to the life of action and held back from it by a deep distrust of worldly commitment. In the early stages of his career he devoted himself almost exclusively to the criticism of German literature and philosophy, but soon his temperamental impatience made such work uncongenial to him, and as the political temperature of pre-Reform England mounted, he found himself increasingly drawn toward the flames. In the polemical review essay he found a temporary resolution of his problem, for in essays such as "Signs of the Times" and "Characteristics" he was able to play, to some extent, the roles of both the critical analyst and the polemicist. For fifteen years after the appearance of the first of these essays Carlyle continued to balance the demands of these contradictory roles, and to balance them so well that it is generally the case that he can most fully realize one side of his literary nature only when he simultaneously gives free rein to the other. Thus, for example, his *History of the French Revolution* is at once his most brilliant work of scholarship and perhaps the most inflammatory expression of his radical creed.

The publication of *Past and Present* in 1843 marks the culmination of Carlyle's literary career, and in the thirty-eight years of life that were left to him he continued to grind out works that revealed more and more clearly his pathetically diminishing creative powers. His ambitious plans for a life of Cromwell, which was to have been the capstone of his career, gradually evaporated until he settled for an edition of Cromwell's letters which, despite its value in helping to bring about a historical reassessment of the Lord Protector, scarcely measures up to the standards Carlyle had set in *The French Revolution, Chartism*, and *Past and Present*. Subsequently, fourteen years went into the production of his *History of Frederick the Great*, a sprawling structure in eight volumes which stands as the tomb of Carlyle's once mighty talent. These two works, plus the rather puzzling *Latter-Day Pamphlets* of 1850, a frail biography of his friend John Sterling, and a few individual essays, constitute the bulk of his work after 1843, and it is a dreary bulk.

Critics of Carlyle generally speak of a "souring" process that set in somewhere in the 1840s and that accounts for the nature of his later works. In a sense they are right, and certainly a reading of the biographies of Carlyle reveals increasing signs of bitterness, anger, and frustration as Carlyle moved toward and into old age. But the trouble with such accounts, it seems to me, is that they imply some change in Carlyle's thought, some development in his intellectual system, which simply is not there. It is not so much that Carlyle developed harsher, more "sour" ideas after the 1840s as that he ceased to develop at all. His later works are marked, more than anything else, by their dull repetitiousness, and even the style becomes a hollow aping of itself. There are no new insights, no new ideas; indeed, Carlyle's letters, as he worked on *Frederick*, show clearly his weariness with the project and his desire simply to get done with it and to fulfill the commitment he had made with himself to write the thing. This weariness is detectable almost everywhere in his later writings, and only when he deals with what were always the harsher elements of his thought is he able to summon up the energy to write with anything like the old fire.

The work that follows, therefore, deals with Carlyle's writings only during the fifteen productive years that ended with *Past and Present*. Personally, I do not find the question of why Carlyle "soured," of what went wrong with his later writings, an interesting one; these writings seem to me scarcely worth reading and even less worth writing about. If Carlyle had gone off on some new track, had developed some new insight, even a deplorable one, the works in which he did so would present a problem one would feel one had to deal with; as it is, they contain only a one-sided repetition of ideas which, in their proper place in his earlier works, truly deserve our close attention.

From time to time I feel, I must confess, a certain sadness about having come to the conclusion that only a decade and a half of worthwhile work is all that remains of Carlyle's sixty years of painful endeavor. But on the other hand, when I consider how low Carlyle's reputation has sunk in the past forty years, how completely irrelevant to modern political thought his ideas have come to seem, it becomes clear to me that rescuing fifteen years of Carlyle's career from oblivion is no disservice to his achievement. During those fifteen years he struggled with problems that still confront radical intellectuals today, and he did so with such passion and intelligence that even his failures are paradigmatic.

For the contemporary radical intellectual Carlyle can well serve as what his friend Emerson would have called a "representative man," for he embodied within himself the tensions and ambivalences inherent in the radical intellectual's position vis-à-vis his twofold commitment. Moreover, Carlyle is significant not only because his intellectual development is instructive as a case history but also because his mature thought constitutes a valuable contribution to radical political theory. Indeed, it is one of the primary purposes of this volume to demonstrate that Carlyle's writings, if properly interpreted, can be of considerable use in the development of a theory of radical activism at a time when, after the diffuse and unfocused activism of the 1960s, such a theory is badly needed.

In the course of preparing this study I have benefitted from the assistance of numerous people, to whom I owe a deep debt of gratitude. Above all, I should like to thank Steven Marcus, whose unerring sense of what was missing helped strengthen the argument in countless places. I am grateful also to Lionel Trilling for his generous assistance and to Jacques Barzun, who had the patience to read at least three versions of the manuscript, who found the time to discuss them with me at considerable length, and whose encouragement I valued greatly. In addition, John D. Rosenberg was kind enough to contribute a healthy sheaf of valuable suggestions and Herman Ausubel also read the manuscript and commented helpfully.

To my brother, Stuart, who argued and edited the book into a shape it never could have achieved without him, and to my wife, Charlotte, whose detailed suggestions helped me clarify both my thinking and my writing, I am more profoundly grateful than I suspect either of them realizes, for I do not think they can possibly appreciate as fully as I do the magnitude of their contributions. In addition, special thanks are due to Mark Zussman, who heard most of this at a stage when one wasn't thinking yet of writing it down, and to James Monaco for ten years of valued conversations on these matters. I should like also to thank Nancy Clemente for an exceptionally fine job of editing. Finally, let me thank Shandy, who provided the occasion on long walks in Riverside Park for some good quiet thinking.

P.R.

New York
December 1973

Contents

I   The Rejection of Self   1

    1. The Self-Centered Universe
    2. Knowledge in the Self-Centered Universe
    3. The Self and History

II   The Borders of the Public World   15

    1. Mysticism and Withdrawal
    2. Action and the Cosmic Perspective
    3. The Signs of the Times

III The Annihilation of Self   45

    1. Carlyle's Religion
    2. Action and Work

IV   The Making of History   63

    1. Revolution and History
    2. Historical Causation
    3. Historical Rationality and the Philosophy of History

V   Sinews and Indignation   77

    1. The Causes of the French Revolution
    2. "An Eloquent Reminiscence"
    3. "Sansculottism Accoutred"
    4. The Reign of Terror

VI   Revolution and the State   108

    1. The Constitutional State
    2. Legitimacy and Force
    3. Revolutionary Organicism

VII The English Revolution 128
  1. The Condition of England
  2. Political Reform, Social Reform, and the "Reform of the Heart"
  3. A Note on the "New Mythus"

VIII Wealth and Power 146
  1. Medievalism
  2. Carlyle's Critique of Political Economy
  3. The Cash Nexus

IX A Whole World of Heroes 176
  1. Radical and Bourgeois Democracy
  2. The Hero in Carlylean History
  3. "But I Say Unto You . . ."
  4. The Seventh Hero

  Notes 205

  Index 231

Politics are vulgar when they are not liberalised by history, and history fades into mere literature when it loses sight of its relation to practical politics.—Sir John Seeley

I

The Rejection of Self

1. The Self-Centered Universe

The modern period in Western European culture has witnessed significant changes in the conception of the "self." "There have always been selves," Lionel Trilling has observed, "or at least ever since the oracle at Delphi began to advise every man to know his own. And whoever has read any European history at all knows that the self emerges (as the historians say) at pretty frequent intervals. Yet the self that makes itself manifest at the end of the eighteenth century is different in kind, and in effect, from any self that had ever before emerged." [1] These differences, in kind and in effect, will serve as the starting point of my analysis of the modern self.

Until the onset of the modern age, the term "self" indicated what later would be identified by psychoanalytic theory as the ego and what traditionally had been identified in the moralistic literature of Western Europe as "character" or "personality"—both usages referring to those aspects of man's psychic makeup which manifest themselves in interactive behavior. In this sense the self may be compared with what, in religious terminology, is called the "soul," for both the soul and the self were seen as mere aspects of the total man, although, to be sure, the soul was, for the religious mind, the only aspect that mattered ultimately. What is more, both the premodern self and the soul were always conceived of as subordinate to larger cosmic forces—particularly the deity. Just as all the faculties of man, including his self, were to subserve the well-being of his immortal soul, so his soul was always in the service of god.

The tendency of religious systems to divide man up into "faculties" such as the worldly self and the god-oriented soul had begun, as early as the Renaissance, to generate doubts about the adequacy of religion for dealing with the full nature of man. By the nineteenth century the response to these doubts had produced what may be called the Kierkegaardian or existential sense of man, of which the central feature was an expanded sense of self. In this Kierkegaardian sense the term "self" has come to stand for the total reality of man, and its fullest meaning is no less than his absolute ontological being. In contrast to the premodern self, which was a fragment of man, this modern self is a totality of unprecedented proportions.

Moreover, implicit in the definitional expansion of what is to be included in the self is an equally significant expansion of the role of this self in the cosmic system. Precisely because the premodern self had been a fragment of man, having no wholeness in its own right, it could readily be subordinated to the wholeness and totality of god. The existential self, however, is a whole and total entity, and as such can confront god as an equal. Kierkegaard, who was both an existentialist and a Christian, recognized the danger that the modern self posed to religious belief and warned that consciousness of self could be healthy "only when . . . grounded transparently in God." Inevitably, this warning fell on deaf ears, for from the moment it was realized that the total self stood on an equal footing with god, it followed, by the law of parsimony, that the self would usurp the place of god and come to stand forth as its own absolute, its own god-term. Indeed, the danger against which Kierkegaard warned was latent in his own thinking all along, for the Kierkegaardian self is already capable of being its own absolute, of defining itself in terms of itself: "Generally speaking," Kierkegaard writes, "consciousness, i.e., consciousness of self, is the decisive criterion of the self." [2]

Already in the 1820s Thomas Carlyle had set himself in opposition to this emerging ideology of self, recognizing that it was thoroughly incompatible with the concept of a limited self, a subservient self or soul, which was the foundation of his Scottish Calvinist heritage. This recognition set the terms of what proved to be a major dilemma for Carlyle but of course could not solve it. Although he attacked the modern ideology of self, he had been so deeply influenced by modern thought that he found himself unable to reject and repudiate it. Certainly he would have preferred to have been able to believe in a traditional universe in which the limited self recognized its subordination to a superior and absolute being. But such a belief was not possible in a skeptical and positivistic age unless one was willing to turn one's back on modernity and live by values in whose validity one could no longer believe. Carlyle had no alternative but to acquiesce in the modern perception of the self; although he despised this imperious self, he could not deny its reality.

This conflict between preference and perception has gone unnoticed by most students of Carlyle, who tend in consequence to see his longing for a god-centered universe as the totality of his thought on this matter. In fact, however, Carlyle's belief that the self should be subordinate to some higher force in no way altered his perception of the fact that it was not. The sense of the self we find in his writings is decidedly of the modern, Kierkegaardian sort despite the fact that his sense of what that self should be was appropriate to more traditional conceptions of a god-centered universe. It is interesting to note that his thought here symbolically figures his relationship to his own father, a man whom, like god, Carlyle yearned to believe in, even believed he believed in. As we shall see in the discussion of *Sartor Resartus* in Chapter III, the upshot was that, in proportion as Carlyle recognized the self to be none other than the absolute, ontological self of the modern world, he saw it as a parricidal self in that it overthrew god to stand forth as its own absolute, and he sought relief from this guilt-ridden perception by sentencing that self—no less than the whole of his being—to death and destruction. The "Annihilation of Self" was to be, on the philosophical level, the suicidal program expressing the suicidal urges felt, conquered, and described in *Sartor*.[3]

Of course, in his early essays Caryle had not yet worked these ideas into their final consummation of self-loathing. He was at this point sensible only of a certain vague wrongness whenever he contemplated the self-centered universe of skeptical rationalism; yet at the same time he was powerfully tempted to hold such a conception himself. In the essays written during what he recognized to be his literary apprenticeship, Carlyle dealt with and expressed the tensions which resulted from his inability either to deny or to accept openly a self-centered universe.

Unfortunately for students of Carlyle, these early essays are not in the least systematic examinations of the problem of the self. On the contrary, they are a group of wordy and convoluted studies of German literature with only tangential relevance to our purposes and, it should be candidly confessed, little intrinsic interest. Because their connection with Carlyle's later works is far from apparent, they have been on the whole either treated separately as works of philosophy or critical theory—a treatment they hardly merit—or ignored by students who wish to begin with the far more promising *Sartor*.

Both of these approaches are mistaken, the former because it is a waste of time and the latter because it ignores essential evidence as to the nature of the problems with which Carlyle was concerned from *Sartor* onward. In this chapter, therefore, I shall examine the early essays, not by starting out cold and approaching them as independent literary productions in their own right, but by reading them as it were backward, knowing what to look for and disregarding the rest.

To be sure, this method inevitably produces a certain sort of distortion, so that one cannot pretend that the resulting study actually describes what these early essays are "about" in the usual sense of the word. To make matters worse, this body of essays is disproportionately large relative to the value of what one finds there. On the other hand, if the toilsome first steps involved in undertaking a study of the early essays can prevent one from getting off on the wrong foot, as is bound to happen if one starts with *Sartor*, then it is essential that one take them. And if in doing so one focuses on matters that are peripheral to the essays themselves but that are to become important in Carlyle's later writings, one does so because it is these mature writings that are, after all, what one wants to understand. In short, I will be considering the early essays simply as progress reports of the early stages of what was to become for Carlyle a continuous battle with the imperious self.

2. Knowledge in the Self-Centered Universe

In his essay on Goethe (1828) Carlyle identifies the greatness of the German poet as his ability to stand, in a positivist age, as a synthesis of perfect knowledge and perfect faith. Indeed, for the rest of the century almost all the myriad journalists who concerned themselves with the eclipse of faith in Victorian England would have recognized just such a synthesis as the solution they were looking for. The nostalgia for religion characteristic of the period led a host of uneasy thinkers into attempts at balancing the benefits of modern positive science against the consolations of faith, apostasy against obscurantism. If knowledge and faith somehow could be reconciled, the dilemma would be avoided. But finding such a reconciliation proved a most difficult task, so that the history of nineteenth-century thought records a chronic vacillation between the opposing claims of the religious and secular orders.

This typical vacillation, however, though widely recognized, is not easily explained. Just what was being placed in the two scales, what were the poles one wavered between? What, to put it most bluntly, would have been lost if one had gone over wholeheartedly to the side of the skeptics? G. M. Young observes among the Victorians an "unwillingness to quit, and . . . [an] incapacity to follow, any chain of reasoning which seems likely to result in an unpleasant conclusion." [4] But what was the unpleasant conclusion in this case? Surely religion itself was not the issue. The loss of faith is of consequence only if one accepts the truth value of the religion at stake, and Carlyle, Tennyson, Arnold, and others in the same boat certainly did not accept it in any simple sense. Indeed, if they had, there would have been no problem, for if "faith" were "true" they would not have had to worry that "knowledge" would contradict it.

Carlyle's early essays are more revealing on this score than are his later, more sophisticated examinations of the problem. In a famous passage from *Sartor Resartus* Carlyle obscures the issue by characterizing the godless world as "one huge, dead, immeasurable Steam-engine, rolling on, in its dead indifference, to grind me limb from limb." [5] Seen in this way, the horrible result of the loss of faith is the emergence of a positivistic, mechanical conception of a world in which there is no place for human value. But in his earlier writings Carlyle does not seem to be troubled by the mechanical nature or the dehumanizing effect of the universe as conceived by modern science. On the contrary, it is relativism or even solipsism rather than positivism that he singles out as the danger inherent in the rationalist attitude.

The issue goes deeper than a simple opposition of religious faith to scientific knowledge, for, as Carlyle analyzes the problem in his early writings, the highly touted certainties of the scientific mind are, far from being a form of knowledge at all, merely what he was later to call "scientific hearsays." [6] Based upon a methodology of doubt, the scientific spirit anchors itself, as in Descartes' equation, to the self. Because of this self-centeredness at the very bottom of rationalist epistemology, the scientific enterprise is incapable of achieving certainty. Instead, it produces a system of doubt which encompasses not merely religious beliefs, not merely accepted political and social attitudes, but ultimately the very subject matter of science itself. Whether one sees science as an empirical or as a deductive discipline, the scientific frame of reference can never extend beyond Descartes' *cogito:* like perspective in painting, it sets the thinking and observing mind at the center of a universe in which all else is problematic. As Hannah Arendt has observed, "The modern astrophysical world view, which began with Galileo, and its challenge to the adequacy of the senses to reveal reality, have left us a universe of whose qualities we know no more than the way they affect our measuring instruments. . . . Instead of objective qualities, in other words, we find instruments, and instead of nature or the universe—in the words of Heisenberg—man encounters only himself." [7] This is necessarily the case because, as Kant explained, science can study nature only "in accordance with what reason itself has originally placed into nature." [8] Thus the very mathematical foundations of science turn out to be nothing other than "the science of the structure of the human mind." [9]

In this sense all science is psychology, for sooner or later it must concern itself not with the known but with the knower and the knowing. This is why the English positivists put a psychological theory—Hartleyan associationism—at the center of their entire system, and this is why James Mill devoted several decades of his life to the task of making *"the human mind as plain as the road from Charing Cross to St Paul's."* [10] Carlyle too was well aware of the crucial importance of knowledge of the human mind, for in a letter to his friend Robert Mitchell he asked, "When *will* there arise a man who will do for the science of Mind what Newton did for that of Matter—establish its fundamental laws on the firm basis of induction—and discard for ever those absurd theories that so many dreamers have devised? I believe this is a foolish question, for its answer is—never." [11] Carlyle recognized this answer to be inevitable because when one places the self at the center of the cosmos, one annihilates the unitary solidity of the traditional cosmic system, for there are then as many universes as there are selves. He thereupon abandoned his flirtation with positive science, which, even if it could make the human mind "plain," could do so only at the cost of raising fundamental doubts about the road from Charing Cross to St. Paul's. The inescapable nature of the problem was now clear to Carlyle: on the one hand, "reality," whether one meant thereby the ontologically absolute or the pragmatically present, was unknowable save as it was refracted through the human mind; on the other hand, accepting this epistemological limit relegated all knowledge to the sphere of subjective, and therefore relative and pluralistic, data.

In this context the synthesis Goethe achieved—the synthesis of understanding and faith—can best be understood by comparing it with Carlyle's sense of what its antithesis would be. Goethe's Mephistopheles, whom Carlyle calls "the best and only genuine Devil of these latter times," is a "combination of perfect Understanding with perfect Selfishness." [12] These pairs—understanding and faith versus understanding and selfishness—point to a perception of the modern crisis as having nothing whatever to do with the putative certainties of a mechanistic world view. Carlyle is less afraid that the universe is fundamentally a "dead, immeasurable Steam-engine" than he is afraid that it is fundamentally nothing but a projection of himself.

In German literature and philosophy Carlyle thought he saw a way to avoid the danger of a self-centered universe. But, as Charles Frederick Harrold shows, Carlyle never gained more than a sloganistic, haphazard understanding of German metaphysics, so that, while the general drift of his ideas is more or less clear, his early essays are often confused and perplexing in their specific points.[13] For example, he is at times unwilling to admit that absolute and knowable truth is not to be found in a work of literary art; at such times he speaks in terms that echo eighteenth-century certainties about the "True": "There are rays of the keenest truth, nay, steady pillars of scientific light rising through this chaos," he writes of Richter's prose in his first essay on Richter (1827). "Is it in fact a chaos; or may it be that our eyes are of finite, not of infinite vision, and have only missed the plan?" [14] In a passage such as this, Carlyle falls back on a neoclassical commonplace by claiming that man's inability to know the universe, though inevitable, is not radical and fundamental. That is to say, the unknowableness of the universe is held to derive from the nature of man, not from the nature of the universe itself. Just as a nearsighted man looking for a distant object would not be justified in saying that the object was invisible simply because he could not see it, so we would not be justified in saying that Truth does not exist simply because our "finite vision" makes it impossible for us to apprehend it.

But coupled with such passages, in which Carlyle refuses to accept the idea of radical unknowableness, are others in which he abandons all claims about the existence of "truth" or "pillars of scientific light" outside and superior to the finite mind—in which he admits, as it were, that the object itself is invisible. Thus one must look for truth, Carlyle says, not by testing whether Richter's statements correspond to "reality," however conceived, but by ascertaining whether they are consistent with themselves. "The secret of the matter is," he patiently explains, ". . . [that] in the man's own sphere there is consistency; the farther we advance into it, we see confusion more and more unfold itself into order, till at last, *viewed from its proper centre*, his intellectual universe, no longer a distorted incoherent series of air-landscapes, coalesces into compact expansion. . . ." [15]

Despite the outlandish phraseology—could any other author in English have written "coalesces into compact expansion"?—the implications of this passage should be apparent. Carlyle is here performing an intellectual trick common among the English Romantics and not far removed from what Kant was doing in a more serious way in Germany. In Kant Carlyle could discover a technique for avoiding the dilemma of the radical unknowableness of ultimate value by the simple expedient of identifying the location of these absolutes in the human mind itself. Thus the upsetting implications of Cartesianism vanish and Descartes' discovery that the only knowable entity is the self can be made to serve as the basis of a new sort of certainty. (Although this analysis is a gross oversimplification of Kant, there is every reason to believe that just such an oversimplification was all Carlyle ever made of him. "I began with Hume and Diderot," he wrote, "and as long as I was with them I ran at Atheism, at blackness, at materialism of all kinds. If I read Kant, I arrived at precisely opposite conclusions, that all the world was spirit namely, that there was nothing material at all anywhere. . . ." [16])

What Kant was doing in ways mostly unfathomable to Carlyle, Shelley and a number of lesser English Romantic aestheticians were doing by means of a simplified new Platonism which, as M. H. Abrams explains, locates the realm of Ideas "both behind the veil of the material world and in the minds of men. . . ." [17] In the second of the passages on Richter quoted above, Carlyle approaches such a position, for he claims that in this incoherent universe one can locate a "compact expansion" of coherence in the mind of the author, which he calls the "proper centre" of meaning in a work of art.

Carlyle's attempt to find a realm of absolute value within the mind itself initiates an analysis of this problem which may be either dialectical or merely ambiguous. Carlyle possessed a very un-British sensitivity to dialectical modes of thought, but the carelessness with which he handled concepts makes it altogether possible that his subsequent thinking on this matter was the result not so much of dialectical reasoning as of an inability to take a firm stance. Whichever way one has it, the idea that the mind itself is the locus of ontological absolutes meant that Carlyle was alternately preoccupied with the psychology of the creative process, insofar as these absolutes were "bodied forth" through such a process, and with the realm of Truth itself, and with the mind only insofar as it happened to be the locus of such Truth.[18]

Thus we find that at times Carlyle can be quite explicit on the point that he will not allow a psychologistic perspective to undermine his faith in the existence of an absolute realm behind the purely personal. The mind of the artist, he writes in "Goethe's Helena" (1828), exercises sovereignty only over the "manner" in which it deals with upper-case Truths: "If an artist has conceived his subject in the secret shrine of his own mind, and knows, with a knowledge beyond all power of cavil, that it is true and pure, he may choose his own manner of exhibiting it, and will generally be the fittest to choose it well. . . . In fact, the grand point is to *have* a meaning, a genuine, deep and noble one; the proper form for embodying this, the form best suited to the subject and to the author, will gather round it almost of its own accord. We profess ourselves unfriendly to no mode of communicating Truth. . . ."[19]

At other times, however, Carlyle leans in the opposite direction. For example, within a page or two of the passage from "Goethe's Helena" just quoted, Carlyle clearly reverses his absolutist position and opens the Pandora's box of psychologistically based relativism. When he turns his attention from the author's creation of a work to the reader's response to it, he finds this response to be totally experiential and subjective. Merely to receive Truth from the hands of an author, Carlyle argues, would be a "passive pleasure" which could neither last long nor be worth much. Not until "we have seen his object, whatever it is, as *he* saw it" do we get at the true meaning of a poet's work. Here Carlyle accepts the full relativistic implications of perspective in art: for if "that Hill of Vision where the poet stood" were an objectively realizable realm of Truth, then it would not be the case that the passive reception of the poet's message would be less valuable than the active (though vicarious) climbing of the hill for oneself. Not the view itself but the experience of climbing to gain it is here named as the true value of art: "Everywhere in life, the true question is, not what we *gain*, but what we *do*. . . ."[20]

Throughout these tortuous reflections on the nature of Truth, especially truth in art, Carlyle has been laboring, sometimes successfully, more often not, to transcend rather than merely to reject doubt and skepticism. Although frequently he seems to be fighting a rearguard action by simply asserting the existence of a realm of absolute and knowable truth, for the most part he had absorbed enough of the values and beliefs of "these hard, unbelieving utilitarian days"[21] to make an out-and-out dismissal of their egocentric and skeptical epistemology impossible for him. The history of Goethe he takes as a pattern, a pattern which indeed seems to mock the shabby dissembling efforts which were produced throughout the nineteenth century by Carlyle himself and numerous other moralists who wrestled with the problems of doubt and faith. "At one time, we found him in darkness, and now he is in light," Carlyle writes of Goethe; "he was once an Unbeliever, and now he is a Believer; and he believes, moreover, not by denying his unbelief, but by following it out; not by stopping short, still less turning back, in his inquiries, but by resolutely prosecuting them."[22]

3. *The Self and History*

Carlyle's grapplings with the problem of relativism versus absolutism would be of little interest if they were only a philosophic issue, for Carlyle's philosophizing was never more than amateurish, despite his pretensions to serious philosophical status in works like *Sartor Resartus*. But the problem of relativism is of crucial importance when one comes to consider Carlyle as a historian. Carlyle's development as a writer coincided with the development in European thought of a new sense of history;[23] Scott and Hegel were just beginning their careers when Carlyle was born, and the heightened interest in history which started with them continued to be a major preoccupation among intellectuals throughout the nineteenth century. Along with interest in the writing of history came inevitable questions on the nature of the historical enterprise—questions about historical methodology, the philosophy of history, and the nature of historical truth. The growth of this modern historical sense is intimately related to the very questions with which Carlyle was puzzling himself in his early writings, for the element which made this new history new was precisely the introduction of a pluralistic and relativistic spirit into historical discourse.

In *Mimesis* Erich Auerbach devotes a chapter to distinguishing between Judaic and Homeric types of narration. "[T]he basic impulse of the Homeric style," Auerbach says, is the desire "to represent phenomena in a fully externalized form, visible and palpable in all their parts, and completely fixed in their spatial and temporal relations." Completely absent are any signs of a "subjectivistic-perspectivistic procedure . . . [which would result] in the present lying open to the depths of the past. . . ." [24] Biblical narrative, on the other hand, does not flatten out time; rather, it completely subordinates historical time to an overriding teleological scheme. "The Old Testament . . . presents universal history: it begins with the beginning of time, with the creation of the world, and will end with the Last Days, the fulfilling of the Covenant, with which the world will come to an end. Everything else that happens in the world can only be conceived as an element in this sequence. . . ." [25]

Between the Homeric mode, with its chronicle-like sequence of isolatable events, and the Hebraic mode, with its strict subordination of historical sequence to teleology, one can more or less sum up Western attitudes toward history for over two thousand years. No other significant pattern of narration was available for the writing of history until the sudden appearance early in the nineteenth century of a new mode of conceiving events in time—until the advent, that is, of the Hegelian system of historical exegesis. What differentiated the Hegelian sense of history from all previous historical thought was Hegel's conception of time as process rather than as purpose. To be sure, Hegel himself did not forthrightly abandon teleological thinking, for the "end" of Hegel's history—human freedom—is conceived of as something eternal and absolute, inasmuch as any end, any *teleos*, logically must be coexistent with the entire duration of the events for which it is the determination.[26] But the fact remains that, despite the perpetuation of teleological modes of thought in Hegel, the thrust of Hegelian thinking was to relativize history. "It is no accident," as Karl Löwith points out, "that only after Hegel do we have an historical aspect of the systems of philosophy, a so-called history of ideas and problems." [27] Hegel's philosophy of history looks backward toward older schools of historiography insofar as it subsumes history under the absolutizing category of philosophy, but it looks boldly forward toward the twentieth century insofar as it subjects philosophy to the relativizing discipline of history. It is both a *philosophy* of history and a philosophy of *history*.

Carlyle was very slow to recognize the implications of antiabsolutist thought for the writing of history; but by the same token he was slow to recognize his own calling as a historian. For all his reading in German literature and philosophy, he has strikingly little to say about the work of Hegel; his essays and Journals abound with references to now forgotten German authors, but they mention Hegel's name only one or two times, in contexts which give no sense at all that Carlyle had any knowledge of Hegel's contribution to the philosophy of history. Indeed, history itself seems to have been far from Carlyle's mind at this time. In his *Life of Schiller* (1825) he pictures Schiller, already a successful playwright, "growing tired of fictitious writing. . . . To a mind . . . so earnest, the love of truth was sure to be among its strongest passions"; and so Schiller casts about for a new career. "[A]t length he began to think of History." [28] One wonders what Carlyle himself was waiting for.

He seems at this point in his career not yet to have grasped that there was a new historiography abroad. Indeed, he explicitly denies the widely circulated notion that there is anything "radically new" in modern attitudes toward history. He maintains, on the contrary, that "In the hands of a thinking writer history has always been 'philosophy teaching by experience'. . . ." [29] There are in his scattered early comments on history no hints that the peculiaristic element —the "accidental" and unique, which he occasionally recognizes in his literary criticism—has a role to play in history, no sense at all of the modern notion that history needs to be understood in its own terms rather than in terms imported into it from theology, metaphysics, or ethics. With Richter's prose he found consistency "in the man's own sphere," which was the "proper centre" from which to view his work. There is no analogous concession about history, no willingness to admit that events have a consistency within their own sphere, have a proper center which is not tied to some larger realm of meaning.

The absence of any such historicistic viewpoint may seem surprising when one considers that Carlyle was quite sympathetic to the nationalist attitudes which were then one of the main avenues of the peculiaristic strain of thought. Nationalism is, after all, to the political scene what Romantic individualism is on a narrower stage; each leads toward the abandonment of universal values, the latter in terms of the uniqueness of individual self-cultivation, the former in terms of cultural relativism. In "The State of German Literature" (1827) Carlyle speaks of the inner "life and secret mechanism" of the German national character, just as throughout the essays on German subjects he deals in terms of national rather than world literatures. Literary production is intimately tied, he maintains, not to some general or universal aspect of mankind, but to some national strength and unity in the country of its origin, to the "feeling of itself as of a nation" the country can manifest. In other words, Carlyle sees the value of any national culture in the way it expresses the unique identity of a nation, rather than in its expression of absolute truth values. Indeed, the whole purpose of studying foreign literature is to engage in a sort of free trade in ideas, a "free intercourse . . . in the commerce of the mind."[30] With mind as with matter, the principle of free trade is predicated on the assumption of differentiation of function.

Carlyle's use of nationalistic arguments is nowhere more clear than in his essay on Burns, the great poet of his own national literature, for it is precisely the "remarkable increase of nationality" that Carlyle singles out as Burns's major contribution to the poetic tradition. Writing at a time when "a certain attentuated cosmopolitanism" had come to dominate intellectual life, Burns set himself counter to the neoclassical tendency of writing "not . . . so much for Englishmen, as for men; or rather, which is the inevitable result of this, for certain Generalisations which philosophy termed men."[31]

Yet Carlyle's use of the pluralistic arguments of nationalist thought is, like many of the more "advanced" elements in his early essays, a sign merely of the fact that he had assimilated the vocabulary of modernism. He scoffs at the absolutistic generalizations of the eighteenth century, but after all it is just such a generalization, an ideal world of general men, that he imagined Burns to be finding behind the local color of his subject matter: "for him the Ideal world is not remote from the Actual, but under it and within it: nay, he is a poet, precisely because he can discern it there."[32]

If Carlyle had written history at this point in his career, he would have written rather old-fashioned history, for the pluralistic and relativistic emphases of the modernist movement in historiography were part and parcel of the self-centered, antiabsolutist conception of the universe put forth by modern skepticism and attacked by

Carlyle whenever he was aware of its presence. Wilhelm Dilthey has credited Carlyle with having pioneered the biographical approach to history, with its emphasis on the unique rather than the general, the idiosyncratic rather than the abstract, the Actual rather than the Ideal.[33] But at the time of his German essays Carlyle's commitments were still running in the opposite direction. Indeed, whenever he finds himself confronting an Actual he is quick to assure himself that there is an Ideal behind it. Behind the Ideal is god, whereas behind the Actual is the modern Mephistopheles, who boasts the ability to understand the world with reference only to its own particularities. To explain the world in terms of itself is, by the solipsism of science, to explain it in terms of oneself—to combine "perfect Understanding with perfect Selfishness." To avoid this Carlyle avoided writing history, confining himself to the more rarefied "air-landscapes" of arcane German literature. Even after he had lost all interest in this subject and had come to recognize that his writings on it were mere hackwork which prevented him from striking out on his own, he kept at it with stubborn persistence, prolonging an already overlong apprenticeship. In 1829, when he was thirty-four years old, Carlyle's apprenticeship ended and he found himself facing the actuality of contemporary England. His first important essay, "Signs of the Times," is followed, significantly enough, by an essay "On History," just as "Characteristics," his second major excursion into the actual, is followed by the piece called "Biography."

II

The Borders of the Public World

Toward the end of the preceding chapter I observed that Carlyle was slow to realize his calling as a historian, without pausing to explain why I believe he had any such calling. In the 1840s, after he had written *Past and Present*, he would remember with surprise and amusement that his friend John Sterling had noted years before that "my nature was Political." [1] His remarks to Sterling indicate both that he then recognized his development as a historian and a political polemicist to be a fulfillment of that nature, and that through the 1830s he had been unaware of the direction in which he was moving even when it had become apparent to others.

Only after he was established in his career as a political writer did Carlyle realize that some aspect of his psychological constitution, some element of his "nature," had drawn him toward involvement with the historico-political dimension of activity. This self-impelling tendency toward history, which amounts to what is usually described as a calling, eventually led Carlyle from the criticism of Continental literature to the study of history and the criticism of his own society. Three of the transitional works that mark this developmental process—"Signs of the Times" (1829), "Characteristics" (1831), and "Corn-Law Rhymes" (1832)—will be analyzed in this chapter to determine the specific nature both of the factors that motivated him toward political involvement and of the factors that tended to retard his development in this direction.

Throughout Carlyle's career there is a sense of reluctant purposefulness about each of the new departures he takes on the way to developing his mature thought; he enters his career as a political essayist like a man toe-testing cold ocean water: we can tell that he wants to go in by the way he stays close to the water's edge, and when he finally is fully immersed we know that we had divined his intentions correctly. But for a long time he hardly seems to get wet at all.

1. Mysticism and Withdrawal

In the late 1820s and early 1830s Carlyle found himself increasingly drawn toward a career involving historical writing and political journalism. There were, however, elements within his thinking which cautioned him against such a commitment and urged him not to enter the public space of political action or, once it was too late for that, to withdraw from it. We know of course that his final choice was for a career as a social and political commentator and as a historian with an instinct for historical issues of a hotly controversial nature, so it comes as rather a surprise to find that in many ways the tendency making for commitment seems to be greatly outweighed by that making for retreat. In fact, the latter is so considerable that we can hardly afford to ignore it or to pass it off as simply a phase Carlyle had to go through on his way to staking out his own position in English letters. On the contrary, we must pay close attention to the antipolitical and quietistic elements in Carlyle's thought because their importance to him was so great that they remained largely intact and colored his judgments and attitudes even after he had established himself as a political polemicist.

Carlyle's background was not one to predispose him to any sort of political involvement. Scotland as a whole played little role and had little interest in English parliamentary matters, for the nature of Scottish representation at Westminster was not such as would inspire an active and concerned electorate. "All Scottish seats, boroughs as well as counties, were indeed utterly venal," G. D. H. Cole and Raymond Postgate observe. "Their introduction into the English Parliament under Anne had merely been an introduction of 45 purchasable seats, of which 39 were steadily in the possession of the Government or the King. For all practical purposes, Scotland had no representation at all." [2] At least in part as a result of this situation, although there certainly were other factors also at work, Scotland remained largely apathetic toward the political controversies that had been agitating England since before the turn of the nineteenth century. Especially in the more remote areas of the country was this the case, and the political indifference of Carlyle's family accurately reflected the prevalent attitudes of the rural community in which they lived.

Carlyle's father was a man who, his son reported, "never meddled with Politics," [3] although he was not insensitive to the sufferings of the poor and the deteriorating condition of the village workingmen. He had himself been forced to give up his trade as a mason and turn to a very meager form of near-subsistence farming when he was in his late fifties. "I have heard him say in late years, with an impressiveness which all his perceptions carried with them," Carlyle wrote in his Reminiscence of James Carlyle, " 'that the lot of a poor man was growing worse and worse; that the world could not and would not last as it was. . . .' " [4]

The notion that the world could not last as it was, however, did not move the elder Carlyle to change his principles about meddling with politics. Economically backward, Scotland shared with the less advanced sections of England a tradition of modest cooperation between farmers, landlords, and working people. In England the increasing capitalization of agriculture, combined late in the eighteenth century with the Speenhamland system of poor relief, had served to break down some of the traditional attachment between farmers and agrarian laborers, but in Scotland capitalism made headway only slowly on the farms and there was no Speenhamland system—indeed, there were no poor laws at all in various parts of the country until well into the nineteenth century. Thus poverty, the poor, and poor relief, one of the perennial issues of modern politics, was in Scotland not a political issue at all, but essentially a private matter between the indigent, their families, and their community. [5] On his rural rides through England William Cobbett had always kept his eyes open for any traces of this cooperative spirit but very rarely found any signs of it, and the *Rural Rides* contain few stories like this one, which James Carlyle wrote to his son in February 1817: "Times is very bad here for labourers—work is no brisker and living is high. There have been meetings held by the lairds and farmers to assist them in getting meal. They propose to take all the meal that can be sold in the parish to Ecclefechan, for which they shall have full price, and there they sign another paper telling how much money they will give to reduce the price." [6]

Growing up in a setting in which a sense of cooperation and community were still actively at work, Carlyle would find little in his background to foster that keen sense of class antagonism that is often one of the chief ingredients in the growth of a radical political consciousness. As a stonemason, his father worked in a trade which often was conducted on a contract basis; the master who secured one contract frequently found himself as a workman on the next job, and as a result the distinction between wage workers and employers was minimal. Compare for a moment the smoldering network of resentment one sees between master and worker in Dickens' *Barnaby Rudge*, which is undoubtedly an accurate picture of the London situation somewhere between the Gordon Riots and Dickens' own youth. It is just such a sense of class hostility that made London, with its Corresponding Society dating back to 1792, an early and intense source of radical sentiments, whereas Scotland, except for Edinburgh and the agriculturally and industrially "modernized" parts of the lowlands, developed in this direction scarcely at all.

Further, and perhaps even more important, there was much in Carlyle's religious background that would have militated strongly against political involvement. Calvinism, with its complex attitudes about the nature of the relationship between the individual believer and the secular powers that be, provided a context in which the question of one's involvement with worldly principalities and powers was extremely problematic.[7] The militant brand of Protestantism in which Carlyle was raised was both intensely secular and intensely pietistic. On the one hand, its secularism, as has been widely observed, provided the Reformation with the ideological tool which ultimately helped the private citizen break the shackles which had kept him from playing a historical role. History in the Christian world always had been the plaything of the political classes, but after the Reformation it became, in principle at least, the property of the common man. The fruits of this Calvinistic secularism can be seen in Carlyle's often quoted assertion that the history of the world is "the essence of innumerable Biographies."[8]

This spirit, which Max Weber has described most thoroughly in his account of "inner-worldly asceticism," later provided the foundation for the best of Carlyle's historical writings, and it does his Calvinistic heritage a disservice if one does not acknowledge that there was much in it to make for active engagement with the world. Inner-worldly asceticism, Weber tells us, "reached its most consistent development" in Calvinism, and there is much in his analysis of this religious type that quite accurately describes Carlyle's mature attitudes toward political commitment. "The [inner-worldly] ascetic," Weber writes, "rejects the world's empirical character of creatureliness and ethical irrationality, and rejects its ethical temptations to sensual indulgence, to epicurean satisfaction, and to reliance upon natural joys and gifts. But at the same time he affirms individual rational activity within the institutional framework of the world, affirming it to be his responsibility as well as his means for securing certification of his state of grace." [9] Interested primarily in the question of his own salvation, the inner-worldly ascetic recognizes that "salvation may require [his] participation within the world (or more precisely: within the institutions of the world but in opposition to them). . . . He may have the obligation to transform the world in accordance with his ascetic ideals, in which case the ascetic will become a rational reformer or revolutionary on the basis of a theory of natural rights." [10]

Even in its commitment to acting in the world, however, inner-worldly asceticism is fundamentally a "world-rejecting" attitude, for it derives its commitment to action from the necessity to oppose worldly institutions which may otherwise stand in the way of personal salvation. The worldly ascetic's commitment to action is thus in an important sense accidental, for his ultimate goals can be achieved quite as well by an alternative route—that of contemplative mysticism. Although Carlyle never even approached the pure type of contemplative mysticism described by Weber, it is interesting to note that during the period in his life in which he weighed the competing claims of commitment and withdrawal, he developed a fondness for referring to himself as a mystic; [11] the famous "conversion" which he experienced in the 1820s and later described in *Sartor* has a distinctly mystical flavor, resulting in the "deliverance" of his soul "from the Devil and the pit. . . . And there burnt accordingly a sacred flame of joy in me, silent in my inmost being, as of one henceforth superior to fate, able to look down on its stupid injuries, with contempt, pardon, and almost with a kind of thanks and pity." [12]

Although Carlyle certainly would not qualify as a genuine mystic, his description of himself as one is not completely fanciful. We can see traces of mysticism in his frequent calls for silence and meditation and in his antiintellectual conviction that the ways of god are directly discernible to the properly receptive mind. Weber himself points out that "the distinction between world-rejecting asceticism and world-fleeing [mystical] contemplation is fluid," and this certainly seems to have been the case with Carlyle. He had what Weber describes as the mystic's fear of activity, "which [was] regarded as the most dangerous form of secularization." [13] For him the secularistic, worldly aspect of Calvinism was matched by a pietistic emphasis which militated strongly against involvement with the political collectivity, both insofar as that was a realm of corruption and godless power and insofar as it was totally irrelevant to the private salvational drama, the acting out of which is man's primary mission. Thus Karl Löwith, expressing a Protestant point of view which would have been familiar to Carlyle, announces "that one true God, revealed by one single event at one definite time, has established the historical process for one single purpose—to bring man back to his creator"; further, Löwith argues that "only *one* inference as to the meaning of history" is possible—namely, "that history is a discipline of suffering, an opportunity for the creature to return to its creator—no more and no less." [14]

For one holding such intensely pietistic attitudes, the only appropriate form of the polity would be a theocracy, and a highly personalized theocracy at that, in which god held his kingship as a system of direct relationships to each citizen of the kingdom rather than as an overriding relationship to the community as a whole. Nietzsche points to just such an individualistic, anticollective conception of the community of believers when he writes that, in the Christian world view, "for each soul, the gravitational center of valuation was placed within itself: salvation or damnation!" [15] With the passing of time, this individualistic emphasis, this "extremest form of personalization," was replaced among Christian sects more moderate than Scottish Calvinism by a collectivistic sense which moved the "gravitational center" from the individual believer to generic Man—but this was a change with which the Carlyles would have been unfamiliar.

The contrast Nietzsche posits between the private and religious world of personal salvation and the secular world of collective progress weighed on Carlyle's mind as he watched friends like John Stuart Mill plunge into the political vortex, and he was forced to ask himself whether or not such activity would provide an opportunity for him to return to his creator.[16] "Politics are angry, agitating . . . ," he wrote in his Journal at the height of the Reform Bill agitation in 1831: "what have I to do with it? Will any Parliamentary Reform ever reform *me?*" [17]

Carlyle spent about five years trying to answer these questions. On the one hand he was certain, as he wrote in his diary in 1829, that "Politics are not our Life (which is the practice and contemplation of Goodness), but only the *house* wherein that Life is led." [18] On the other hand he was beset by a growing suspicion that, as we shall see, it was not contemplation but action that his own being needed in order to achieve some sort of wholeness. What is more, the objective conditions of Britain seemed to cry out for some sort of action, and as the political situation deteriorated in the early 1830s, Carlyle began to balance the private duty to attend to one's own salvation against the historical demands put forward by one's own time and place in the world. No longer so confident that "Politics are not our Life," he now asks: "Meanwhile *what* was the true duty of a man; were it to stand utterly aloof from Politics (not ephemeral only, for that of course, but generally from all speculation about social systems &c. &c.); or is not perhaps the very want of this time, an infinite want of Governors, of Knowledge how to govern itself?" Still uncertain as to the answer, he counsels himself only *"Denk' und schweig!"* (*"Think and be silent."*) [19]

Within ten months, however, he is no longer asking himself whether he should involve himself in politics; the question has become one of what form that involvement should take: "Politics confuse me—what my duties are therein?" he wrote in his Journal in August 1832. "As yet I have *stood* apart, and till quite new aspects of the matter turn up, shall continue to do so." [20] By 1833 his period of "standing apart" was coming to an end. No longer debating the issue in the privacy of his Journal, he writes to John Stuart Mill that he contemplates the "Hell and Hunger" of contemporary England with a feeling of "powerless pity which really amounts to pain." The aloof stance he so long maintained has become, he now realizes, impossible to maintain any longer: "One cannot look at it without a mixture of horror and contempt," he says of the political scene. "I declare my prayer was that I should hide altogether from hearing of it; but that may not be." [21]

The prayer which Carlyle expressed here privately to Mill, together with his saddened recognition that it "may not be," adds up to a complex attitude toward the world around him and his own role in it. If his internal debate on this matter had ended when he realized that quietism and resigned withdrawal were not possible for him—if, that is, one could say that his reluctance about political involvement formed an early chapter in his life which ended when he decided to direct his literary career into political channels— then Carlyle's attitude toward politics could be easily explained. Such is, indeed, the impression one gets from reading the literature on Carlyle, for it is natural among literary critics to try to divide a man up into "periods." But it will not do to treat Carlyle—or any author for that matter—as though he were an engine which runs on either one set of tracks or another. His reluctance to get involved in the political world is a part of the meaning of the work he did there once he was involved. Carlyle dragged his quietistic impulses along with him into his career as a political essayist, and traces of them are to be found on practically every page he wrote. Especially is this the case with the works he produced between 1828 and 1833, when he was most actively engaged in the internal debate between commitment and withdrawal.

Weighing the claims of the profoundly unworldly Calvinism of his youth, which constantly reminded him of the trap set by the secular principalities and powers, against the growing recognition that mystical withdrawal was not possible for him in the face of the "Hell and Hunger" that called upon him to act, Carlyle could bring himself, as we shall see, only to the borders of the public world, from where he sent forth social and political essays in which public matters are discussed in an essentially private, inward-looking vocabulary. Significantly, many of his essays on arcane German literature were written in London, whereas his studies of contemporary England were worked out in retreat on a remote farm in Scotland which he himself described as a "desert." [22]

2. Action and the Cosmic Perspective

The ambivalent and perplexing nature of Carlyle's ideas about political involvement did not go unobserved by the more astute of his contemporaries. In 1844 Giuseppe Mazzini was to ask, not without a trace of bitterness: "Wherefore does he speak to us at times in such beautiful passages of hope and faith, of the divine principle that is within us, of the duty which calls us to act, and the next instant smile with pity upon all that we attempt,—and point out to us the night, the vast night of extinction, swallowing up all our efforts?" [23] A few years earlier Mazzini already had found occasion to complain that in Carlyle's writings, "The eternal *cursus et recursus* inexorably devours ideas, creeds, daring, and devotedness. The infinite takes, to him, the form of Nihilation." [24]

Mazzini's coupling of Carlyle's sense of "the duty which calls us to act" with his awareness of the "night, the vast night of extinction, swallowing up all our efforts," brings us very close to the heart of the matter, for Carlyle tends to see human struggle not as a battle waged against the forces of annihilation, but rather as a campaign which it is our duty to take up even in the face of the certainty that the forces of annihilation ultimately must triumph. Mazzini is correct in remarking that the nihilistic strain in Carlyle is somehow tied up with his sense of "eternity." Carlyle was fond of defining historical man as a creature who lives at "the conflux of two eternities." Just what this phrase may mean will vary, of course, according to whether the emphasis is placed on the conflux or on the eternities. In the former case attention will be directed to the historical moment, the scene of action, whereas in the latter we find ourselves contemplating the field of action in cosmic terms that tend to diminish the meaningfulness of whatever action unfolds upon that field. The important point, though, is that Carlyle did not find it necessary to choose between these two meanings. Just as, in his early essays, he had wavered between theories of absolute value and the principles of subjectivism, so now the same antinomic terms reappear in a new form. The realm of the absolute emerges in the guise of the cosmic theater in which human actors perform, and because the absolute is by its nature unchanging and unchangeable, action in such a context must be meaningless. But at the same time the subjective element reappears in the conflux, the moment, the point in time and space that is immediately recognizable as what I have been calling the self. "The conflux of two eternities" is a Carlylean trope which simultaneously postulates a self-centered universe and a god-centered universe, which combine to form a world of human action in the context of universal stasis. What Mazzini saw in Carlyle as a troubling contradiction was for Carlyle one of the cardinal truths of the human condition.

No phrase is so often repeated in Carlyle's writings as the Biblical text which couples the idea of duty with the idea of annihilation in just the way Mazzini describes. "Work while it is yet day, for the night cometh in which no man may work" was one of Thomas Carlyle's favorite texts—a text in which the conjunction between the two clauses serves as an unstable bridge thrown over a chasm of absurdity. No grammar can give the meaning of that conjunction, for it calls upon us to enter the finite world of action both because of and in spite of the fact that this world exists in a universe of infinite space and time which can know nothing of human action and purpose.

This metaphysical perception is apparent in both "Signs of the Times" and "Characteristics," where Carlyle attempts to diagnose the spiritual malaise from which England as a whole was suffering at that particular historical juncture. Carlyle was not alone in observing that one of the most salient features of the period of the Regency and the reign of George IV was an intense preoccupation with the present moment. Modern historians of the nineteenth century tend to overlook this preoccupation with the present because it was flanked on the one side by the fascination with the past which is characteristic of much of the Romantic movement and, on the other, by the orientation toward the future which manifested itself in the Victorian cult of progress. In the 1820s and early 1830s, however, a number of commentators felt that questions about both the past and the future would have to wait. Carlyle's first major essay, "Signs of the Times," was published within months of John Stuart Mill's analogous piece, "The Spirit of the Age," and the two of them are surrounded in the literary journals of the time by numerous similarly titled essays, all of which give the unmistakable sense that nothing could have been more pressing than determining the nature of the present moment.

In his contribution to this subgenre Mill observes that the idea of examining the spirit of the age is a novelty: "I do not believe that it is to be met with in any work exceeding fifty years in antiquity," he notes, and goes on to add that, while the idea of comparing one's age to other ages both past and to come "had occurred to philosophers" at other times, "it never before was itself the dominant idea of any age." In attempting to explain why the present age should be so obsessed with itself, Mill suggests that such a tendency is inevitable in "an age of change. Before men begin to think much and long on the peculiarities of their own times, they must have begun to think that those times are, or are destined to be, distinguished in a very remarkable manner from the times which preceded them. . . . The first of the leading peculiarities of the present age is, that it is an age of transition." [25]

The sense of being in an age of transition is quite unlike the sense of living in a period of progress. Progress implies a process of growth, a natural and inevitable development of tendencies already apparent, so that the future will in some way be a true heir to the present, which has not yet fully realized its own potentialities. But being in an age of transition implies living through an anomic time in which the connections to past and future are at best tenuous. Carlyle himself was to become brilliantly adept at portraying the transitional man's foreboding and lonely sense of his place in time, for the most memorable passages of his histories often come at those moments when a man stands alone, cut off from past and future, faced with a momentous decision. For Carlyle the pun that plays between *moment* and *momentous* is perhaps the most important truth of history, a truth appropriate to a transitional age in which historical sequence tends to dissolve into a succession of discontinuous moments.

To be sure, the sense of being transitional sometimes gives place, especially in lesser writers, to an optimistic faith that new institutions and new values are immediately forthcoming, and that one may well live to be present at the creation of the new order. But for the most part the feeling of living in a crack in the façade of time is, emotionally, never very far removed from the grim perception that one is caught

> . . . between two worlds, one dead
> The other powerless to be born.

The sense of transition, then, unlike the sense of progress, bespeaks a mood of apprehension. Both Carlyle and Mill take this apprehension as their starting point, immediately translating it, as one might expect, into the terms of their own major preoccupations. For his part Carlyle lets the emphasis fall not on the rootless, transitional nature of the age, but upon the intense self-contemplation that results from its attempts to come to terms with itself. "Never since the beginning of Time was there, that we hear or read of, so intensely self-conscious a Society," he writes.[26] Taking his metaphor from the vocabulary of contemporary medical technology, which saw fever both as the most important symptom of disease and as the process by which the body heals itself, Carlyle sees in the epidemic of self-consciousness a case of "a disease expelling a disease," for the cult of self-examination and self-questioning is an unhealthy condition which arises precisely when man's position in the world in fact becomes questionable.[27]

In his attempt to discover the origin of contemporary society's inability to come to terms with its condition, and its consequent plunge into skeptical self-absorption, Carlyle came to recognize what he felt to be an inadequacy of conventional historical explanations. To say that the contemporary sense of anomie, the feeling of being transitional, arose because the early nineteenth century was indeed a transitional period in the course of the industrial revolution would merely beg the question. It would not do to point out that the anomic spirit arose because the times had changed and old patterns of social and political relations had collapsed, for it was this very loss of contact with meaningful ways of life that was in need of explanation. Thus Carlyle argues that to attribute the contemporary malaise to particularly modern historical conditions inevitably would leave the sources of these historical conditions unexplained.

Moving outside history, Carlyle argues that the psychosocial disease of the modern world must be seen in relation to the perennial nature of man. Such an approach allows one to trace the problems of the modern world back to the "perpetual Contradiction [that] dwells in us," a contradiction which Carlyle defines as the "diseased mixture and conflict of life and death." [28] As Carlyle develops his thinking, this inherent polarity of man's nature comes to play a constantly increasing role as an explanatory device. Like the Hegelian dialectic, the "perpetual Contradiction" of human life is a cosmic principle which can stand outside history as an unmoved mover explaining historical change; unlike the dialectic, however, the Carlylean view of history as an unending warfare between the forces of death and the forces of life is completely nonteleological, for it has no component part capable of performing the progressive function of the dialectical synthesis. This feature of Carlyle's thought accounts for the tendency, more or less present in all of his historical writings, to combine a vivid apprehension of the historical process with a relative ignorance of or indifference to the long-term direction of historical development.

Thus in "Characteristics," where Carlyle offers a quasi-historical explanation for the growth of the modern materialistic and skeptical world view, he attempts to deal with historical phenomena completely in terms of the timeless constants of human nature. With an excitingly bold willingness to deal with paradoxes, Carlyle acutely suggests that the roots of the problem reach all the way back to the primitive religious distinction between body and soul: "is not that very division of the unity, Man, into a dualism of Soul and Body, itself the symptom of disease," he declares. Indeed, looked at in this light, materialistic skepticism, in suggesting that man is "but a Body, and therefore, at least, once more a unity, may be . . . the beginning of cure!" [29] By this unique twist of reasoning, the roles of materialism and religious faith seem to cross as materialism is assigned the function of healing the rift in man's being caused by religion's bifurcation of man into body and soul. Just for a moment, though—for when one looks at materialism historically, one begins to see problems. Materialism is inextricably tied to the belief that the world is rational and knowable. When materialism says that man is Body rather than Soul, it means thereby that he is Mind, for materialist philosophy is historically a response to man's quest for intellectual comprehension of his universe, and this quest in turn is itself a symptom of the inescapable disease—the lack of oneness with the self. "The beginning of Inquiry is Disease: all Science, if we consider well, as it must have originated in the feeling of something being wrong, so it is and continues to be but Division, Dismemberment, and partial healing of the wrong." Hence, Carlyle points out, in the Book of Genesis "the Tree of Knowledge springs from a root of evil." [30]

Not content with this simple antiintellectualism, Carlyle goes on to argue that, even though knowledge is itself "the symptom of Derangement," we must use this diseased rationality to "do our best to restore a little Order." [31] In other words, we must use knowledge to transcend knowledge. But how is this possible? Carlyle describes the efforts philosophy has made in this direction. Focusing on Cartesian skepticism, the parent of all modern skeptical thought and the antithesis of the earlier "dogmatical" religious metaphysic which it superseded, Carlyle describes the task of modern philosophy as the effort "to educe Conviction out of Negation," just as Descartes had deduced the certainty of his own existence from his doubt.[32]

The problem with such a dialectic, Carlyle says, is that it is insufficiently dialectical. It fails to solve the problem at hand inasmuch as it does not take us out of the realm of thought; it can give us only a new idea, a new knowledge, but it cannot transcend knowledge. Just as Marx was to amend Hegel by insisting that the dialectical negation of an idea is not an idea but a *praxis*, so Carlyle repeatedly insists that "Doubt of any sort cannot be removed except by Action." [33] "Consider it well," he says of the Cartesian dialectic, "Metaphysics is the attempt of the mind to rise above the mind; to environ and shut in, or as we say, *comprehend* the mind. Hopeless struggle, for the wisest, as for the foolishest! What strength of sinew, or athletic skill, will enable the stoutest athlete to fold his own body in his arms, and, by lifting, lift up *himself*? The Irish Saint swam the Channel, 'carrying his head in his teeth'; but the feat has never been imitated." [34]

To a considerable extent, Carlyle's use of the term "action" as the way of transcending the contemplative self-involvement which results both from a state of rootlessness and from the skeptical-rational spirit is a call specifically for political action, inasmuch as political action is, as both Hannah Arendt and Karl Mannheim have shown, the primary meaning of the concept of action. Indeed, in Arendt's specialized neo-Hegelian vocabulary it is the only meaning, for she distinguishes between "labor," which is activity directed toward things for the purpose of satisfying man's biological needs; "work," which is activity directed toward things for the purpose of creating and shaping man's physical and social environment; and "action," which is activity directed toward other men for the purpose of creating the political realm of human interaction in which alone man can fully realize himself and attain freedom.[35] Similarly, Mannheim, in *Ideology and Utopia*, postulates a distinction between the "political" realm in which true action is to be found and the "administrative" realm in which the individual's relationship to his environment is established beforehand and in which activity takes the form of routinized transactions. "Every social process may be divided into a rationalized sphere consisting of settled and routinized procedures in dealing with situations that recur in an orderly fashion, and the 'irrational' by which it is surrounded," Mannheim writes.[36] Both Mannheim's and Arendt's distinctions between action as a political concept and "work," "labor," or "administration" as nonpolitical forms of activity depend of course on the Hegelian analysis of free and servile action, the latter of which, confined to man's acting on things, is capable of transcending the self only in the negative sense of abolishing the self by projecting it outward into the object one is acting on, where it reappears in objective form as "alien, external reality," as not-self.[37]

Carlyle, of course, does not draw Hegel's, Arendt's, or Mannheim's distinctions, and he often seems to use the terms "action" and "work" interchangeably. At the very least, however, his idea of action must involve interaction or transaction between the actor and something external to himself, for the concept is by its nature transitive; if this were not the case Carlyle hardly could claim that in action lies a means of getting outside the self. There are two possibilities here, and Carlyle seems to waver between them. Insofar as Carlylean "action" means interaction between the subject and his fellow men, we have what Arendt and Mannheim were to call political action, and the possibility of freedom and self-realization; insofar as Carlyle chooses merely interaction of the subject with the natural, nonhuman world around him, we have Hegel's servile labor, Arendt's labor and work, or Mannheim's administration, offering only negative freedom from self in the form of an alienation of the self. As we shall see in Chapter III, *Sartor Resartus*, with its famous

"Gospel of Work" aimed at what Carlyle called the "annihilation of Self," represents that phase in Carlyle's thinking when he fell short of a true conception of action and chose instead self-destruction as an antidote to self-absorption. Conversely, his historical writings and his theories of the heroic actor in history represent that phase in his thinking when he realized that genuine action—political action —offers the possibility of a positive transcendence of self.

In the early thirties Carlyle tended to waver between these two formulations. Leaving the negative side of his thinking for the highly personal and self-involved exegeses of *Sartor*, he tended in his periodical writings to lean toward an awareness that true action would lead to salvation from the diseased introspection which characterizes an age at odds with itself. Yet even here Carlyle's sense of the needfulness of action was unable to provide him with a content to complete his idea. Firmly convinced that both the particular historical crisis of doubt and self-questioning through which England was passing at that time and the perennial struggle of life and death at the deepest level of man's psyche could find resolution in action, Carlyle nevertheless had no conception whatsoever about what kind of action would be needed. Indeed, the answer to this question seems not to have mattered to him. "Whatsoever thy hand findeth to do, do it with thy whole might," [38] is as specific as he is able to get, and he confesses that, although the most important question is, "What is to be done; and How is it to be done?" he as yet has no answer.[39]

Carlyle's inability to give any specific content to his activist doctrine results, as Mazzini noted, in a tone of lofty indifference to the outcome of action, even when he exhorts his readers to act and seems to be quite passionately involved in the issues. Thus R. H. Horne complained in 1843 about Carlyle's "contradictory tone concerning all work, as unavailing and yet a necessity," just as John Sterling lamented "his characteristic tendency to sympathize with every struggle, and turn away from the fruits of every victory." [40] Indeed, Horne, Mazzini, and Sterling all seemed well aware that the result of Carlyle's thinking on work often took shape as a world-weary, even nihilistic defense of the status quo, for which they took him to task.[41] For all his reputation as an outspoken man and a literary firebrand—a reputation he had earned even as early as the date of the essays under consideration here—Carlyle was in fact rather timid, until much later in his career, about putting forth opinions on anything more specific than the general need for moral reform in England. Indeed, whenever he found himself forced to deal with a potentially controversial subject, his tendency was to depoliticize it. For example, in his essay on the poetry of Ebenezer Elliott, the so-called Corn-Law Rhymer, Carlyle is not reluctant to depoliticize a body of poetry which is nothing if not political. "To his Political Philosophy there is perhaps no great importance attachable," Carlyle writes of Elliott, a major political controversialist of his day.[42] As a result, Carlyle's "Corn-Law Rhymes" essay seems, perversely, to be intended as a record of its author's indifference to his subject matter.

To be sure, there were bona fide reasons for not caring one way or the other about corn-law repeal. The militant Chartist Feargus O'Connor, a decade later, was to base his indifference to repeal upon the belief that lowered wheat prices would serve as a pretext for lowering wages, so that, by the free traders' own Ricardian principles, the workers would not be better off with bread cheap than with it dear. But Carlyle uses no such arguments. Will the worker be economically in a better position after repeal? Will he eat better or live better? Carlyle does not say. What will be the effect of the government's maintaining or changing its policy with respect to the corn trade? So far as Carlyle can see, there will be no effect worth considering. "That the 'Bread-tax,' with various other taxes, may ere long be altered and abrogated, and the Corn-Trade become as free as the poorest 'bread-taxed drudge' could wish it, or the richest 'satrap bread-tax-fed' could fear it, seems no extravagant hypothesis," he observes matter-of-factly, but then adds, with a touch of cynicism: "would that the mad Time could by such simple hellebore-dose, be healed!"[43]

What is significant here is that Carlyle's coolness to the corn-law question is not based, as O'Connor's was to be, on a belief that repeal, as a political and economic measure, would not have the effects the repealers foresaw. Rather, Carlyle is claiming that the vagaries of trade policy are a matter of indifference because political policy in general is powerless to alter the times. Of course, writing in 1832, before the Anti–Corn Law League had been formed and before the issue of corn-law repeal had captured the center of the political stage, Carlyle cannot reasonably be expected to have given the subject the careful consideration political thinkers would be giving it a decade later. Nevertheless, the fact remains that he had chosen to write on repeal and the works of a repealer, and that he had voiced a principled disinterest in the outcome of Elliott's political struggle on the grounds that governmental policy was inherently meaningless. This was not to be the last time Carlyle adopted such a quietistic position, for the term "hellebore-dose" should call to the mind of anyone familiar with his writings the various phrases and formulas he used throughout his career to denounce all specific policy recommendations that caught his attention, ranging from copyright bills [44] to universal suffrage. Throughout his writings, Carlyle's political judgments are those of a man half of whose mind is committed to an apolitical view of things.

The most famous instance of this syndrome was still twelve years ahead of him when he wrote his essay on the Corn-Law Rhymes, but it is worth considering here for what it tells us about his attitude toward politics. In *Past and Present*, which Carlyle wrote in 1843 after observing at first hand the deplorable conditions in the workhouses established under the New Poor Law of 1834, Carlyle invented the epithet "Morrison's Pill" as a term of political opprobrium. Briefly, he defines a "Morrison's Pill" as any "remedial measure" by which it is hoped the social ills of the day can be cured. The term is taken from the name of a highly advertised patent medicine, and the point is, quite simply, that the social maladies of England lie far deeper than any patent medicine can hope to reach; further, that anyone who imagines the problems can be solved by a simple remedy and offers such a remedy to the public is more than likely a quack. "It seems to be taken for granted," Carlyle wrote in *Past and Present*, ". . . that there is some 'thing,' or handful of 'things,' which could be done; some Act of Parliament, 'remedial measure' or the like, which could be passed, whereby the social malady were fairly fronted, conquered, put an end to; so that, with your remedial measure in your pocket, you could then go on triumphant, and be troubled no farther." [45]

Certainly there is much good sense here, and Carlyle is accurately diagnosing one of the most significant defects of the reforming spirit in nineteenth-century England. Shaw's famous praise for Dickens —that he taught us to see that it is not our disorder but our order that is at fault—comes to mind here, and we can see that perhaps Carlyle deserved this praise more than Dickens. For it was Carlyle who, more clearly than any other British author of the period, excepting only his disciple Ruskin, saw that the specific-grievance radicalism which passed for advanced political opinion in his day was a dead-end street. While Parliament looked into the conditions in the cotton mills and got up Blue Books on sanitary conditions, while

Dickens exposed the courts of Chancery and the Yorkshire schools, Carlyle insisted that all this would come to naught unless more fundamental changes were realized in the very structure of British society.

Such a position cannot but seem uncompromisingly radical. And, within certain all too confining limits, it was.

Brothers, [Carlyle wrote,] I am sorry I have got no Morrison's Pill for curing the maladies of Society. It were infinitely handier if we had a Morrison's Pill, Act of Parliament, or remedial measure, which men could swallow, one good time, and then go on in their old courses, cleared from all miseries and mischiefs! Unluckily we have none such; unluckily the Heavens themselves, in their rich pharmacopœia, contain none such. There will no 'thing' be done that will cure you. There will a radical universal alteration of your regimen and way of life take place; there will a most agonising divorce between you and your chimeras, luxuries and falsities, take place; a most toilsome, all-but 'impossible' return to Nature, and her veracities and integrities, take place: that so the inner fountains of life may again begin, like eternal Light-fountains, to irradiate and purify your bloated, swollen, foul existence, drawing nigh, as at present, to nameless death! Either death, or else all this will take place. Judge if, with such diagnosis, any Morrison's Pill is like to be discoverable! [46]

When I come to examine *Past and Present* in Chapter VIII, I shall be concerned with the radical content of this message, the nature of the "radical universal alteration" Carlyle sees as necessary. Here I am more concerned with the limitations which hedge Carlyle's radicalism—limitations beyond which he never fully passed. The nature of these limitations can be understood if we realize that, although Carlyle's injunctions against "remedial measures" are, formally considered, tantamount to a radical political position, they are, in their etiology, not political at all. Rather, they are an inevitable result of the cosmic perspective Carlyle adopts—a result, that is, of his tendency to look at the historical moment from the vantage point of the two "eternities" that he sees surrounding it.

Two examples clearly show the effect of this cosmic perspective on his political imagination. The first comes from his *History of the French Revolution*, where Carlyle offers the following profoundly ambiguous apostrophe to the common citizen of France: "Louis was a Ruler; but art thou not also one? His wide France, look at it from the Fixed Stars . . . , is no wider than the narrow brickfield, where thou too didst faithfully, or didst unfaithfully." [47] At first glance, this statement is radically democratic, egalitarian, proclaiming that at the profoundest level all men are equal. But the problem is that if one takes the "Fixed Stars" as one's vantage point, human action shrinks to infinitesimal proportions, so that the political result of such a cosmic perspective is likely to be a sublime indifference to social inequalities: if men are *essentially* equal, then veridical inequalities cease to matter.

Similarly, the passage in the "Corn-Law Rhymes" essay in which Carlyle deals with the democratic content of Elliott's political message shows the same effects of the cosmic perspective in action: ". . . is not the Corn-Law Rhymer already a king . . . king of his own mind and faculty; and what man in the long-run is king of more?" [48] True enough. But the use of such a long run as part of one's political time scheme can lead only to distortion and confusion. "Might and Right," Carlyle wrote elsewhere, "do differ frightfully from hour to hour; but give them centuries to try it in, and they are found to be identical." [49] This would be wise counsel among the Struldbruggs, but among mortals the experiment cannot even be attempted. We are all familiar with Shelley's sonnet mocking the pretensions of worldly power; but if we realize that Ozymandias ruled for sixty-seven years, perhaps we will recognize that the joke is finally on Shelley, and that any sense of the historical that tries to shrink two thirds of a century in the life of a great empire into insignificance, that can ignore the difference between a starving peasant and the king of France, is only fooling itself.

One would like to be kinder about this limitation as it appears in Carlyle's work, but it does, in the final analysis, severely debilitate the value of his contribution to the political and social development of nineteenth-century England. If one takes Carlyle's work in large doses, the feeling one comes out with at the end—at least I do— is frustration amounting at times almost to anger. It is not just that his sympathies were so often on the right side; more than that, he contributed—indeed, as we shall see, so far as England was concerned we might say he created—the intellectual tools that would make possible a radical critique of modern industrial society while at the same time staying remarkably free of the reactionary tendency which cast so much of English antiliberalism in an implacably Tory-conservative mold. G. K. Chesterton once expressed doubts about the authenticity of Carlyle's radicalism because it was willing to come to terms with the industrial system; Carlyle, he said, "never contradicted the whole trend of the age as Cobbett did." [50] Chesterton's point is well taken, but his conclusion is unrealistic, for the value of Carlyle's contribution was to lie precisely in the fact that at a time when the alternatives seemed to be either acquiescence in the system of industrial capitalism, as with the Westminster radicals and the Manchester liberals, or a quixotic and reactionary rejection of it, Carlyle was able to forge an attack on liberalism without lapsing into the machine-breaking attitudes that so often mar the works of men like Ruskin, Morris, and even Cobbett. Even when he seems closest to the conservative ideology—in parts of *Past and Present*, for example, as we shall see in Chapter VIII—there is scarcely a trace of Tory reaction in his thinking. This in itself is a remarkable feat, matched only by Robert Owen among English authors of the time. Hence the sense of frustration is bound to be acute when one realizes that Carlyle's uncompromising attitude toward all "remedial measures" adds up to a rejection of politics as a mode of human action and a grim passivity in the face of the sufferings of the working classes.

I do not mean to suggest that Carlyle should have gone on record as favoring whatever the solution of the day happened to be. But certainly he should have made distinctions. All Morrison's Pills are not created equal, yet Carlyle fails to make even so fundamental a distinction as that between government measures like the Poor Law Amendment Act of 1834, Factory Acts, and Corn-Law Repeal, on the one hand, and working-class self-help initiatives like the Cooperative and Trades Union movements on the other. In terms of what they indicate about the development of political consciousness among the English common people, the great strikes of 1829–30 are not to be classed with petitions to Parliament for various reliefs. Yet to Carlyle they are all the same—all "remedial measures." Even dogmatic Marxists, a group as hostile to ameliorative policies as any to be found anywhere, admitted that genuine parliamentary democracy would be a step forward. But the very concept of a political step forward seems incomprehensible to Carlyle, who shrugs off all suggestions as though they equally lead nowhere.

To be sure, Carlyle's passivity was more or less inevitable for him. In the first place, it is not unconnected with his personal pathology, and anyone with a mind to do so can easily trace the connection between the self-loathing which, as we shall see in the next chapter, manifests itself in a doctrine of work as *Selbst-tödtung* ("Annihilation of Self"), a faintly sublimated suicide wish, and his invariable denunciations of the futility of all the positive work he saw around him.

In the second place, any course other than Carlyle's is most difficult for an intellectual to take. After all, the literary man who deals with politics in a radical cause has, insofar as he is to remain an intellectual, only three possibilities open to him. The first two give him the choice between pointing to an overriding failure of his society and attempting to mend it by pushing a favored scheme of regeneration, or pointing to as many problems as he sees and offering as many solutions as he can come up with. In the first case he becomes a crank, at least as far as his literary career is concerned, and if his career is completely literary he becomes completely a crank. This can be seen clearly in the case of Robert Owen: when his life work is examined through the perspective afforded by his writings, as in Crane Brinton's essay on him,[51] the man seems to be riding a hobbyhorse, whereas in fact there was nothing at all cranky about the Grand National Consolidated Trades Union or the Cooperative movement, as is apparent to those who deal with Owen otherwise than through his writings.[52] On the other hand, if the intellectual takes the second path, offering as many solutions as there are problems, he will be dismissed as a "tinkerer" as soon as there arises a movement no more radical but more single-minded than he.[53]

The third course, then, is Carlyle's, and it is in many ways the natural one for an intellectual to take. Indeed, the detachment demanded of an intellectual makes it almost inevitable that anyone choosing the role of the intellectual will be one who finds commitment to a particular course of action uncongenial. This was precisely Carlyle's position, for he recognized in principle the necessity for action but did not recognize that the principle of action will not get one very far unless it is coupled with an awareness of the need for *taking* action. As Hegel noted, a principle, "even if it is true, is yet none the less false just because and in so far as it is merely a . . . principle."[54] In this sense Carlyle's principles are false, for he coupled his fervor for the radical cause with an inability to come to terms with the necessity for taking action. He thus relegated himself to the role of a cheerleader for the radical spirit, who is at the same time profoundly cynical about his team's chances. As a result we find him repeatedly applauding the appearance of radical consciousness among the lower classes while at the same time professing disdain for or indifference to the specific forms this consciousness takes. Hence the disparity between his praise for the Corn-Law Rhymes insofar as they help to mold the working-class consciousness and provide an "intelligible voice . . . from the deep Cyclopean forges, where Labour . . . [does] personal battle with Necessity, . . ." and his opinion that "there is perhaps no great importance attachable" to the form this consciousness takes as a political program.[55]

The essay on the Corn-Law Rhymes is, then, a harbinger of much that is to come in Carlyle's later work, for we can see here an ominous instance of the failure of will and commitment which tended to keep Carlyle from using his radical principles as the foundation for a radical politics. In a perfect world, I suppose, a principle should be a starting point—a principium or first thing; but for Carlyle, with the intellectual's typical idealism, his principles were all too often where he stopped.

3. The Signs of the Times

The sixteenth chapter of the Gospel according to St. Matthew tells how the Pharisees and the Sadducees tempted Jesus by asking him to show them a sign from heaven. "He answered and said unto them, When it is evening, ye say, It will be fair weather: for the sky is red. And in the morning, It will be foul weather to-day: for the sky is red and lowering. O ye hypocrites, ye can discern the face of the sky; but can ye not discern the signs of the times?"

It is on the basis of this distinction between reading the face of the sky and reading the signs of the times that Carlyle launched his career as a political polemicist. Wasting no further time, he plunged into the vortex of political controversy by denouncing at once all the diagnoses of England's political malaise offered by conservatives and radicals alike. "Signs of the Times" is a rather alarmist essay, filled with gloomy forebodings about England's future, but it opens with a brief introductory section in which Carlyle ridicules the sense of crisis he detects in the cultural atmosphere. "How often have we heard, for the last fifty years, that the country was wrecked, and fast sinking; whereas, up to this date, the country is entire and afloat! The 'State in Danger' is a condition of things, which we have witnessed a hundred times; and as for the Church, it has seldom been out of 'danger' since we can remember it." [56]

Carlyle, who had as lively a sense of impending catastrophe as even the most panicky of his contemporaries, is satirizing the alarmists not because they are wrong in apprehending danger, but because they are fearful of the wrong danger. On the political right, the repeal of the Test Acts and of Catholic disabilities, followed by the threat of a radical reform of Parliament, has convinced the conservative mind that the institutions of Church and State are crumbling: "Our worthy friends mistook the slumbering Leviathan for an island; . . . and so, mooring under the lee, they had anchored comfortably in his scaly rind, thinking to take good cheer; as for some space they did. But now their Leviathan has suddenly dived under; and they can no longer be fastened in the stream of time; but must drift forward on it, even like the rest of the world. . . . Their cherished little haven is gone, and they will not be comforted! And therefore, day after day, in all manner of periodical or perennial publications, the most lugubrious predictions are sent forth." [57]

Dismissing the panic of the conservatives with these satirical reflections, Carlyle commences his own reading of the signs of the times. The principal charge in his indictment of the world around him denounces the contemporary epoch as an "Age of Machinery, in every outward and inward sense of that word. . . ." Politically, this line of attack, which has become one of the staples of cultural criticism over the last century and a half, indicates Carlyle's crucial premise that both the contemporary radical movement and the political establishment against which it was directed must be seen as parts of the problem rather than as aspects of the solution, for in his analysis of the modern cult of machinery Carlyle traces the origins of the "Mechanical Age" back to John Locke, the ideological architect of the Revolution of 1688, and concludes therefrom that Whiggism and radicalism, both of which derive from Lockean arguments, share the same mechanistic understanding of the function of government: "To both parties it is emphatically a machine: to the discontented, a 'taxing-machine'; to the contented, a 'machine for securing property.' " [58]

Extending his analysis, Carlyle shows that although both the Whig tradition of Locke and the radical school of Bentham profess due respect for the individual, neither is in fact a genuinely individualistic ideology. The rationalist tradition, in both its Lockean and its Benthamite versions, is founded upon the postulate that "Men are to be guided only by their self-interests," and on the basis of this postulate it calls itself individualistic. But self-interest should not be confused with self, Carlyle argues, pointing to the way in which the school of Locke and Bentham has directed attention away from the individual self and toward that which is of benefit to the self. Proclaiming that a man's home is his castle, rationalist individualism forgets that the man who inhabits a castle should be a king; thus it asserts man's sovereignty over his furniture while neglecting his sovereignty over himself. By means of this deflection, rationalist individualism has focused on what is external to man's own being—on his interests rather than on his actions—and as a result has ended with the lugubrious belief "that our happiness depends entirely on external circumstances." [59]

Considering the individualist philosophy as an ontological system, Carlyle had some time earlier concluded, as we saw in Chapter I, that it was dangerous and destructive because it tended to place the self at the center of the universe, and thereby obliterated the entire supraindividual dimension in which man finds meaning and purpose. Now, looking at the same individualist ideology with a view toward its practical and political implications, Carlyle sees that it is not only destructive but also self-destructive, for it ends in its own negation. Having destroyed the cosmic order of which man is a part, it turns its virulent force against man himself, whom it tends to see in atomistic terms; having denuded man of meaning and purpose, individualist thought inevitably goes on to strip him also of force and power. Ironically, man becomes impotent exactly in proportion as he is important, and each atom is the victim of the little universe which surrounds it. "[W]e have argued away all force from ourselves," Carlyle writes; "and stand leashed together, uniform in dress and movement, like the rowers of some boundless galley." [60]

As Carlyle sees it, Benthamite philosophy is the terminal phase of the empirico-rationalist tradition, for it openly acknowledges that power and force have passed from man to his environment. It is therefore inevitable that Benthamism should be exclusively concerned with adjusting that environment so that it can best care for the interests of the infinitesimal beings at its center. Thus in "Signs of the Times" the followers of Bentham emerge less as corrosive, skeptical individualists (as even today we are wont to see them) than as system-builders, "codifiers," in Carlyle's terminology, men who merely seek to replace a decayed and outworn set of institutions with a new set of institutions. The radicals are, Carlyle insists, obsessed with *"mere political arrangements."* [61]

To a large extent this analysis is correct. We are today too prone to imagine that the laissez-faire program of the Political Economists committed Philosophical Radicalism to the principles of "small government," whereas in truth nothing could be further from the case. Benthamism is the ideology of the bureaucratic state, and far from being the ideologue of small government, Jeremy Bentham was the architect of the Chrestomethia, the Panopticon model prison system, the New Poor Law, and factory inspection. As E. P. Thompson observes, "the main protagonists of the State, in its political and administrative authority, were the middle-class Utilitarians, on the other side of whose Statist banners were inscribed the doctrines of economic *laissez faire*." [62] Economically, Benthamism differs from Whiggism in having as its clientele the manufacturing and commercial interests, whereas the Whigs were identified with the landed connection. But politically they differ only in that Benthamism would replace the decentralized machinery of the squirearchy with the centralized and bureaucratic machinery of the state. The difference is very much the same as that between modern American liberalism and conservatism, and Carlyle was having none of either.

Thus in "Signs of the Times" Carlyle is concerned almost exclusively with rejecting the political philosophies of both the Sadducees of Lockean Whiggery and the Pharisees of Benthamite Radicalism. These critiques leave us, however, with the still unanswered question of where Carlyle himself stands. And with this question one comes to the crux of the entire clouded issue of Carlyle's politics and the even more important issue of the nature of political possibilities.

The most common assumption with regard to Carlyle's politics has been that his attack on Benthamite Radicalism comes from the right rather than from the left. From Emery Neff, a distinguished Carlylean of forty years ago who found traces of conservatism in Carlyle's earliest writings and a growing conservatism throughout his career, to Eric Bentley, who sees Carlyle as almost an architect of the Third Reich, the idea of a right-wing Carlyle has been predominant in the literature. [63]

The problem with such an interpretation is that Carlyle has very little in common with conservative ideology. Not only did he ridicule the conservative reading of the signs of the times, but, what is more, he explicitly extended the meaning of his pejorative term "Mechanism" to include all "political, ecclesiastical or other outward establishments." With this stroke Carlyle cut himself off completely from the great conservative tradition, for it is most fundamentally in its insistence on the value of "establishments" or "corporations" that English conservatism distinguished itself from individualistic, rationalistic radicalism. Coleridge and Burke both insist that the various corporate entities of English social and political life are the true seats of national greatness and national identity, but for Carlyle corporate institutions are just another form of machinery: "No individual now hopes to accomplish the poorest enterprise single-handed and without mechanical aids," he complains; "he must make interest with some existing corporation, and till his field with their oxen." [64]

Carlyle himself laughed at the delusion of a number of conservatives who had jumped to the conclusion that he was one of them because he shared their antipathy to Whiggery and radicalism. "They knew me to be no Whig and fondly trusted I might stand by altar and throne," he wrote to Mill in 1833, adding that such was far from his intention.[65] Indeed, if we remember that for the British conservative the Established Church was one third of the sacrosanct triad of Crown, Land, and Church, the impassable distance between Carlyle and the conservative position is nowhere more unmistakable than in his arch-Protestant affirmation of the irreconcilability of religion with any institutions whatever. "How did Christianity arise and spread abroad among men?" he asks. "Was it by institutions, and establishments and well-arranged systems of mechanism? Not so; on the contrary, in all past and existing institutions for those ends, its divine spirit has invariably been found to languish and decay." [66] In politics as in religion, the corporate forms into which society is arranged were the mainstay of English conservatism and were less than useless to Carlyle. Thus, under the rubric of "Machinery" Carlyle included the Lockean view of the state as a machine for protecting property, the Benthamite view of it as a machine for forwarding the Greatest Happiness Principle, and the Tory view of it as a complex machine containing political, ecclesiastical, and other submachines.

If, then, Carlyle is in agreement with neither the conservatives nor the Whigs nor the Philosophical Radicals, it might be possible to make a case for identifying his dissent from all of these alternatives as stemming from a type of popular (proletarian- or peasant-based) radicalism. Indeed, throughout his career, in such works as *Chartism*, *Past and Present*, and *The French Revolution*, one can identify numerous passages indicating a deepfelt sympathy for the situation of the propertyless. Although twentieth-century critical literature on Carlyle is nearly unanimous in seeing him as conservative or even reactionary, the idea that Carlyle's politics had affinities with popular radicalism is not without historical precedent. Both Friedrich Engels and Giuseppe Mazzini, the exiled leader of the Young Italy movement, saw Carlyle as a spiritual kinsman, and their testimony weighs heavily in favor of a radical Carlyle.[67] Unfortunately, aside from the general drift of his sympathies, there is little in either Carlyle's published writings or his letters and journals to connect him with the popular radicals, and one must conclude that Carlyle cannot be classed as a supporter of their cause for the simple but compelling reason that he never gave any indication of wanting to be so classed. Yet one cannot adduce any ideological reason why he did not. As I have already remarked, his sympathies disposed him that way and he seems to have held no body of beliefs which would have kept him from espousing some form of popular radicalism. Even the supposed authoritarianism of his so-called hero theory would not in principle disqualify him from the radical left, for, as Barrington Moore points out, there are no historical grounds for assuming that authoritarianism is necessarily a right-wing, reactionary phenomenon or that egalitarianism is necessarily left-wing and progressive.[68] History provides examples of authoritarians of the left as well as of egalitarians of the right, for the insistence on formal and absolute egalitarianism is the property of liberalism but not necessarily of radicalism. We can translate this generalization into terms appropriate to Carlyle's case by noting that he found no inconsistency in championing both the authoritarianism of Oliver Cromwell and the radicalism of the O'Connorite Chartists; indeed, years later he was to describe himself as a man who "believe[d] both in the French Revolution and in . . . Kingship. . . ." [69]

Carlyle's relationship to popular radicalism is quite unlike his position with regard to conservatism and Benthamite liberalism, to both of which he was implacably antagonistic for principled reasons. But it was not so much the case that Carlyle was opposed to the burgeoning radical movement as that he failed to take a stand with it, and this failure seems to have been a result more of ignorance and indifference than of antagonism. He seems never to have entertained seriously the possibility of a mass radical movement. This failure undoubtedly has something to do with a certain quality of visibility or saliency which can be ascribed to political movements. What were the radical movements in England of which Carlyle could have been aware from his youth through the late 1820s, the period I am now dealing with, and how would he have perceived them?

The London Corresponding Society was founded three years before Carlyle was born and had been active in generating sister societies throughout Great Britain in the last decade of the eighteenth century. But this source of active working-class jacobinism had gone underground before Carlyle had reached his teens and had disappeared altogether some time in the early part of the nineteenth century. There was a labor movement of some dimensions, but it was scarcely political. The trade unions of the "labor aristocracy" produced a number of politically conscious labor leaders, but for the most part these men—for example, Francis Place, William Lovett, and John Gast—took on the task of spreading Benthamism to the working class. On the whole, then, the labor movement, insofar as it was political at all, was completely in the hands of the bourgeois reformers and totally "free from anything that could now be conceived as political sedition," as Sidney and Beatrice Webb have pointed out.[70] Thus the labor movement, limited for the most part to the skilled artisans and craftsmen of the labor aristocracy, did not present any alternative to the policies of the bourgeois reformers, and was not to do so, except for a brief period in the middle 1830s when it adopted an Owenite socialist position, until much later in the century. Among the lower strata of the working class there was scarcely any organized labor movement and even less of a political program.

There was, indeed, through the 1810s and even into the 1820s a working-class movement of some political pretensions, but it was even less visible than the trade unions, which in the years before repeal of the Combination Acts were forced either to go underground or to masquerade as burial or friendly societies. I am referring of course to Luddism and the related phenomena which punctuated the history of rural England from the time Carlyle was about twenty years old through the next decade. E. P. Thompson, in *The Making of the English Working Class*, argues very convincingly about the revolutionary political purposes of the Luddites and describes, for example, the abortive "Pentridge rising" of 1817 as "one of the first attempts in history to mount a wholly proletarian insurrection, without any middle-class support." [71] Here, then, was an alternative to Philosophical Radicalism which offered radical objectives more far-reaching than parliamentary reform and which expressed popular dissent from the politics of the "political classes." But the fact is that it would have been almost inconceivable for Carlyle—or any of his contemporaries for that matter—to have perceived it as such. The saliency of Luddism as a political movement was so low, and has remained so to the present day, that except for the work of Thompson and perhaps to an even greater extent that of E. J. Hobsbawm, no account of the period takes note of its political dimension.[72] Like the Webbs almost a century later, Carlyle would have seen in Luddism an expression of the torment of the workers but not a political movement aiming at the amelioration of their condition.

Just as today it does not necessarily follow that a person adopting a critical stance toward the current political scene would be led by his dissatisfaction with the available legitimate political options into perceiving the New Left as a bona fide alternative, so it was possible for Carlyle to reject the entire political *mise en scène* from Toryism to Benthamism and also to overlook the working-class revolutionary movement—which was soon to die out anyway. With Whiggism, Toryism, and Benthamite Radicalism unacceptable to him, and popular radicalism, the only position he might have found congenial, for various reasons unavailable to him, Carlyle thus was left without a position to take.

With the political turmoil of the reform agitation about to erupt, England was as close to revolution as she was to come throughout the nineteenth century; even so temperate a reformer as Francis Place felt that a revolutionary "convulsion should be risked rather than have the boroughmongering system continued," and in 1832 plans were underway for an armed insurrection in case the Duke of Wellington formed a government unpledged to reform. "If we have money we shall have the power to lead and feed the people, and in less than five days we shall have the soldiers with us . . . ," Place predicted, and reform, he promised, would be only "the first step in the British revolution." [73] But on all this Carlyle was silent. Taking the high road of cultural criticism, he kept himself free to criticize broadly without feeling compelled to make political choices of his own. Such politics as he had took shape only in the vague and contentless activism I have examined in the preceding section of this chapter.

By the time he wrote "Characteristics" Carlyle had tied together the two strands of his critique of rationalist individualism. In the early essays, as we saw in Chapter I, it was primarily to the solipsistic or self-centered aspect of the rationalist creed that he had directed his attention, and in "Signs of the Times" he had addressed himself to the mechanistic implications of the same body of thought. "Characteristics" fuses these two lines of reasoning and concludes that rational examination itself—the demand that all phenomena and all action be submitted to testing by the rational mind of man—is merely the other side of the coin on whose face is stamped the image of man as a thinking machine in a machinelike universe. To such a man only motion is possible, but never action, to use Kenneth Burke's fine formulation of the distinction Carlyle is making.[74]

"Action is paralysed," Carlyle concludes, and argues convincingly that it is to the task of restoring the possibility of action that any meaningful reform of contemporary society must address itself. Unfortunately, the idea of action has become for Carlyle a sort of closed circle. I have examined already the chain of reasoning that led him to recognize that he must enter the world of public action. Yet his actions in that world consist, in "Characteristics," primarily of making public the need for action. Action has become for him a principle of first importance, and in this lies the paradox of his thought, for a principle is a standing-place from which one may act but it is not itself an act. Indeed, Carlyle at times seems to be gropingly aware that there is a problem here, for he cites the proliferation of readers and writers of review articles as a cardinal symptom of the diseased introspection of modern times, and then wryly adds, "Far be it from us to disparage our own craft, whereby we have our living!" [75] Clearly, Carlyle has not yet fully realized that the idea of action is an idea and not an action. He was a man whose "nature was Political," but he had no politics.

III

The Annihilation of Self

Sartor Resartus is a thoroughly eccentric book. In the guise of an extended commentary on an actually nonexistent German treatise on clothes, the book gave full scope to Carlyle's insolent crankiness of temper, and he greatly relished the fact that at least in the hinterlands it succeeded as a hoax. He quoted with delight the North American reviewer who cautiously announced that "After a careful survey of the whole ground, our belief is that no such persons as Professor Teufelsdröck [*sic*] or Counsellor Heuschrecke ever existed; . . . that the 'present Editor' is the only person who has ever written upon the Philosophy of Clothes; and that the *Sartor Resartus* is the only treatise that has yet appeared upon that subject. . . ." [1] The North American reviewer need not have been so pleased with himself, for few people could have been taken in by the hoax. Compared with such masterpieces of the genre as Swift's Bickerstaff papers it is a transparent performance: Carlyle had merely elevated into a principle the habit of self-quotation he had practiced even in his earliest works and would continue to practice both in season and out for the rest of his career. *Sartor Resartus* is an exercise in just how far Carlyle's canniness would let him get with the authorial tic which had led him to insert in his 1828 essay on Goethe an extended passage from his own introduction to his translation of *Wilhelm Meister* as the observation of "a writer on this subject." [2]

What gives *Sartor* its peculiar flavor, more than anything else, is the latitude which this seemingly unpromising trick allowed Carlyle in expressing his ideas. By consistently mocking Teufelsdröckh's excesses, Carlyle is able to disown his own thinking and thus to feel free to put forward ideas for which he did not want to be held responsible. This somewhat schizophrenic technique apparently derived from a habit in the Carlyle household of speaking with mocking irony about what really was taken most seriously. Carlyle, it seems, used irony where more straightforward writers would use italics. The result is a most elusive book—its meaning hard to pin down, the serious difficult to separate from the joke.

Ralph Waldo Emerson, who had a great fondness for *Sartor Resartus* and whose salesmanship was responsible for the book's success in America long before it gained readers in England, felt that the barbarities of the style did the ideas scant justice. He suspected, he told Carlyle, that the grotesqueness of the work came from Carlyle's bitter notion that, inasmuch as no one was going to read it anyway, he might as well indulge himself as he saw fit. And Carlyle answered that this was in fact the case.[3] To John Stuart Mill, who also raised objections about his ironic mode of writing, Carlyle explained: "I cannot justify, yet can too well explain what sets me so often on it of late: it is my singularly anomalous position to the world,—and, if you will, my own singularly unreasonable temper. I never know or can even guess what or who my audience is, or whether I have any audience: thus too naturally I adjust myself on the Devil-may-care principle." [4] *Sartor* is, in many ways, not the book of a man who expects to be read much.[5]

One may well be puzzled about why Carlyle felt this way. Certainly his name was not a household word among the English reading public when he sat down to write *Sartor*, but he had gained himself a rather solid reputation as a contributor to the more influential periodicals. People recognized his work when it appeared and there was a ready market for his essays. Yet Carlyle himself carefully cultivated the image of a Carlyle ignored by the bookselling establishment—perhaps because, as Lytton Strachey wryly remarks, Carlyle aspired to the status of a latter-day prophet and therefore needed to feel himself dishonored in his own country.[6] In any case, if Carlyle liked to fancy that he was unappreciated by the British reading public, the publication of *Sartor* gave him every opportunity to do so. "It issued thro' one of the main *cloacas* of Periodical Literature," Carlyle complained by way of explaining why the book received so little attention.[7] To this we should add that it is a singularly unprepossessing work; with its wild humor, its personal allusions, its private jokes, and its lawless syntax, *Sartor Resartus* is a sort of jeu d'esprit, but it is the jeu d'esprit of a man in very bad spirits.

1. Carlyle's Religion

The very private nature of *Sartor Resartus* is, in a sense, an aspect of its meaning. It is, after all, an autobiography, and although it is autobiographical in a concealed way, Carlyle made no secret of its personal significance. In the small details of childhood and education, as well as in the larger narrative of the crisis of faith and the final "conversion," there can be no doubt that Teufelsdröckh is Carlyle. Yet for a work whose impulse is autobiographical, *Sartor Resartus* takes great pains to be unrevealing about its author. The impulse behind it often seems to be one of concealment rather than one of revelation. For our purposes, fortunately, the purely personal dimensions of the book, which often take the form of a parable of lost and found faith, do not require much attention.

As we already have seen in Chapter II, the concept of the struggle of life and death—"the diseased mixture and conflict of life and death"—was central to Carlyle's thought at this time. In *Sartor Resartus*, as in so much of Carlyle's other writing, the forces of negation, denial, reticence, and death are lined up against the forces of creation, affirmation, spontaneity, and life. In passage after passage Carlyle's Manichean demonology calls attention to the presence of the divine and the diabolical in human affairs. Yet these images can never crystallize into a polarized vision because Carlyle seems unable to tell his demons apart: "either diabolical or divine," he is likely to say, as though there were only a hairline of difference between them. Even his style expresses the tension behind this tentatively poised polarization, this vision of a satanic-divine. On the one hand, the style is spontaneous, unfettered, eccentric, and expressive; on the other hand, it is an instrument of concealment, a measure of the author's aloofness and indifference toward his audience and his distance from them. Carlyle professes himself unable to decide whether his prose is "the Song of Spirits, or else the shrill mockery of Fiends. . . . Up to this hour we have never fully satisfied ourselves whether it [Teufelsdröckh's style] is a tone and hum of real Humour, which we reckon among the very highest qualities of genius, or some echo of mere Insanity and Inanity, which doubtless ranks below the very lowest." [8] At times, indeed, Carlyle, with an unfailingly accurate self-awareness, senses in the style such a "malign coolness towards all that men strive after . . . that you look on [the author] almost with a shudder, as on some incarnate Mephistopheles. . . ." [9]

The frequency with which Carlyle has recourse to such images of the satanic-divine is an index of the extent to which he was preoccupied with questions of faith and doubt. It does not, however, indicate that Carlyle in any very important way managed to hang onto the religious beliefs of his childhood. This is an important point because it is often maintained that Carlyle always remained somewhat of a preacher, taking through literature the role of a secular minister after he had turned his back on the clerical calling his parents always imagined to be his.[10] In 1829 he wrote that "The true Church of England, at this moment, lies in the Editors of its Newspapers," and in that church Carlyle chose to become a lay preacher.[11] Further, the idea that, at least as far as religion was concerned, the Carlylean apple did not fall far from the parental tree is given added credence by his attempts to allay his mother's fears about his growing apostasy by explaining to her that "fundamentally our [religious] sentiments are completely the same."[12] The curious contradiction between the adverbs here renders the attempt at reassurance less than convincing, however. Carlyle was not reticent about asserting that his beliefs were those of his parents, and he often protested that he remained pious "at bottom," as though at some deep level of intent he could hold onto the religious convictions of his parents in spite of innumerable strata of difference.[13]

Certainly the faith in god Carlyle insisted he never lost is not an insignificant part of his belief system. Yet it seems to me completely artificial, something he vehemently asserted in an attempt to coach it into existence, something he said not because it was true but because he wanted to make it come true. In his private Journal, Carlyle's protestations of his faith invariably are accompanied by phrases that remind us—and himself—how far from such faith he truly was: "Nothing can exceed the *gravity* of my situation here," he wrote in July 1834. ". . . I have no practical friend, no confidant, properly no companion. . . . Alone! alone! 'May we say' (my good father used to pray), 'may we say we are not alone, for the Lord is with us.' True! true! Keep thy heart resolute and still; look prudently out, take diligent advantage of what time and chance *will* offer (to thee as to all); toil along and fear nothing. Oh thou of little faith! Weak of faith indeed! God help me!"[14]

One could, I think, debate the question of Carlyle's religion at some length, setting his preacherliness, his belief in some sort of godly power of nemesis at work in the world, his devotion to his deeply religious mother (who survived until Carlyle was fifty-eight years old) on one side, and his denunciations of Christianity as an outworn mythus and his abandonment of his career in the church on the other. Such a debate, however, would be sterile, except from a narrowly biographical point of view. Of far more importance is the role which the admittedly present religious element played in his intellectual system. It goes without saying that religious or quasi-religious rhetoric bulks large in the volume of his writings, but whether or not it has much of a dynamic role to play there is another matter. When one tries to hunt out the theological principle as an active ingredient of Carlyle's world view, one does not come back with many trophies. In *Sartor Resartus*, the only place where Carlyle gave any systematic attention to the explication of his own religious beliefs, one finds hints that he was moving toward something like pantheism or a "Religion of Man." Especially prevalent in Germany, theological movements of this nature served as halfway houses between traditional Christianity and naturalism or positivism, and Carlyle, who was steeped in German philosophy, could easily have adapted them to his own purposes.

Ludwig Feuerbach wrote, "The divine essence is nothing else than the human essence, or, better stated, the essence of man. . . . Thus all the attributes of the divine essence are attributes of the essence of man." [15] Carlyle's Clothes Philosophy says much the same thing, with its repeated insistence that god is "bodied forth" in the spatio-temporal world, and more particularly in the structures of human society and the patterns of human action. This is an ambiguous formulation, susceptible of both traditional and radical interpretations. Characteristically, Carlyle plays it both ways. On the one hand, he confines himself to the relatively modest assertion that the "bodies-forth" principle means that the physical world is the manifestation by which god makes himself visible and palpable to the limited minds of men. On the other hand, he pushes the trope further, seeing in the universe the realized body of god—a conception not far removed from the Spinozistic identification of god with nature. Seen in this light, god and the world are, if not identical, at least isomorphic—that is, they are functionally identical if not ontologically so. If they are not the same thing, at any rate, as Feuerbach put it, the attributes of one are the attributes of the other.

Each of these two formulations—the world as a manifestation of god [16] and the world as the body of god—comes into play at a crucial moment in *Sartor Resartus*. Teufelsdröckh's spiritual crisis, we may recall, was precipitated by his apprehension that there was no god; it was resolved when he recognized that "The Universe is not dead and demoniacal, a charnel-house with spectres; but godlike, and my Father's!" [17] Against this recognition of the world as like and belonging to god, we may set another passage in which the world itself becomes god: "He [Teufelsdröckh] gazed over those stupendous masses [of mountains] with wonder, almost with longing desire; never till this hour had he known Nature, that she was One, that she was his Mother and divine. And as the ruddy glow was fading into clearness in the sky, and the Sun had now departed, a murmur of Eternity and Immensity, of Death and of Life, stole through his soul; and he felt as if Death and Life were one, as if the Earth were not dead, as if the Spirit of the Earth had its throne in that splendour, and his own spirit were therewith holding communion." [18]

Here, side by side, are the two competing visions: god-as-the-father, who is not directly perceptible except insofar as the world is recognized to be his and he is recognized to be behind it; and god-as-the-mother, who is identical with the world her son wonders over. God in the guise of the "sternly loving father" whom the young Carlyle said he "*durst not* freely love," whose "heart seemed as if walled in" to his son, is a god present in the world as a proprietor, with all the rich world unambiguously subordinate to him: "The Universe is . . . my Father's!" But god is also seen in the guise of the tender, loving mother, with whom one could be open, natural, oneself, of whom Carlyle wrote: "my heart and tongue played freely only with my Mother." [19] This god as nature and as mother creates a complex set of identities behind which no further god-term is necessary, for the god of the world is the world itself.

To make such an identification of god and the world is to create a situation in which one of the terms is redundant. If the natural world is the embodiment of god, then god is not really a necessary hypothesis for understanding the universe, which is what Laplace tried to explain to Napoleon. In his *Grammar of Motives* Kenneth Burke calls the formation of just such an equation "the great watershed moment in Western thought when men were narrowing the scope of their terminologies as *per* the Occamite law of parsimony. Theologically, this amounted to the narrowing of the circumference from a scene comprising both creation and creator to a scene comprising creation alone." Burke goes on to counsel that, whenever we are confronted with such identities, we should always ask: "Which of the two equal terms was foremost?" [20] In Carlyle's case the answer is not simple, but then it probably never is. Beyond a doubt there was a large atavistic element in Carlyle that would have answered unhesitatingly: God; if one of the terms must go, let it be man and nature. Yet there is no reason why we need accept that answer for ourselves. If the idea of god was important to Thomas Carlyle, so be it; for us it is only a distraction, for from the moment he asserted the transcendental identity of god and the forces at work in the natural, historical world, his theology became a redundancy which we can well afford to ignore.

2. Action and Work

There is a sense in which Carlyle's career, especially the early phases of it, forms a continuous series of treatments of the same problem. His development as a thinker—and it is a very real development—consists for the most part of progressive changes in the terminologies he uses. In Chapter I we observed his involvement with the issues of modern egocentric philosophy and his alarm lest the self-centered universe of rationalist thought cut man off from his connection with the absolute and the godlike. In Chapter II we saw that, as Carlyle begins to approach the world of human historical action, he reformulates the god-centered versus self-centered antinomy in terms of the cosmic scene in which man lives and the momentary conflux in which he acts. Similarly, in *Sartor Resartus*, as we have just seen, the absolutist religious terminology appears in his conception of the world as belonging to a father deity, whereas the historical and relativistic axis is represented by a world conceived of as being itself the god principle. In each of these terminologies there is an overriding concern with the problem of defining one's own role in relation to a larger context, the nature of which is always problematic. How is man to exist at the center of a self-centered universe? How is he to act at the conflux of two eternities? In *Sartor Resartus*, where the absolutist context—that is, the realm of god—is identical with the human sphere of action—the natural world—the attempt to answer this question cannot be put off. Because of the semi-autobiographical nature of the work, this problem is confronted most directly here, and it is here that one therefore can see most clearly the deeply personal sources of Carlyle's inability to solve it. Just as we saw in Chapter I that the autonomous self is held in check by Carlyle's religiously based attachment to some sort of absolute god principle, and as we saw in Chapter II that the self existing at any given historical moment is stifled in the spaciousness of the cosmic scene around it, so here we should note that Carlyle's inability to extricate the self and free it for historical action can be traced to the personal, private level of his almost suicidal self-loathing, which tormented him most acutely at this time in his life.

Carlyle began his analysis of the nature of man's being in the historical world by attempting to clarify how it is that man acts. All human activity, he wrote, can be divided into three categories, which can be arranged into a hierarchical order. These three modes of human functioning—in an older terminology they would have been called "faculties"—are feeling, intellect, and action. On the most primitive level of organization, "existence [is] all a Feeling, not yet shaped into a Thought. Nevertheless, into a Thought, nay into an Action, it must be shaped. . . ." [21] This passage gives us both the categories and their hierarchical arrangement. We can recognize at once that feeling, as the most elementary unit of the triad and as a simple biological function, belongs to the province of the bodily senses. Intellect or thought belongs to the highest realm of individual capability, the mind. Action is, by its very nature, a supraindividual phenomenon, there being no bodily or personal element which can contain the concept of action in the sense in which feelings are contained in the sensorium and ideas in the mind. Action is always interaction, for one must act on something outside oneself. Even the most seemingly self-contained action has its ramifications outward, so that all action is, at the very least, social, being an event which influences one's fellow men, and, at the most, cosmic: "It is a mathematical fact that the casting of this pebble from my hand alters the centre of gravity of the Universe." [22]

In principle, each of these three modes can serve as the focal point of an ideological system, so that there would be an ideology of man as a sentient being, an ideology of man as a thinking being, and an ideology of man as an actor. In fact, however—and this is one of the most significant failures in the entire history of Western culture —the third ideology had not been developed. The first, the ideology of the feelings, manifested itself in Benthamite rationalism, with its system of motivation based upon the elementary feelings of pleasure and pain. (William Cobbett scornfully termed the Benthamites "feelosofers.") The second, the ideology of thought, is Romanticism, with its insistence on the potency of the individual, idiosyncratic creative mind and its absorption in self-consciousness. It is this ele-

ment of introspection, this focusing of the mind on itself, this "fret-
ting and fuming, and lamenting and self-tormenting," that Carlyle
sees as the danger of Romanticism when he warns, "Close thy
Byron; open thy *Goethe.*" [23]

There is a common tendency to reverse these findings, on the assumption that the emotionalism of the Romantic movement made it
akin to feeling, whereas the dry intellectual approach of Benthamite
rationalism related it to the realm of thought. Such a conclusion is
superficial and mistaken, for it takes into account only the styles of
these two schools rather than the bases upon which they are built.
Bentham's dry intellectual calculations are calculations of the feelings; the emotionalism of Romantic poetry revolves around a belief
in the sovereignty of the mind.

If Benthamism is the ideology of feeling and Romanticism the ideology of mind, then what is the ideology of action? Presumably,
Carlyle hints, it is to be found in Goethe, but this answer is not very
helpful. As we should have come to expect by now, Carlyle sees no
clear channel through which action can flow. Certainly there is no
shortage of human motion—that is, mindless action; people do go
about their business every day. But true action, which, as we already have seen in Chapter II,[24] involves transactions between
human beings in order to shape the raw, unordered data of reality
into a social order, requires the agency of mind if the "irrational"
givens of nature are to be subdued. Thus action must transcend but
remain rooted in intellect just as true intellect must transcend but
remain rooted in feelings. The modern world, however, does not
even remotely provide a context for such a healthy personal integration; on the contrary, it fragments the personality, dissociates, according to T. S. Eliot's formulation, the intellect from the feelings.
For modern man, who cannot reach even this first level of integration, any higher integration is out of the question, and thus, as Carlyle was to write in 1841, "Genuine Acting ceases in all departments
of the world's work; dextrous Similitude of Acting begins." [25]

Carlyle's thought here is distinctly on the modern side of the watershed that divides traditional from modern perceptions of the
relation between thought and action. Just a few decades before Carlyle wrote the passage from *Sartor* under consideration here, Edmund Burke had warned that government must attempt to control
thought because of the intimate connection between thought and
action, "because, as opinions soon combine with passions, even when
they do not produce them, they have much influence on actions." [26]

But with Carlyle this connection has become problematic, or at least is no longer to be taken for granted; indeed, some of his best efforts involve the search for ways in which it can be made. And today it is not even problematic, but practically nonexistent. The result is that where Burke was worried about the way opinions inevitably influence action, men like Paul Goodman recently have worried about how nearly impossible it has become to forge just such a connection between thought and action. Ironically, Burke's words come to sound like those of a Philistine who does not properly understand that it is the nature of intellect to issue in nothing.[27]

Be that as it may, what Carlyle is struggling with here is a problem of integration, of integrity, of identity, which he conceptualizes in terms of an integration of feeling, thought, and action—in terms, that is, of finding the thoughts appropriate to one's feelings and the actions appropriate to one's thoughts. If Erik Erikson is correct in distinguishing between the sociopolitical milieu of the Freudian age and that of today by saying that "the patient of today suffers most under the problem of what he should believe in and who he should—or, indeed, might—be or become; while the patient of early psychoanalysis suffered most under inhibitions which prevented him from being what and who he thought he knew he was," then Carlyle is very much a twentieth-century figure.[28] In an age when bourgeois liberals of the Westminster school were still denouncing what Bentham termed the "feudal" remnants that kept English society from achieving true freedom, Carlyle was decades ahead of them, recognizing from his own sense of lonely isolation that the real task of the time was to combat the anomie and indecisiveness that beset a formally liberated people who have not learned what sorts of action are possible for them.

Although Carlyle, unfortunately, does not make much progress in delineating the possibilities of action in the modern world, he does recognize that truly meaningful action must be a transcedence or a realization of thought. It must be action that somehow serves as an extension outward of man's mind into the historical realm in which we pass our lives. Just as thought without action is merely a self-indulgence that leads ultimately to the despair of solipsism, so action without thought is a brutality. Thus at the apex of Carlyle's hierarchy one finds not merely the actor, but the "Ideopraxist"—the man whose actions generate concretizations of his thought, much as Hegel's "World-historical man" works through the medium of the "creating Idea."[29] "Inventive spiritualism" is the label Carlyle gives to this highest mode of functioning, in which ideas reach into the realm of action and action becomes the bringing into being of idea.

According to Carlyle's ontology of action, it is primarily to the sociopolitical world that one must turn to find a scene that gives ample scope to the force of inventive spiritualism, for the sociopolitical world is itself a system of ideas and actions. Society is an idea, Carlyle tells us, in the sense that the concept *society* is a mental construct created by philosophers to account for the way in which men actually act in relation to each other. In other words, society itself is an ideopraxis: as an idea, it is the idea of human action; and as a way of acting, it is acting patterned by social ideas. In marked contrast to the social theories of the Hobbesian and Lockean tradition of contractualist thought, which saw society as a more or less reified entity and the polity as a *body* politic, Carlyle insists that there is nothing in any sense "real" about the mental construct termed "society"; what is real are the interactions this construct is used to describe. Carlyle counters the rationalistic tendency to hypostatize society by arguing that "Of Man's Activity and Attainment the chief results are aeriform, mystic, and preserved in Tradition only: such are his Forms of Government, with the Authority they rest on; his Customs, or Fashions both of Cloth-habits and of Soul-habits; much more his collective stock of Handicrafts, the whole Faculty he has acquired of manipulating Nature. . . ." [30]

It is important to translate Carlyle's ideas here into the relatively more level-headed terminology of political science in order to make clear that the criticism commonly leveled at him as a mystagogue is quite beside the point. After all, society *is* an idea, and there is nothing very mystical about saying so. It is an idea in the relatively straightforward sense that the truly important things we think about when we think about society are not physical, spatial entities, like books, parliaments, and clusters of buildings; rather, they are patterns of arrangement generated in the minds of men and radiating outward through action to affect the spatio-temporal world— patterns such as literary conceptions and the technology of printing, the idea of government, the city as a way of organizing space. Thus society is an idea for Carlyle in much the same sense as it is for Max Weber, who was so scrupulous about avoiding the hypostatization of society that he generally avoided using the substantive term "society" altogether, and spoke instead of "social action," "social relationships," and "social organization." "Even in such forms of social organization as a state, church, association, or marriage,"

Weber wrote, "the social relationship consists exclusively in the fact that there has existed, exists, or will exist a probability of action in some definite way appropriate to this meaning. It is vital to be continually clear about this in order to avoid the 'reification' of these concepts." [31]

Carlyle, who was as continually clear on this point as Weber could have wished, concluded that, precisely because the sociopolitical world was itself an ideopraxis, an ordered pattern of action, it is to the sociopolitical world that the ideopraxist must turn for an appropriate scene in which to operate. Conversely, because society is by definition the pattern traced by man's ideas as they extend into action, the practical application of any meaningful idea will be reflected in changes in the social system. "He who first shortened the labour of Copyists by device of *Movable Types* was disbanding hired Armies, and cashiering most Kings and Senates, and creating a whole new Democratic world," Carlyle wrote in a hyperbole which has the merit of adumbrating the necessary connections between thought, practice, and social structure.[32] "It is said," he wrote elsewhere, "ideas produce revolutions; and truly so they do; not spiritual ideas only, but even mechanical. In this clanging clashing universal Sword-dance that the European world now dances for the last half-century, Voltaire is but one choragus, where Richard Arkwright is another." [33]

Thus Carlyle's attempt to transcend the self through the medium of action leads him to recognize both that it is in the sociopolitical world that one must act and that the pure type of such action is revolutionary action, whether of the political or the technological sort. Revolution being to politics what creativity is to art, Carlyle has no doubts that the ideopraxist, whatever else he may do, must in one sense or another be a revolutionary. Indeed, *Sartor Resartus* ends with dim hints that both Carlyle and Teufelsdröckh are moving in this direction. Teufelsdröckh, the author reports, has disappeared from his apartment in Weissnichtwo and there are indications that he may be somewhere in Europe, probably Paris, engaged in underground revolutionary work. Before he disappeared he was last seen sitting quietly in a tavern while his compatriots exchanged gossip about the Paris revolution of 1830; he listened as they talked, without speaking "for a whole week, any syllable except once these three: *Es geht an* (It is beginning)." [34]

Ending this way, with a beginning, *Sartor Resartus* leaves us with a feeling of incompleteness which is not quite like and not quite unlike the open-endedness we always sense at the end of a work that concludes with a promise. Behind *Sartor* we are aware of that "austere and serious girding of the loins in youth" which Walter Pater tells us is the sign of growth, and at its conclusion we are promised that Carlyle-Teufelsdröckh, like Joyce-Dedalus at the conclusion of the *Portrait of the Artist*, will now begin the work for which we have watched him prepare. But where Joyce and Dedalus, as it were, went to Paris together, Carlyle stayed in Cheyne Row and let Teufelsdröckh go alone. Once again, Carlyle had substituted the idea of action for action itself, and in this sense *Sartor* records the incomplete, truncated development of its author's thought, which was necessarily incomplete insofar as it remained purely thought.

To understand more fully why Carlyle should have failed in this way, we must go back into the book in order to find what it was that kept Carlyle from doing more than merely adumbrating the idea of sociopolitical action. Here we may notice that, although Carlyle was quite capable of conceptualizing true action when he dealt in generalities, the moment he approaches the subject on the personal-biographical level he pulls up short. We saw in Chapter II that Carlyle did not distinguish carefully between the closely related but nonetheless distinct concepts of "labor," "work," and "action." Because of the vague, contentless way in which he discussed this matter in his essays from the late twenties and early thirties, and because he used the terms "action" and "work" interchangeably, it was not possible to determine the specific nature of the mode of activity he had in mind. With *Sartor Resartus* a precise definition of Carlyle's conception of action becomes possible.

Before proceeding with my analysis, however, I should pause to put the distinction at issue once more clearly in mind.[35] Recall that, following Hannah Arendt, I distinguished conceptually between "labor" as activity directed toward things for the purpose of satisfying man's biological needs; "work" as activity directed toward things for the purpose of creating and shaping man's physical and social environment; and "action" as activity directed toward other men for the purpose of creating the political realm in which alone full self-realization is possible. The first, labor, Arendt writes, "is the activity which corresponds to the biological process of the human body, whose spontaneous growth, metabolism, and eventual decay are bound to the vital necessities produced and fed into the life process by labor." [36] The second, work, corresponds to the Hegelian conception of servile labor; in contrast to Arendtian labor, which has as its object merely the transient biological life of the subject, work (servile labor) creates more or less permanent external objects onto which the subject, the worker, projects his own self-consciousness, so that, as Hegel wrote, his self-consciousness "is externalized and passes into the condition of permanence." In doing this, however, work makes possible only a negative transcendence of self-consciousness, "for in shaping the thing it [self-consciousness] only becomes aware of its own proper negativity, its existence on its own account, as an object, through the fact that it cancels the actual form [i.e., of the raw materials on which it works] confronting it. But this objective negative element is precisely the alien, external reality, before which it trembled." [37] Hence the self is objectified to itself, through work, as something alien, something other.

Finally, in the third mode of activity, which Arendt calls "action" and which corresponds to the activity of the "creating Idea" in Hegel, a full realization of the self is possible, for through action man realizes not only his biological life, not only his individual existence "as an object," but also his full nature both as a subjective being capable of applying his will to reality and as a *human* being who is part of a larger community of beings who share the human condition with him. "Action," Arendt writes, "the only activity that goes on directly between men without the intermediary of things or matter, corresponds to the human condition of plurality, to the fact that men, not Man, live on the earth and inhabit the world. While all aspects of the human condition are somehow related to politics, this plurality is specifically *the* condition . . . of all political life." [38]

Now if one examines *Sartor Resartus* with these distinctions in mind, one finds that, although Carlyle did not explicitly disaggregate the concepts of labor, work, and action, precisely such a separation is effectively in operation in the book, shaping the choices he makes.

Like Carlyle himself, Diogenes Teufelsdröckh suffers an eclipse of faith which precipitates in him the most abject psychic torments. After a disastrous love affair he reaches a point where there seem to be only three possibilities open to him: "Establish himself in Bedlam; begin writing Satanic Poetry; or blow-out his brains." [39] Yet he manages to avoid doing any of these. Paradoxically, it is his poverty that keeps him from suicide: "That I had my Living to seek saved me from dying . . . ," he explains in a cryptic but significant utterance.[40] Here Teufelsdröckh, who is just at the point of regaining a measure of psychic health after a period of almost suicidal depression, takes on the simple task of labor, the most primitive and fundamental of the three modes of activity. The biological limits of labor stand out clearly in this formulation, in which Teufelsdröckh's "Living," in the sense of livelihood, is also quite literally "living," in the sense that it is the antithesis of "dying."

Carlyle, of course, does not long remain content with the simple, biological mode of labor, for labor, even though it can assure the temporary biological survival of the subject, cannot secure any lasting triumph over death, which still awaits man despite his efforts to make a "Living." To be sure, neither science nor philosophy has discovered an objective way to triumph over death, but, subjectively, it is possible to rise above the fear of death, which can make death not only the factual end of biological existence but also the central feature of life itself. Obsessed with death, Teufelsdröckh lived, Carlyle tell us, "in a continual, indefinite, pining fear; tremulous, pusillanimous, apprehensive of I knew not what. . . ."[41]

Indeed, so completely was his psychic being shaped by his obsession with death that the longing for his own death which seemingly he had overcome when he renounced suicide can be seen to be still present in him, only now in a new form. Teufelsdröckh's decision to "seek a Living" marked the moment when he turned away from willing his own death, but we find now that he has merely projected the will toward his death out onto the universe, which at this stage he imagines to be seeking his destruction. Thus, although he admits that a "Universe . . . all void of Life, of Purpose, of Volition," must be also a universe void "even of Hostility" to him, nevertheless he projects his own suicidal impulses outward so that, even while he acknowledges the universe's ultimate indifference to him, he speaks of it as though it were in fact malign: "it seemed as if all things in the Heavens above and the Earth beneath would hurt me; as if the Heavens and the Earth were but boundless jaws of a devouring monster, wherein I, palpitating, waited to be devoured."[42] In that "diseased mixture and conflict of life and death" that Carlyle elsewhere tells us is the perennial condition of the human psyche,[43] the death principle has asserted its sovereignty and put the stamp of its image upon the whole cosmic system, as though the death one feared were something external and not a part of one's own being.

Suddenly, in an inexplicable moment of conversion, which may be unconvincing as a fictional device but which seems to correspond to Carlyle's own experience, Teufelsdröckh realizes that his "continual, indefinite, pining fear" has no relation to objective reality. It becomes luminously clear to him that the objective fact of death is not to be feared: "what is the sum-total of the worst that lies before thee?" he asks himself. "Death? Well, death. . . ." Although he cannot deny the objective reality of death, he can purge himself of that internal death that is at the root of his fearful and apprehensive mode of living: "and I shook base Fear away from me forever. I was strong, of unknown strength; a spirit, almost a god." [44] At this moment he feels he has overcome that sense of objectless anxiety which made him feel a rejected outcast, living the life of "ancient Cain, or of the modern Wandering Jew,—save only that he feels himself not guilty and but suffering the pains of guilt. . . ." [45] Death no longer frightens him: "Let it come, then; I will meet it and defy it!" [46]

To defy death, one first must realize what it is. Quite simply, death is time: "It continues ever true . . . that Saturn, or Chronos, or what we call TIME, devours all his Children"; the answer, then, is to get outside time: "only by incessant Running, by incessant Working, may you (for some threescore-and-ten years) escape him. . . ." [47] With this repudiation of the internal principle of death, Teufelsdröckh passes beyond the level of simple labor and reaches the level of work, where the self can realize itself in a form that enjoys, in Hegel's words, "the condition of permanence." After all, time is, as Carlyle had learned from Kant,[48] only a condition or form of human thought processes, a "superficial terrestrial adhesion . . . to thought," and in that sense a part of the self but not of the world outside the self.[49] To get outside time, then, one must get outside the self, an aim realizable through the medium of work— for it is in work that one objectifies and reifies oneself, Carlyle realized in a Hegelian solution to a Kantian problem. Thus Carlyle replaces the classical dictum "Know thyself" with "Know what thou canst work at," for it is only through its objects that the self can become real to itself. Without work, "How then could I believe in my Strength, when there was as yet no mirror to see it in?" [50]

Carlyle's conception of work as a mirror wherein the self becomes real to itself corresponds very closely to the "duplication of himself . . . in reality" that, a few years later, Marx was to describe as the ultimate product of the worker's efforts. Indeed, Marx's writings on work can throw considerable light on Carlyle's handling of the subject. "It is," Marx was to write in the *Economic and Philosophic Manuscripts of 1844*, "just in his work upon the objective world

. . . that man first really proves himself to be a *species being*. This production is his active species life. Through and because of this production, nature appears as *his* work and his reality. The object of labor is, therefore, the *objectification of man's species life:* for he duplicates himself not only, as in consciousness, intellectually, but also actively, in reality, and therefore he contemplates himself in a world that he has created." [51]

By far the most striking difference between Carlyle's treatment of work as a mirror wherein man sees himself and Marx's roughly similar explication of work as a medium through which man "duplicates himself" is that the Marxian mirror shows man his "species nature"—that is, his generic quality as a member of a class of beings larger than himself—whereas the Carlylean mirror shows man only his individual self. "When the labourer co-operates systematically with others," Marx wrote in *Capital*, "he strips off the fetters of his individuality, and develops the capabilities of his species." [52] But because Carlyle was preoccupied with work as a purely therapeutic device, he saw in it merely a personal regimen. For a long while he did not comprehend the social aspects of work, and hence was unable to put together the two intense needs his writing is most often about—the individual's need for work to do and society's need for work to be done upon it. He was intensely aware both of contemporary society's desperate need for the application of heroic efforts at regeneration and of the individual's need to find the work he can do, but he was unable until much later in his career to make what seems such an obvious connection. Thus in *Sartor Resartus* he failed to recognize that the "work at hand" may be precisely the task of molding a new society—that is, precisely what I have been describing with the term "action." Had he been able to see in work anything other than a strategy for a purely personal salvation, he might not have been so ready to answer in the negative the forlorn question, "Will any Parliamentary Reform ever reform *me?*"

What is more, because work was for Carlyle an objectification of man's personal self rather than of his species being, it was simultaneously an alienation of that self in that it made the self perceptible to itself as an *other*—that is, as not self. Of course, Carlyle realized this; it is, sadly, just what he wanted. Thus, again unwittingly echoing Hegel's distinction between servile labor and creative action, Carlyle explicitly describes work not as a realization of the self, but as an "Annihilation of Self (*Selbst-tödtung*)," which he tells us is "The first preliminary moral Act" after the denial of death. [53] Elsewhere he terms it "Renunciation" and quotes Goethe to the effect that "It is only with Renunciation (*Entsagen*) that Life, properly speaking, can be said to begin." [54] By calling the process whereby man projects his self out into the external world to become objectified there an "Annihilation of Self," Carlyle makes explicit what had been implicit in his writings as early as the essays on German literature. As we saw in Chapter I, it was the self that Carlyle recognized as the true enemy of modern man. Indeed, the self, it now becomes apparent, is for Carlyle merely another name for the disease of modern society and at times even for death itself, as in the following apposition from *Sartor:* "the Self in thee needed to be annihilated. By benignant fever-paroxysms is Life rooting out the deep-seated chronic Disease, and triumphs over Death." [55]

Because of this essentially negative attitude toward the self, Carlyle chooses to come to rest here. He had, after all, been combatting the self in his writings since the first essays. His ideas about the danger posed by the modern self had not changed, and neither had the personal self-loathing which manifested itself psychopathologically in his own life. In *Sartor* he had taken a considerable step forward, for where he had been on the verge of suicidally sentencing himself to death, he now commutes that sentence to banishment. But he is not yet ready to lift the sentence entirely and offer the self the freedom that comes through action. Nineteenth-century readers who read Carlyle for moral uplift and imagined they saw in his "Gospel of Work" a noble expression of the belief that hard work can cure excessive egoism and take one's mind off one's problems were grotesquely wrong about Carlyle. The fact is that in *Sartor Resartus* the purpose of work is an "Annihilation of Self" that borders on the suicidal, serving as the final stage in the metamorphoses of the desire for self-murder that Carlyle-Teufelsdröckh tells us he felt. In his "Gospel of Work" Carlyle had not fully overcome his self-loathing, his sense of himself as "devil's dung"; he had, rather, reached a *modus vivendi* with his self-tormenting perceptions: only by courting the most extreme form of alienation—alienation from self— could he come to terms with himself. And with the act of self-annihilation, he deluded himself into believing, "I directly thereupon began to be a Man." [56]

IV

The Making of History

1. Revolution and History

The modern sense of history and the modern sense of revolution are siblings not widely separated in age. Although one cannot fix a very precise date for the origin of what we can readily recognize as a "new" spirit of historiography, certainly it would not be an error to place the date somewhere in the last quarter of the eighteenth century—that is, in the decades around the French Revolution. "Theoretically, the most far-reaching consequence of the French Revolution was the birth of the modern concept of history . . . ," Hannah Arendt well observes.[1] As a profound historical event, the Revolution called out for explication and generated inquiries into the nature of historical processes. No event so profoundly touches the depths of man's understanding of himself as a historical creature as does a revolution. Indeed, were there no revolutions there probably would be no history, for without sudden change the need for explanations of human movements in time would be wanting. Just as metaphysics and structural-functional sociology, to name only two examples, are intellectual systems designed to explain stasis and status, so history and related disciplines stand as attempts of the mind to comprehend action and change.

Furthermore, few historical phenomena are so intimately involved with a sense of history as are revolutions, and revolutionaries are often more addicted to the study of history than are conservatives. For example, Friedrich Engels wrote *The Origin of the Family, Private Property and the State* in an attempt to focus on the system of primitive communism which is said to have been the economic system prevalent before the advent of private property. "[T]o reconquer [this system of primitive communism], but on the basis of the gigantic control of nature now achieved by man and of the free association now made possible, will be the task of the next generations," Engels wrote, revealing how closely he imagined the revolutionary future to be tied to the historical or even prehistorical past.[2] Similarly, when William Cobbett, shortly before his death, proclaimed that English workingmen had the right to expropriate the land if the owners of it could not arrange things for the workers' welfare, he based his claim on the system of land tenure believed to have been in effect at the time of the Norman conquest.[3] For much the same reasons, English radical movements from well before Cromwell's time into the nineteenth century had been steeped in Saxon lore. As Christopher Hill points out in his essay "The Norman Yoke," from the seventeenth century onward we find that popular revolutionary movements in England tended to base their claims to a large extent on historical precedents from Saxon history, in contrast to the bourgeois reformers, who tended to lean more heavily on abstract, rational criteria of justice.[4] The "rights of Englishmen," E. P. Thompson shows, were far more important to early laboring-class radicalism than were the "rights of man," and the former were always understood in historical terms.[5]

Examples of this practice of combining a backward-looking idiom with a revolutionary intent could be multiplied beyond number. I mention them because it is often imagined that the interest in history which flourishes during revolutionary times is spurred by the desire of people who are appalled by the revolution to turn backward in an effort to find some source of stability, some roots. This may have happened, I suppose, but I think at least as often the interest in the past is to be found among partisans or at least fellow travelers of revolution. This is the case because, as Karl Mannheim has shown, the utopian spirit, which must be present in all revolutionary movements, derives a considerable portion of its coherence from its sense of the historical past. It is through "the sense of historical time as a meaningful totality which orders events . . . [that] we first truly understand the total course of events and our place in it," Mannheim writes, and only with such an understanding of one's place in the course of events is meaningful action possible.[6] The utopian order toward which revolutionary movements aim derives from history, for, as Hobbes remarked, "No man can have in his mind a conception of the future, for the future is not yet. But of our conceptions of the past, we make a future. . . ."[7] In this sense, revolutionary movements, far from being, as Edmund Burke imagined, thoroughgoing breaks with the past, generally are oriented toward the past in very fundamental ways. In the words of Benedetto Croce, "only one who hopes and works for the future looks backwards." [8]

What is more, a sense of one's place in history is crucially important not only to those who are to make a revolution but also to those who come after them, for the generation that must live in the aftermath of a revolution often finds itself at loose ends when faced with a situation that seems disturbingly at odds with the world order its fathers knew. At this point it is likely that those who favor the new revolutionary order will find their experience more profoundly unsettling than those who are hostile to it. For the men who find the new order abhorrent, it is, as far as one's own adjustment is concerned, an easy matter to regard it as illegal and criminal; no effort at historical comprehension is necessary or even desirable. Those who find it attractive, on the other hand, must make an effort to justify and legitimate it, lest it and they along with it be exiled into a rootless, existential, and anomic vacuum. History provides the tool with which a postrevolutionary world can reconcile permanence and change, with which it can make itself at home in the new. In a period of cultural dislocation, the study of history teaches that, even though, as Carlyle observed, "[I]n this Time-World of ours there is properly nothing else but revolution and mutation, and even nothing else conceivable," it nevertheless remains true that the generations of man "stand indissolubly woven together." [9]

2. Historical Causation

In a very real way, Carlyle's declaration that history records a continuous process of revolution and mutation expresses one of the most significant insights of the new historical spirit, but before we can understand the nature of this new historiography we must pause to delineate briefly the older attitudes toward history it superseded.

Traditionally, Western European culture has seen history as essentially a linear affair in which the dynastic metaphor of succession could be applied to historical epochs. The dynastic metaphor was perfectly suited to the needs of pre-Hegelian historians, for it provided a model of the historical process quite appropriate for explaining how change arises out of the context of permanence.

With the onset of a period of profound and continuous change, however, the historian's task undergoes a far-reaching alteration. Historical explanation no longer seems to be aimed at clarifying how change occurs in a stable system. On the contrary, the question now becomes one of discovering how stability is possible in the context of never-ending change. The technological, social, and political revolutions of late eighteenth-century Europe produced changes broad and deep enough to lead to just such a reversal of figure and ground. In a "Time-World" in which "there is properly nothing else but revolution and mutation," the metaphor of linear succession is no longer appropriate, for what now puzzles the student of history is not how new historical orders arise from time to time but how the old order can exist from day to day.

In 1830, when Carlyle addressed himself to explicating the new historical spirit abroad in Europe, it was precisely the old historiography's commitment to a linear pattern of explanation that he singled out for attack. Five years earlier, in his *Life of Schiller*, he had denied that there was any such new spirit. History is what it has always been, he wrote—philosophy teaching by experience; all that has changed are the values with which modern history works and by which it measures experiences.[10] But by 1830, half a decade of thought on the subject had convinced him that philosophy, far from being in a position to teach by experience, would have to learn from it. "Truly, if History is Philosophy teaching by Experience, the writer fitted to compose History is hitherto an unknown man," he says, recanting his earlier view. "[E]very single event," he explains, "is the offspring not of one, but of all other events, prior or contemporaneous, and will in its turn combine with all others to give birth to new. . . ."[11]

The belief that this thickness of history, this weblike complexity of the historical process, renders any linear account of history inadequate had been the principal creed of the Hegelian revolution in historiography and lay at the heart of what I have been calling the new spirit of history. Writing of Hegel's philosophy of history, Sir Isaiah Berlin observes that "if the historian is fully to realize his task, to rise above the chronicler and the antiquary, he must endeavour to paint a portrait of an age in movement. . . . The historian . . . must see and describe phenomena in their fullest context, against the background of the past and the foreground of the future, as being organically related to all other phenomena which spring from the same cultural impulse."[12] In exactly this spirit, Carlyle argues that "our 'chains,' or chainlets, of 'causes and effects,' which we so assiduously track through certain hand-breadths of years and square miles," are inappropriate for explaining a system in which "each atom is 'chained' and complected with all!" [13]

Despite what he sees as the failure of the principle of linear causality to explain history, Carlyle is far from ready to conclude that history is essentially inexplicable. To be sure, it is inexplicable by conventional narrative techniques, inasmuch as "Narrative is *linear*, Action is *solid*." [14] But this does not preclude the possibility of constructing some sort of verbal account of the complex and solid materials from which history is made. Such an account, Carlyle reasons, will have to be based on nonlinear narrative techniques appropriate to his modern, somewhat Bergsonian sense of time. In his own work as a historian, particularly in his *History of the French Revolution*, which I shall examine in the next chapter, Carlyle boldly and on the whole rather successfully created a model of nonlinear technique suitable for conveying the solidity of action. Indeed, a large part of the effect of the work, as we shall see, derives from Carlyle's turning away from simple sequence and causality to paint instead a rich impasto of sociological detail, of which we can say, as Franz Neumann has said of Vico, "no isolated element can be held responsible for the occurrence of social change; it is the totality of interrelationships between social relations and [social] superstructures that determines change." [15] Thus if we look in the pages of Carlyle's *French Revolution* for an explanation of the causes of the Revolution, we will find only a mass of sociological detail in which the chain of causal relationships, if we can find one at all, is circular and continually turning in on itself. [16]

Carlyle's refusal to treat history in terms of linear causality places him firmly in the mainstream of modern historiography, as exemplified preeminently in Hegel and Marx. Although Hegel claims that the course of history is "the rational necessary course of the World-Spirit—that Spirit whose nature is always one and the same, but which unfolds this its one nature in the phenomena of the World's existence," we should recognize that, as an explanatory device, the "World-Spirit" is obviously an evasion, for it means only that history will go in the direction in which it will go. [17] Even when Hegel attributes a specific content to this World-Spirit— "The History of the world is none other than the progress of the consciousness of Freedom" [18]—he is able thereby to explain the growing liberalization of European political institutions only in terms of the tendency of such institutions toward liberalization. In this sense, then, one cannot attribute a belief in linear causation to Hegel, for in the final analysis his history knows no causes at all—an idea Hegel expresses tautologically by describing history as its own cause.

Similarly, Marx is willing to speak of causality only when he is dealing with the evolutionary developments which unfold within a social structure; such developments, he says, are limited by the structure of the society in which they occur and aim toward "a *definite predetermined objective* existence." [19] But, once the evolutionary process has brought us beyond the limits of the social structures in existence at a given point in time, the limits which define an evolutionary process have been passed and the process accordingly becomes revolutionary and indeterminate. At this point Marx feels the need to use the catch-phrase "historical process" for much the same purpose as Hegel used the "World-Spirit"—namely, to give a sense of having explained the essentially inexplicable.

Just as Hegel speaks of the "World-Spirit" and Marx speaks of the "historical process," so Carlyle develops a theory of the spontaneous growth and decay of social, political, and intellectual systems. In doing so, he finally frees history from its dependence on the non-historical, absolutistic categories of thought to which heretofore it had been subjected in his thought. The idea that history determines itself represents for Carlyle the application to history of the relativistic arguments he had been willing, years earlier, to apply only to literary productions.[20] The famous analogy from *Sartor Resartus* comparing social ideas and arrangements to clothes which tend to wear out over the course of time is an example of this conceit, for it means that the wearing out of these systems is in need of no explanation other than their own inherent proclivity for wearing out. Transported out of the rarefied atmosphere of the speculative *Sartor* and into the denser medium of *The French Revolution*, this conception of ideas as having their own fatality reappears as the dictum that "All grows and dies, each by its own wondrous laws, in wondrous fashion of its own; spiritual things most wondrously of all." [21]

The net effect of this rejection of causal explanation is, paradoxically, a heightened sense of the inevitability of the historical events at issue. The philosophical literature on causation holds that any event which is caused is necessary, and, conversely, that to speak of necessity is to speak of the causes which determine that necessity. This conclusion has been inescapable ever since Aristotle demonstrated that the only free being would be a being who had no causes—an unmoved mover. Yet despite the inescapable logic of this argument, it certainly seems that when men are faced with the problem of understanding historical situations, they handle the question of causality just the other way around. Generally speaking, when historians point to a cause, they do so to call attention to a pivotal moment at which things could have been done differently. Thus if a historian were to say, for example, that the French Revolution were to an important extent "caused" by the incompetence of Louis XVI, he would be saying that, had Louis been a different sort of person, things would have gone quite differently. To be sure, Louis' being the way he was had causes of its own, but the fact remains that one cites a cause in order to evoke the sense of indeterminacy. This becomes especially obvious when the strategic purposes of a piece of historical writing are near the surface. For example, when Edmund Burke contends that the revolutionary drive of the philosophes was generated by the "censurable degree" to which the government opened itself to the spirit of reform, he means thereby to call attention to the fact that the Revolution might have been avoided had the government exercised its option to deal harshly with its critics.[22] Conversely, when Carlyle refuses to deal in causes, which is in effect what he is doing when he claims that each event unfolds "by its own wondrous laws, in wondrous fashion of its own," he generates a sense not of accident but of inevitability. Aristotle notwithstanding, to find no cause is to find no handle by which one could twist things another way. To say that an act or event is indeterminate (or overdetermined, for they come to the same thing) is to say that it has no *terminus*, no borders or limits; it is therefore determined only by itself (or by everything), if one can speak of its being determined at all. Furthermore, the fact that it would be meaningless to speak of an undetermined event as contingent brings us to the same conclusion: that cause creates the impression of contingency, whereas the causeless tends to seem self-generated and inevitable.

There is, I might note, a certain existential quality in this picture of spontaneous, self-generating revolution. The actors in Carlyle's revolutionary drama seem to be functioning somewhere outside the parameters defined by traditional concepts of purposive action. This is not to say that Carlyle sees the characters in his *French Revolution* as behaving in aimless and random ways; on the contrary, the book is filled with portraits of men conducting themselves with a singlemindedness that can come only from purposive action. But their purposes do not seem to lie anywhere beyond the actions themselves, so that there is in Carlyle's writing a tremendous involvement with the gestural aspects of how men conduct themselves. This is a subject to which I shall return in Chapter IX when I come to examine Carlyle's theory of the hero as a historical actor. For the time being it is important to keep in mind only Carlyle's conception of history as a nonlinear, overdetermined, and inevitable process.

3. Historical Rationality and the Philosophy of History

If one is to realize the scope of the revolution in historical thought of which Carlyle was a part, one must recognize that the narrative techniques he developed for depicting history as a sociologically complex, nonlinear pattern imply a profound dissatisfaction not only with traditional attitudes toward the practice of writing history, but with traditional philosophies of history as well. Western culture has had a number of deductive philosophies of history which analyze the nature of the historical process by fitting it into rational explanatory schemes. "All states and dominions which hold or have held sway over mankind are either republics or monarchies. Monarchies are either hereditary in which the rulers have been for many years of the same family, or else they are of recent foundation. The newly founded ones are either entirely new, . . . or else they are, as it were, new members grafted on to the hereditary possessions of the prince that annexes them. . . ." And so on. This passage superbly illustrates the stepwise technique of "exhaustive bifurcation" which had dominated theories of history for over three centuries when Carlyle wrote. Hobbes reasoned thus, and so did Locke. Today the chief use of this Machiavellian technique—for the passage just quoted is taken from the first chapter of *The Prince* [23]—is in the scenarios of Herman Kahn and the matrices of game theorists and systems analysts.

The important point to notice is not simply that Machiavelli applied the linear method of exhaustive bifurcation to the philosophy of history; far more crucial is the fact that such a rationalistic approach is inherently Machiavellian. Such a system of rationalistic explanation is suited to a perception of historical events as the outcomes of numerous implicit or explicit policy decisions where the choices must be made in the context: if A, then A_1 or A_2; if A_1, then B_1 or B_2; if A_2, then C_1 or C_2, . . . I call this rational approach "Machiavellian" because it sees history as above all a political process, taking "political" strictly in the sense implied in the word "policy." That is to say, in the rationalistic view, history is seen as the outcome of an endless series of strategic decisions.

From Machiavelli until the rise of the new "Romantic" historiography late in the eighteenth century, European historians were concerned primarily with applying their rational-deductive method to the rational pattern of decision-making which they assumed constituted history. Indeed, that the methods of the historian were more or less modeled on the processes he was describing was so universal an assumption that even today we have only one word, "history," to denote both the products and the subject matter of the historian's efforts. This confusion of history as a product of intellectual analysis and history as a process of events in time—a confusion which led Marx to insist that it was about time a distinction were made between understanding history and making it—stems from the fact that the Machiavellian methodology of rational-deductive history writing was for three centuries held to be a mirror image of the historical process itself.

We also might notice in passing that this Machiavellian or rationalist attitude toward history is in fact quite unhistorical. Any randomly selected pages of *The Prince* or the *Discourses* can convince one of this. The reasoning always comes first, and the historical examples are put in merely as illustrations. Essentially, Machiavelli is involved in a speculative enterprise, which leaves the study and enters the historical world only for corroboration. In this sense his approach to history is rather idealistic, and insofar as this is the case, he handles history with the intention of dehistoricizing it by emphasizing what is timeless and unchanging in it.

For thinkers like Carlyle, however, what was disturbing in such a sense of history was not merely the fact that it inappropriately attempted to reduce history to a rational scheme. Even more objectionable was the nature of the rationality it claimed to find in history. Returning again to Machiavelli as the source of the rationalist tradition at issue here, we can see that, despite the common assumption that Machiavelli brought about the separation of politics from morality, his actual accomplishment was more nearly the reverse of this. Machiavelli, we should recall, wrote at a time when reason and morality were still inseparably linked as cognate human faculties. In this context, Machiavelli maintained the traditional unity of morality and politics but formulated it in such a way that the heretofore moral faculty of reason became subordinate to political aims, became in fact a technique of politics and no longer an agency of man's moral being. In doing this he exploded the entire Western tradition of what constituted rationality, changing the rational from an ethical principle into a methodological instrument. It is not merely the case that, as Harold J. Laski has said, "the whole of the Renaissance is in Machiavelli," [24] for indeed the whole liberal, rationalist, and humanistic tradition from the Renaissance to today is adumbrated there.

From Machiavelli's day to the present, rational conduct generally has been defined as conduct efficiently in the service of goal attainment. The desire to maximize pleasure and minimize pain—translated into economic terms as the desire to maximize profit and minimize loss—has been held to be the quintessence of rational behavior, and the rationalist tradition consists for the most part of an endless series of elaborations on the idea that any being enlightened as to his own self-interest, insofar as he acts rationally, will act so as to maximize the benefits to himself. There is nothing very abstruse about this theory; indeed, its simplicity is universally recognized as its most outstanding feature. But we might pause to consider the juxtaposition of its two key terms, *maximize* and *rational*. Two considerations are relevant here. In the first place, we can note that the foregoing definition of rationality is in stark contrast with the classical Greek definition of the rational which governed Western thought for perhaps two millennia and which insisted that the hallmark of rational conduct is its location at some golden mean between the relevant polar extremes. To the Socratic tradition, the desire to maximize pleasure would have been hardly less irrational than the desire to maximize pain. Second, we can note that the rationalist definition of rationality is markedly different from the scholastic understanding of the term, which saw rationality as a standard by which one measured the accuracy of intellectual methods; that is to say, medieval philosophers would have judged a thought process rational if it followed certain rules of logic, regardless of the course of action into which it issued.

These two considerations—that rationalist rationality differs from the traditional rationality of Western culture in being a goal-oriented rather than a process-oriented concept, and in being aimed at maximization rather than at harmonization—lead to an important conclusion wholly neglected by the antirationalist tradition of the last few centuries: namely, that the whole structure of rationalist thought was erected on the foundation of a highly limited and really quite vulnerable sense of what constitutes the rational.

Among modern social and political thinkers only Max Weber has noticed that this identification of rationality and maximization is the Achilles heel of rationalism. With the insight that made him a great moralist as well as a great sociologist, Weber recognized that there is something perverse about calling the Faustian quest for limitless pleasure and limitless profits rational. Thus he introduced the distinction between the "formal rationality" of maximization and the "substantive rationality" of value-oriented activity.[25] Unfortunately, he has not been followed in this by modern social analysts who, in their quest for a "value-free" sociology, have resolved to ignore the "substantive rationality" of human values while giving exclusive attention to the "formal rationality" of policies of maximization. Thus one highly respected contemporary social thinker, Joseph Schumpeter, asserts that he has "no hesitation in saying that all logic is derived from the pattern of the economic decision"—that is, that the only rationality is the rationality of calculation.[26]

It is, therefore, lamentably true that no equivalent of Weber's insight is to be found in the literature of English-speaking antirationalism. From the eighteenth to the twentieth century, English literature is almost uniform in its unremitting attack on the rationalist spirit. From Edmund Burke, who felt that "politics ought to be adjusted, not to human reasonings, but to human nature, of which the reason is but a part, and by no means the greatest part";[27] to Coleridge, who led the most complete, systematic attack on rationalism; from Blake, Ruskin, Dickens, Newman, and even, reluctantly, John Stuart Mill, down through Morris, Yeats, and Shaw, the mainstream of English literature has been staunchly antirationalist. For the most part, however, the main issue in such attacks on rationalism has been whether or not the rationalist model of the world presents an adequate picture of human history, human nature, and the human mind.

William James has given us the essential features of this approach when, in *The Varieties of Religious Experience*, he scorns rationalism on the grounds of its inability to account for the experiences we all have of the irrational. "If you have intuitions at all," James wrote, "they come from a deeper level of your nature than the loquacious level which rationalism inhabits. Your whole subconscious life, your impulses, your faiths, your needs, your divinations, have prepared the premises, of which your consciousness now feels the weight of the result; and something in you absolutely *knows* that that result must be truer than any logic-chopping rationalistic talk, however clever, that may contradict it." [28] This essentially religious line has been followed even in the more concrete realms of political and economic thought, and the result has been that rationalism has been criticized almost exclusively for being inadequate rather than for being erroneous. Thus John Stuart Mill strove to develop "a Radical philosophy, better and more complete than Bentham's, while recognizing and incorporating all of Bentham's which is permanently valuable." [29] When Mill came to part company with Bentham, it was not because he questioned the foundations of Bentham's thought (this he never did) but because he wanted to offer what he imagined to be an extension of Bentham—a correction of the master which would leave room for the human irrational while at the same time leaving intact Bentham's definition of what constituted the rational.

Another example of this typical critique of rationalism—this one taken from the writings of John Ruskin—is of interest because it makes explicit just how much the antirationalists were willing to concede to their opponents. Ruskin argues that the *homo economicus* model of Political Economy, which considers man merely "a covetous machine," errs in its assertion that man is essentially rational with merely an overlay of irrational sentiment. On the contrary, Ruskin says, these irrational elements "alter the essence of the creature under examination the moment they are added. . . ." To set up rationality as a normative model is as absurd, he contends, as it would be to establish a science of gymnastics "which assumed that men had no skeletons. It might be shown, on this supposition, that it would be advantageous to roll the students up into pellets, flatten them into cakes, or stretch them into cables; and that when these results were effected, the re-insertion of the skeleton would be attended with various inconveniences to their constitution." And he concludes this satire on the rationalist theory of human nature by asserting: "I do not deny the truth of this theory: I simply deny its applicability to the present phase of the world." [30]

All of these thinkers—James, Mill, and Ruskin—attacked rationalism only on the grounds of its inadequacy, and in doing so they allowed rationalist thought to hold undisputed possession of the terrain over which they were fighting. That is to say, rationalism was allowed to control the terminology, for its definition of the rational went unquestioned, and the only issue left to fight over was whether or not there was any terrain left outside the frontiers of the rational. The antirationalists, of course, claimed that there was, but by basing their arguments on the importance of the irrational elements omitted from the normative models of the Political Economists, constitutionalists, parliamentary reformers, and so forth, they were surrendering more than they could ever hope to win, for they all admit implicitly, as Ruskin does explicitly, that they "do not deny the truth of this theory."

Needless to say, Carlyle is not exempt from this limitation. He too expresses his dissatisfaction with the rationalist view of history solely on the issue of its adequacy for dealing with historical phenomena. In his work of the 1830s there is nowhere to be found an equivalent of Weber's awareness of an alternative to formal rationality that still can be defined as rational. Where Weber, who was intensely aware of the so-called irrational elements in history, was able to discern the substantively rational behind what, from the formalist's vantage point, looks like simple irrationality, Carlyle was forced by his lack of a concept of substantive rationality to treat anything outside the boundaries laid down by rationalist theory as irrationality *tout simple*. In other words, the idea of substantive rationality allowed Weber to distinguish between the formal and strategic rationality of maximization; the substantive rationality that manifests itself in such seemingly "irrational" forms as religious, traditionary, and charismatic social systems; and the purely irrational which, by all criteria, appears as madness. For Carlyle, however, who was victimized by the rationalist movement's control of the terminological terrain over which he was passing, there was no way to disaggregate the seeming irrationality of the substantively rational from the purely irrational, so that in his hypercharged *History of the French Revolution*, for example, the Revolution often tends to become for him merely the acting out of "the Madness that dwells in the hearts of men." [31] "Alas, then, is man's civilisation only a wrappage, through which the savage nature of him can still burst, infernal as ever?" he asks, and answers with the doleful conclusion that "Nature still makes him [man]: and has an Infernal in her as well as a Celestial." [32] With this Manichean vision, which looks backward toward the satanic psychology of Blake and forward toward that of Freud, Carlyle stares boldly into the face of irrationality and acknowledges its potent role in the making of history.

Nevertheless, behind this façade of irrationality one can discern in

Carlyle's historical writings the presence of an intuitive sense that even the maddest of historical events is explicable by some sort of reason which rationalism cannot comprehend. For Carlyle as for Hegel, there is a "cunning of reason" which "remains in the background, untouched and uninjured," working its will even while madness seems to be in command.[33] Moreover, because Carlyle believed that the French Revolution was a historical judgment pronounced on the ancien régime, he tended to see in even the most irrational manifestations of the Revolution the working out of some scheme which, to say the least, seemed to have an obscure but nonetheless discernible purpose behind it. Perhaps a thoroughgoing diabolist like Blake could have called that scheme itself irrational, but Carlyle, who will not use shock tactics like this when it is god's plan for the world that is at issue, remains convinced that the forces of irrationality unleashed by the Revolution are doing the bidding of some higher rationality. Reality, we are told, always develops according to "its own laws and Nature's," and although these laws are "not . . . the laws of Formula"—that is, of formal rationality—neither are they irrational.[34]

As yet, Carlyle can say no more about the nature of this higher rationality; he can do little more than hint of its existence. By the 1840s, however, with the writing of *Past and Present*, he will begin to come around to the recognition that the root source of this substantive rationality is to be found embedded in the social systems and structures which governed the relationships between men prior to the onslaught of the skeptical spirit and the principle of formal rationality. Then he will turn toward the Middle Ages in search of a model for those principles of moral reasonableness which Weber was to name substantive rationality and which remained unnamed in Carlyle's writings. All this, however, is still ahead of him. Now, after a long apprenticeship, he is, finally, ready to direct his attention to the world of historical action. His thought on history is as yet incomplete; still lacking is that vision of a moral society which will come, a decade later, with *Past and Present*. But, incomplete or not, he has forged a tool with which he will produce a startlingly new kind of historical writing. In it linear narrative is replaced by the polycentric perspective of a sociological sense of history; throne-rooms and assembly halls as scenes of decision-making give place to the street as a scene of action; and rational order is annihilated by the potency of the irrational.

V

Sinews and Indignation

In the 1820s Carlyle referred repeatedly to the French Revolution, although he does not seem to have read much about it at that time or to have formed any very clear opinions. In both "Signs of the Times" and *Sartor Resartus* he had spoken of the Revolution as in some sense incomplete and needing to be completed, but these references seem deliberately cryptic and it is altogether likely that at the time they were made Carlyle had not precisely decided what he meant by them.[1] In the early 1830s, however, he began to read on the subject more persistently, and by September 1833 he was able to write to John Stuart Mill: "[I]n this [the French Revolution], in the right understanding of this, is involved all possible knowledge important for us; and yet at the present hour our ignorance of it in England is probably as bad as total (for Error is infinitely worse than Ignorance). . . . To me, it often seems, as if the right *History* (that impossible thing I mean by History) of the French Revolution were the grand Poem of our Time; as if the man who *could* write the *truth* of that, were worth all other writers and singers. If I were spared alive myself, and had means, why might not I too prepare the way for such a thing? I assure you the attempt often seems among my possibilities." [2]

Carlyle's sense of the importance of the Revolution is easily understandable. From the time of the Revolution through the first decade or so of the nineteenth century, an Englishman's attitude toward the events in France served as a more or less accurate touchstone of his opinions about political matters in England. In this sense, the French Revolution was a domestic rather than a foreign issue in England. Edmund Burke had been provoked into writing his *Reflections on the Revolution in France* by homegrown revolutionaries, such as Dr. Richard Price and Dr. Joseph Priestley, whose applause for the Revolution in France Burke imagined to be an index of their desire to see just such a revolution in England. From the opposite side of the fence, William Cobbett denounced the Napoleonic wars as a trick of the boroughmongering landlords to get free-born Englishmen to fight and die "for Gatton and Old Sarum": "What they wanted, was to prevent the landing, not of Frenchmen, but of French principles; that is to say, to prevent the example of the French from being alluring to the people of England. The devil a bit did they care for the Bourbons." The immense national debt that resulted from the Continental wars moved Cobbett to exclaim: "Poh! These things are the price of efforts to crush freedom in France, *lest the example of France should produce a reform in England.*" [3]

For his own part, Prime Minister William Pitt made no secret of the fact that it was the invasion of revolutionary attitudes more than the danger of an invasion by a revolutionary army that demanded strict countermeasures.[4] The awful wave of political repression— "the English reign of terror," Ebenezer Elliott was to call it [5]—that began with the burning of Priestley's home and library by a Church and King mob in 1791 and continued with only slight abatement into the 1820s was directed against radical leaders who did not hesitate to style themselves Jacobins. "Probably no English Government," J. L. and Barbara Hammond have written, "has ever been quite so near, in spirit and licence, to the atmosphere that we used to associate with the Tsar's government of Russia as the Government that ruled England for the first few years of the peace." [6]

The French Revolution, then, was a topic of far more than academic interest for politically sensitive Englishmen in the first part of the nineteenth century. Curiously enough, Carlyle had little of substance to say on the subject in the 1820s. As I already have remarked, he ended his "Signs of the Times" with a vague prophecy that the development of European politics in the future would in some way involve the completion of the work left unfinished by the Revolution. "There is a deep-lying struggle in the whole fabric of society; a boundless grinding collision of the New with the Old," he wrote. ". . . France was the scene of their fiercest explosion; but the final issue was not unfolded in that country: nay, it is not yet anywhere unfolded. Political freedom is hitherto the object of these efforts; but they will not and cannot stop there." [7] Except for this cryptic utterance and a few others like it, however, he is for the most part silent on the subject.

An 1829 essay on Voltaire hardly qualifies as an exception to the preceding generalization. The essay is a tissue of evasions, and one would scarcely guess from reading it that Voltaire was commonly held to be one of the spiritual fathers of the Revolution. Carlyle starts out ambitiously enough, pointing to the crucial importance of the ideas of such men as Voltaire in shaping political reality: "not by material, but by moral power, are men and their actions governed." [8] Unfortunately, it is precisely Voltaire's political message that Carlyle refuses to deal with: "In interpreting Voltaire, accordingly, it will be needful to bear some things carefully in mind, and to keep many other things as carefully in abeyance. Let us forget that *our* opinions were ever assailed by him, or ever defended; that *we* have to thank him, or upbraid him, for pain or for pleasure; let us forget that we are Deists or Millenarians, Bishops or Radical Reformers, and remember only that we are men." [9]

Obviously, this is not very promising. We should recognize, though, that at the time at which Carlyle was writing, the names of men like Voltaire, Rousseau, and Paine were such powerful talismans that it behooved one to be particularly careful what one said about any of them—especially if one was not quite sure where one stood oneself. Carlyle, this gives us one more opportunity to note, was at this time far from certain of his own political position.

Nevertheless, somewhere between the Voltaire essay of 1829 and the commencement of his studies of the French Revolution a few years later, he came to realize that it would be necessary to understand the Revolution if one were to understand anything at all about the modern world, for, as he observed a few years later, "These Chartisms, Radicalisms, Reform Bill, Tithe Bill, and infinite other discrepancy, and acrid argument and jargon that there is yet to be, are *our* French Revolution. . . ." [10] "I should not have known what to make of this world at all," he told James Anthony Froude, "if it had not been for the French Revolution." [11] This being the case, Carlyle's three-volume *History of the French Revolution* represents his coming to terms with the modern, postrevolutionary world and the clarification of his relationship with events and ideas which, since the Revolution, had been for an Englishman the key to his whole political stance.

1. The Causes of the French Revolution

Carlyle's study of the Revolution begins by contrasting 1744 with 1774. In the thirty years between these two dates a change of cataclysmic proportions had been consummated in the psychosocial attitudes, the institutions, and the political structure of France. When Louis XV, Louis "the Well-Beloved," lay ill in that earlier year, all France grieved and prayed, Paris most intensely. But a few decades later, as he lay dying, Paris was indifferent and Louis was no longer well beloved: "If they hear of his sickness, they will answer with a dull *Tant pis pour lui.*" [12]

Prior to this change in attitude that transformed the king from a venerable figure to an object of indifference, the principle of kingship and of social hierarchy in general had been, Carlyle says, a "realised Ideal."[13] Of course, one would be naive to imagine that kings and aristocrats had then been ideal governors in any normative sense of the term, and Carlyle's conception of kingship as a "realised Ideal" is far from implying any such fatuity. On the contrary, he is well aware that even in their heyday the institutions of royalty and aristocracy generally fell far short of providing the services which were supposed to have justified their existence. "How much the Upper Classes did actually, in any the most perfect Feudal time, return to the Under by way of recompense, in government, guidance, protection, we will not undertake to specify here," he wrote in 1839; ". . . we can well believe the old Feudal Aristocracy not to have surpassed the new."[14] Clearly, then, Carlyle's description of royalty and aristocracy as "realised Ideals" is intended as an analytic rather than as a normative statement; it means that the institutions of kingship and nobility existed and held sway as quasi-tangible incorporations of the principles of hierarchy, faith, and, above all, power.

Although Carlyle is often accused of being morally obtuse on this point, it does not seem to me that he is guilty as charged. By insisting that the ancien régime was once a valid and vital social arrangement, he is not in fact sentimentalizing the past or whitewashing the record of nobility and royalty in the days when their power was unquestioned. On the contrary, he is saying only what we must all admit: that their power was indeed unquestioned; that it was, in a word, power. Wherever it came from and however they used it— well in some cases, in most not—the men of the old order had power. To say of such men that they realized an ideal is to say nothing at all about the moral or ethical worth of their position, as Carlyle makes clear when he tells us that in the old days "a Seigneur, as he returned from hunting, [was authorized] to kill not more than two Serfs, and refresh his feet in their warm blood and bowels. . . ." In the same vein, he quotes with wry compassion the words of a noble lady about a particularly damnable action of a noble lord: "Depend upon it, Sir, God thinks twice before damning a man of that quality." [15] Obviously, there is nothing normative about the ideal in question here. The ideal is power, and Carlyle's point is simply that it used to take the forms of kingship and seigneurship, and that on the eve of the Revolution it no longer did.

To be sure, Carlyle does speak from time to time of a normative ideal behind the institution of kingship. A king is, or should be, the "Acknowledged Strongest (well named King, *Kön-ning*, Can-ning, or Man that was Able)," he writes, relying on a specious etymology.[16] Of late, though, the king of France has been unwilling to provide the service of "true Guidance in return for loving Obedience"; if he is still the shepherd of his people, it is not as the one who protects his flock but as the one who fleeces it.[17]

However, the fact that the king no longer lives up to the normative ideal of kingship, as expressed in the etymology, does not have an essential connection, Carlyle seems to feel, with the fact that he no longer contains, realizes, or symbolizes the ideal in the nonnormative, absolute sense. One cannot help but be surprised at how seldom the import of this position is appreciated. In general, liberal historians have tended to pin the blame for the Revolution on some sort of administrative failure on the part of the government, which led the sheep finally to resist being shorn. The Revolution, then, is caused by the *misuse* of power, whether in the sense of failure to govern or in the sense of arbitrary and baneful exercise of authority, rather than by the *use* of it. It would seem to follow, therefore, that in the past this power was not used improperly—at least not improperly enough to have generated its own overthrow.

Carlyle will have none of this argument. As he sees it, kingship has declined in power, although it cannot be said that kingly power is being used less properly than was formerly the case, for the proper use of power never was a notable quality among European rulers. Thus the new attitude of the people toward their rulers is not necessarily to be seen as a reaction to hypothetically harsher conditions. Rather, a change in the world-historical perspective of the people as a whole has weakened the ideal of power, as manifested in the sovereignty of one man over another. The old order is no longer a legitimate order, in the Weberian sense that there no longer exists an inherent disposition among those subject to the order to accept the validity of its claims to authority.[18] Insofar as this is the case, the fabled incompetence of royal government under Louis XVI and the moribund condition of the aristocracy in the country are as much results as they are causes of the changed attitude of French citizens toward the sociopolitical hierarchy. Thus Carlyle, who does not mince words about how atrocious government was under Louis XVI, insists that the failure to govern does not account for the impending overthrow of the governing classes.

To be sure, if the atrophy of the old order's legitimacy meant that "the French Kingship had not, by course of Nature, long to live," it nevertheless can be said of Louis that "he of all men was the man to accelerate Nature." [19] This is neither here nor there, however, for the old order was caught in a vicious circle in which the absence of ascribed legitimacy meant that it was to a large extent powerless to act, which in turn led to an administrative chaos which further undermined faith in the legitimacy of the order. In this sense, Louis' notorious passivity was all too often an appropriate response to the situations in which he found himself, for there was in fact nothing to be done. "What could poor Louis do?" Carlyle asks. "Abdicate and wash his hands of it. . . ." The collapse of the ancien régime was coming in any case; at best a more capable king could have helped it collapse with more dignity. A statement the hapless monarch made to Madame de Hausset conveys the essence of his predicament: "If *I* were Lieutenant of Police, I would prohibit those Paris cabriolets." [20]

Of course, attributing the dilemma of the French governing classes to a loss of ascribed validity merely pushes the problem to be explained one step further back. What caused the decay of the legitimacy of their order? One common answer has been philosophism, the skeptical spirit. Carlyle, too, gives this answer: "Faith is gone out; Scepticism is come in" is his terse summary of the situation.[21] But it is important to note that Carlyle's use of this argument is markedly different from the uses to which it is most often put. In general, interpretations of the Revolution that emphasize the role of the philosophes have tended to be, to say the least, counterrevolutionary in their sympathies. Whenever one finds an emphasis on the importance of the philosophes as a causal factor in the Revolution, one usually finds it accompanied by a tendency to see the Revolution as a product of the spirit of intellectual adventurousness (or adventurism). Edmund Burke, who pushes this line of reasoning harder than anyone else, concludes that the perpetrators of the Revolution were monsters of ingratitude who were led to their excesses by the very liberality of the government they questioned. The government of Louis XVI, he tells us, "far from refusing itself to reformation, . . .

was open, with a censurable degree of facility, to all sorts of projects and projectors on the subject." [22] The revolutionaries, who had scarcely any legitimate grievances, were nonetheless dissatisfied with the prosperity of the economy, the happiness of the people, and the peace that reigned in civil society. These blessings merely whetted their appetites for more and led them to escalate their demands. Thus a government which existed "as much for the benefit of those whom it must leave in an humble state as those whom it is able to exalt to a condition more splendid, but not more happy," was destroyed by acts which must stand as "the sad, but instructive monuments of rash and ignorant counsel in time of profound peace." [23]

In dealing with such arguments, which in one form or another still dominate the literature on the French Revolution, one should proceed cautiously. When we consider that the *Encyclopédie* was commenced around midcentury, that Rousseau's major works came out in the sixties, and that Voltaire already was finishing his long career by then, we must begin to have doubts about the intimate connection posited between philosophism and the Revolution. Robespierre was four years old when the *Contrat social* was published, Danton three. It was in 1751, not 1789, that the marquis d'Argenson wrote in his *Mémoires*, "Everyone talks of a necessary and imminent revolution"; it was in 1757 that the Assembly of the Clergy bemoaned the fact "that in religion, morals and even politics the spirit of the times reveals a threat of revolution portending complete social destruction." [24] It is all very well to talk about ideas being planted in one generation and harvested in another, as though they were trees, but political movements are rarely led posthumously. It seems to make only slightly more sense to call the philosophes the architects of the Revolution than it would to see the sources of activism today in the works of Upton Sinclair.

Certainly I do not mean to imply that the radical critiques of the old regime leveled against it by the philosophes were without significance for the Revolution. It is widely known, for example, that an influential role in the Revolution was played by provincial lawyers, who, along with their legal training, had been heavily dosed with philosophism. But one must also bear in mind that these lawyers had given a good part of their practice to representing the claims of peasants and small landholders against their lords, and thus had come, by way of their careers rather than by way of philosophism, to entertain grave doubts about the validity of the rights enjoyed by the upper classes, to recognize the shakiness of some of these rights, and to be identified in terms of mutual interest with the lower orders that retained them. What is more, it is not completely clear that these lawyers were instigating their clients in such cases, for it may well have been that the peasants and smallholders who brought their lords to law provided the impetus for these actions. In either case, the existence of such lawsuits argues for the presence among the provincial population of both hostility toward the seigneurs and the courage to act on this hostility. Surely in this quarter there can be no doubt that the influence of the philosophes was negligible. There is no denying that philosophism helped to give a certain intellectual coherence to the critical positions adopted by the radical provincial lawyers of France, but an explanation of why it was able to do so, as well as of why common people who knew nothing whatever about the literary products of Paris salons should have followed or even led the lawyers in these efforts, must be sought in social history rather than in the intellectual content of philosophism itself. England, we may note, was not without its intellectual equivalent of philosophism, but, as the Hammonds observe, it had nothing like the French provincial lawyers.[25] Philosophism may have adumbrated the Revolution that was to come, but it seems that Michelet may have been speaking very much to the point when he declared: "All had foreseen the Revolution in the middle of the century. Nobody, at the end, believed in it. . . . O ye of little faith, do you not see that as long as it remained among you, philosophers, orators, sophists, it could do nothing?" [26]

Carlyle, it must be admitted, does not provide the analysis of French social history that alone can answer our questions about the early development of disloyal attitudes toward the ancien régime; indeed, considering where and when he was writing, it is hardly to be expected that he could have done so. Nevertheless, in marked contrast to the treatment of this matter by Burke and other counterrevolutionary historians, Carlyle's handling of the issue seems to be at all points informed by an awareness of the existence of social factors behind the rise of philosophism. The development of philosophism, he makes clear for perhaps the first time, must be seen as "the cardinal symptom of the whole widespread malady," but not as the malady itself and still less as the cause of the malady. According to Carlyle, the works of the philosophes essentially are a declaration "That a Lie cannot be believed!" and insofar as this is the case, he sees the intellectual habit of questioning the institutions of the old order as deriving from the presence of skeptical attitudes in society at large, rather than the reverse.[27] Philosophism may have propagandized the new skeptical spirit, but it could not have done so unless, to a considerable extent, its arguments were valid, and its arguments would not have been valid if there had not been already in existence a large measure of doubt about the legitimacy of the ancien régime. In short, the announcement by the philosophes that they could no longer believe a lie would have fallen on deaf ears if the old order were not in fact a lie; they could question the legitimacy of the old order precisely because its legitimacy had become questionable.

Once again we have come round in a circle, in which the decay of legitimacy is held responsible for the rise of the skeptical spirit and the rise of the skeptical spirit is cited in order to account for the decay of the old order's legitimacy. In a sense, then, Carlyle is calling a halt to historical explanation at this point. The various elements that together constitute France on the eve of the Revolution, he says in effect, are involved in a circularly causal system in which each element is to an extent the cause of its own causes. The king fails to govern, and thus breeds disbelief in the institution of kingship; but the king's failure stems from the fact that kingship is already an anachronism, something not to be believed in, and the king himself is an "incarnate Solecism."[28] The philosophes undermine faith in the sociopolitical institutions of France, creating the conditions they describe in the act of describing them. The poor grow poorer, and the peasants especially long to strike out against the absentee landlords who tax them severely while no longer providing the services of government in return; but the landlords have absented themselves from the land precisely because they no longer have any meaningful role to play there, having lost much of their feudal authority to the bureaucratic department administrations.[29]

Because of this complex situation, Carlyle does not rest his explanation of the origins of the Revolution on any of the hard facts of eighteenth-century France, whether political, economic, or intellectual. Rather, he focuses on the "soft" fact of a change in the world-historical disposition of forces. For this reason he is at pains to point out that the collapsing system of social relations is not unique to France, but is, on the contrary, a nearly universal phenomenon. As such, it is an expression of history itself, and therefore beyond historical explanation. As Louis XV lay dying in 1774, his ear could faintly hear the "muffled ominous [sounds], new in our centuries," coming from across the Atlantic. "Boston Harbour is black with unexpected Tea: behold a Pennsylvanian Congress gather; and ere long, on Bunker Hill, DEMOCRACY announcing, in rifle-volleys death-winged, under her Star Banner, to the tune of Yankee-doodle-doo, that she is born, and, whirlwind-like, will envelope the whole world!" [30]

2. *"An Eloquent Reminiscence"*

In Georges Lefebvre's two-volume history of the French Revolution, the phase which he terms the bourgeois revolution gets fourteen pages.[31] In Carlyle's account, the whole course of the Revolution, from the convocation of the Estates General until the fall of the Gironde in June 1793, is seen as rather thoroughly bourgeois.

When the Estates General convened in May 1789, the unresolved question of their constitution kept developments at a standstill for weeks. With ideological support from the duc d'Orléans' *Délibérations*, which insisted, in effect, that "The Third Estate is the Nation," and from the Abbé Sieyès' more famous pamphlet entitled *Qu'est-ce que le Tiers État?* the representatives of the Third finally broke the stalemate by declaring at Versailles on June 17, 1789, "that their name is not *Third Estate*, but—*National Assembly!*" [32] Louis XVI could not let this bold unilateral action go unanswered; on the twentieth of June, using a flimsy pretext, the king ordered the assembly hall used by the former Third Estate, now National Assembly, to be sealed off. The delegates, in a defiant mood, repaired to a nearby tennis court, where they took the celebrated oath and got down to business.

Again it took Louis three days to act, and by the time he came to address the full session of the Estates General, on the twenty-third, a large number of the clergy already had defected to the side of the Third. He offered the Estates a compromise of a sort: on the one hand, he declared that voting shall be by estates, which is what the Third passionately did not want; "On the other hand, France may look for considerable constitutional blessings; as specified in these Five-and-thirty Articles, which Garde-des-Sceaux is waxing hoarse with reading. Which Five-and-thirty Articles, adds his Majesty again rising, if the Three Orders most unfortunately cannot agree together to effect them, I myself will effect: *'seul je ferai le bien de mes peuples.'* . . ." In short, Louis voided the Third Estate's nomination of itself as a National Assembly and offered instead a quasi-constitutional monarchy, or at least a reformed absolute monarchy.

"And herewith King, retinue, Noblesse, majority of Clergy file out, as if the whole matter were satisfactorily completed. These file out; through grim-silent seas of people. Only the Commons Deputies file not out. . . ." [33]

Spurred by the oratory of the comte de Mirabeau, the commons deputies rejected the king's compromise, flatly turning down the thirty-five concessions which a few months earlier would have "filled France with a rejoicing, which might have lasted for several years." [34] Louis responded by turning out the liberal ministry of Jacques Necker and putting in its place a thoroughly reactionary ministry consisting of the duc de Broglie, the "War-god" who had recommended "a whiff of Grapeshot" as the sovereign remedy for popular disturbances; the baron de Breteuil; and Breteuil's father-in-law, Joseph-François Foulon, "who once when it was objected, to some finance-scheme of his, 'What will the people do?'—made answer, in the fire of discussion, 'The people may eat grass.'. . ." [35] The news of this change in ministries became public on July 12, and on the thirteenth Paris, whipped to a frenzy by the cafe oratory of Camille Desmoulins, was in violent rebellion, which culminated in the fall of the Bastille two days later and the invention of an ingenious new use for streetlamp brackets: Foulon, his mouth stuffed with grass, was one of the first to die so.[36] From Louis came the famous exchange with Liancourt which, better than anything else, captures this poor man's inability to comprehend what was going on around him: " '*Mais*,' said poor Louis, '*c'est une révolte*, Why, that is a revolt!'—'Sire,' answered Liancourt, 'it is not a revolt,—it is a revolution.' " [37]

The rising of Paris and the fall of the Bastille thwarted the king at the very moment when he finally had begun to move against the Third Estate and its National Assembly. Thus the bourgeois revolution was saved from defeat by the intervention of the Parisian sans-culottes. It is for this reason that Lefebvre, and most historians with him, date the events of July 13–15 as the end of the bourgeois revolution, inasmuch as whatever authority the Third Estate subsequently enjoyed was based always on the revolutionary muscle of the Fourth.[38]

There is, of course, much to be said for dating the end of the bourgeois phase of the Revolution with the July uprising. Indeed, Carlyle admits one of the main premises behind this historical convention: "the truth is, Patriotism [i.e., the revolutionary movement of the Third Estate] throughout, were it never so white-frilled, logical, respectable, must either lean itself heartily on Sansculottism, the black, bottomless; or else vanish, in the frightfulest way, to Limbo!" [39] But there is a thoroughly different emphasis in Carlyle's account, which is important and perhaps fundamental. Quite simply, the issue here is whether one is to see the Revolution as a popular revolution which the bourgeoisie managed to direct to its own liking, or as a bourgeois revolution which was able to call upon and exploit the revolutionary force of the sansculottic underclass. Carlyle's decision on this matter is clear: neither the year of centralist government under Lafayette nor the convoluted developments of the years during which the Constituent and Legislative Assemblies and the National Convention directed the destiny of France have for him the earmarks of a popular revolution. Only with the fall of the Gironde in June 1793 can the popular revolution, properly so called, be said to begin. Inasmuch as this is the case, the general shape of the Revolution as Carlyle sees it is markedly different from that to be found in liberal and even left-liberal accounts, while it is quite similar to the Revolution as seen through the eyes of a far-left anarchist like Peter Kropotkin, whose judgments throughout his own history of the Revolution are often strikingly like Carlyle's.[40]

Perhaps the most easily recognizable manifestation of this difference between Carlyle and the liberal historians is to be found in their respective treatments of the relationship between the Third and Fourth Estates in the early years of the Revolution. Liberal historians tend to see a very real alliance between these classes, and to see the Revolution, therefore, as a series of developments in which these two social groups work together with common aims until a rupture develops when the underclass attempts to push the Revolution further than the bourgeoisie is willing to go. Indeed, in his *Anatomy of Revolution* Crane Brinton has elevated this scenario to the status of a Law of History: what begins as a "honeymoon" period, in which all classes to the left of the court troglodytes share common aims, ends when the lower classes finally radicalize themselves out beyond the Revolution.[41] Carlyle, in contrast, is very careful to point out that from the start the Third and Fourth Estates had little in common except their hostility to the ancien régime, and that what Brinton was to call the "honeymoon" was merely a moment of domestic tranquility in something that was never more than a highly unstable marriage of convenience. Even before the Estates General met in the spring of 1789, Carlyle contends, to the "Poor Lackalls [of the Fourth Estate] . . . it is clear only that eleutheromaniac Philosophism has yet baked no bread; that Patriot Commit-tee-men will level down to their own level, and no lower." [42]

A few months later, in October 1789, the gulf that separated the bourgeoisie from the sansculottes opened perceptibly when the con-stitutionalist Patrols were forced to declare martial law in order to control the Paris mob, and from this point on the hostility between the two classes that are commonly said to have made the Revolution together was never to be absent from the picture. With his charac-teristic flair for making his points by seizing on particularly repre-sentative moments, Carlyle focuses on the "Day of the Poignards" to underline the fact that the Revolution is not to be seen as the work of two classes—the bourgeoisie and the sansculottes—united against the ancien régime; rather, it is a complex struggle in-volving shifting alliances between three mutually irreconcilable forces. On February 28, 1791, the Paris sansculottes rose and attacked the castle of Vincennes, a Paris prison. Lafayette put down this re-bellion and was still in the streets being hailed as a hero by the con-stitutionalist moderates when word reached him that the National Guard had discovered concealed weapons on the persons of the king's courtiers at Versailles. An ugly scene developed in which the aristocracy was rather roughly handled, and Lafayette rushed imme-diately to Versailles, this time to soothe the National Guard and re-buke the aristocracy. "Thus . . . has the reader seen," Carlyle writes at the end of his narrative of these events, "in an unexpected arena, on this last day of February 1791, the Three long-contending ele-ments of French Society dashed forth into singular comico-tragical collision; acting and reacting openly to the eye. Constitutionalism, at once quelling Sansculottic riot at Vincennes, and Royalist treach-ery in the Tuileries, is great, this day, and prevails. As for poor Royalism, tossed to and fro in that manner, its daggers all left in a heap, what can one think of it? Every dog, the Adage says, has its day: *has* it; has had it; or will have it. For the present, the day is La-fayette's and the Constitution's. Nevertheless Hunger and Jacobin-ism, fast growing fanatical, still work; their day, were they once fanatical, will come." [43]

Indeed, the day for Jacobinism will come after the forces of constitutionalism, of bourgeois revolution, have had theirs and have proven themselves unequal to it. From the moment the Con-stituent Assembly was formed in August 1789 it was faced with the tricky task of dismounting from the tiger it had ridden so far. Four years were spent in drafting a constitution or in trying to make one work. "And such a Constitution; little short of miraculous: one that shall 'consolidate the Revolution'! The Revolution is finished, then? Mayor Bailly and all respectable friends of Freedom would fain think so. Your Revolution, like jelly sufficiently *boiled*, needs only to be poured into *shapes*, of Constitution, and 'consolidated' therein? Could it, indeed, contrive to *cool;* which last, however, is precisely the doubtful thing, or even the not doubtful!" [44]

Cooling the Revolution was to prove a long, arduous, and ultimately impossible task for the bourgeois moderates. In the fall of 1792, after a tortuous history which it is not necessary to trace here, the issue came down to a life-and-death struggle between the constitutionalist Gironde party and the radical Jacobins, or the Mountain, as their parliamentary wing was called, who had over the course of these years become more and more outspokenly the political arm of the Paris sansculotterie. The moderates had failed time after time. In the first place, they were unable to solve the chronic financial crisis of the French government, which had proven itself insoluble over the course of more than half a century. And second, except insofar as they had been able to exploit the mob and the radical representatives to whom the mob would listen, they were unable to mobilize France in the face of Prussian and Austrian invasion. "The truth is, if our Gironde Friends had an understanding of it, where were French Patriotism, with all its eloquence, at this moment, had *not* that same great Nether Deep, of Bedlam, Fanaticism and Popular wrath and madness, risen unfathomable on the Tenth of August? French Patriotism were an eloquent Reminiscence; swinging on Prussian gibbets." [45]

Even as the Austrian armies moved across the frontiers of France, the Gironde-led Assembly could do no more than deal in "Formulas, Philosophies, Respectabilities, what has been written in Books, and admitted by the Cultivated Classes: *this* inadequate *Scheme* of Nature's working is all that Nature, let her work as she will, can reveal to these men. So they perorate and speculate; and call on the Friends of Law, when the question is not Law or No-Law, but Life or No-Life." [46] In the final analysis, their failure was inevitable from the start: their philosophism could bake no bread, and in fact did not even try to. Their efforts, rather, were bent toward exploiting the revolutionary energy of the lower classes, "those brethren whom one often hears of under the collective name of 'the masses,' as if they were not persons at all, but mounds of combustible explosive material, for blowing down Bastilles with!" [47] The leaders of the bourgeois revolution, like Louis before them, had become "solecisms": "they and their Formula are incompatible with the Reality: and, in its dark wrath, the Reality will extinguish it and them!" [48]

After the Paris sections revolted against the Assembly in June 1793, the Gironde was all but dead. Its fled ministers attempted to rally at Caen, a stronghold of constitutionalist sentiment which sent forth Charlotte Corday to martyr herself and Marat. When the constitutionalists in Lyons broke into open civil war against the Revolution, their struggle served only to rally what was left of royalism, for the situation was by then so thoroughly polarized that any force leveled against the Jacobins was a force leveled on behalf of the royalist reactionaries. Yet even this effort collapsed, for "it turns out that Respectabilities, though they will vote, will not fight." [49] Only at this point can the popular revolution be said to begin, for only at this point can the people begin to attempt to establish a revolutionary order, the purpose of which was, they had known all along, to bake bread.

3. "Sansculottism Accoutred"

If it may be said that Carlyle's distrustful critique of the bourgeois-constitutionalist phase of the Revolution put him in a good position for developing a radical analysis of the Revolution—and, by extension, of modern society—it also is unfortunately true that he did not in fact realize the promise held out by such beginnings. For, the moment we turn to his conception of the lower classes and of their role in society and in the Revolution, we enter an area that is at once illuminated by some of his finest insights and obscured by his most persistent blindnesses.

With the fall of the Gironde in June 1793 the direction of the Revolution passed, albeit indirectly, to the hands of the sansculottic underclass. To be sure, proletarians did not gain control of the National Convention, nor did the extreme left Enragés, who undoubtedly were the faction closest to the sentiments of the Paris sections, succeed in coming to power. It was, rather, the Montagnard (Mountain) faction, made up mostly of lawyers from the Jacobin clubs, that inherited the mantle of the discredited Gironde. The Montagnards were a bourgeois party whose primary commitments ran in much the same direction as those of the Girondins they replaced—that is, toward the principles of a free economy and the protection of property. Unlike the Gironde, however, the Mountain was far from doctrinaire on this point. When, in the face of the rising prices and the bad harvests of 1792, the Parisian and provincial sansculottes had begun to reassert their perennial demand for the imposition of price controls on grain and other necessities (the famed "Maximum"), the Jacobins showed themselves flexible enough to take the popular side; and when rioters in Orléans seized the local markets and established their own de facto maximum, the Jacobin Club of Orléans issued circulars supporting their actions, for which they earned the censure of the Girondin minister of the interior, Jean-Marie Roland.[50]

The Montagnards came by their flexibility—or opportunism—primarily because they were led by Maximilien de Robespierre, a superb opportunist who, as Albert Mathiez remarks, "was no visionary, but had a strong sense of reality and followed the slightest manifestations of public opinion with close attention. . . ."[51] Under Robespierre's direction, the Jacobin clubs and the Montagnard faction in the Convention came increasingly to represent the desires of the Paris sansculottes. On April 15, 1793, thirty-five of the forty-eight Paris sections brought to the Convention a petition directed against twenty-two prominent Girondins, and nine days later the Montagnards forgot about their principled objections to trade restrictions and "openly joined with the sans-culottes of the sections and the Cordeliers [a revolutionary club at this point in the hands of radical extremists] in supporting the controlled economy."[52]

With this sort of mutual cooperation—the Montagnards proclaiming themselves in favor of the sansculottic demand for price controls and the sansculottes supporting the Mountain in its parliamentary struggle against the Gironde—the Revolution moved into its popular phase. To be sure, there would be some foot-dragging among the bourgeois politicians now cast, by exigency if by nothing more, into the role of political representatives of the Fourth Estate; but it is nonetheless safe to say that by the time Robespierre had completed his purge of the Girondins in the Convention, the Revolution belonged for all practical purposes to the sansculottes. Hence Peter Kropotkin's judgment that "This period, which lasted from May 31, 1793, to July 27, 1794 (9th Thermidor of the Year II. of the Republic), represents the most important period of the whole Revolution. The great changes in the relations between citizens, the programme which the Assembly had sketched during the night of August 4, 1789, were, after four years of resistance, at last carried out by the purified Convention, under the pressure of the popular revolution. And it was the people—the *sans-culottes*—who not only forced the Convention to legislate in this way, after they had given it the power of doing so by the insurrection of May 31; but it was also they who put these measures into execution locally, by means of the popular societies to whom the commissioned members of the Convention applied, when they had to create local executive power." [53]

If the sansculottes did not come directly into power in June 1793, they were unquestionably the most potent (if not the only potent) political force in France—as they virtually had been from the earliest days of the Revolution. Carlyle's history reflects this fact in the sharp focus with which it always watches the doings of the revolutionary underclass, and for Carlyle the French Revolution means the popular revolution above all else. On his pages the activities of the various bourgeois factions in the Constituent Assembly, the Legislative Assembly, and finally the National Convention are shadowy motions which cease to matter the moment they fail to reflect the revolution unfolding in the streets. "[T]he History of France, one finds, is seldom or never there," he says of these assemblies, for if the Revolution established anything it was that henceforth history would be made out of doors.[54]

The Paris mob first enters Carlyle's history in September 1788 when the king agreed to end the unpopular ministry of Archbishop Loménie de Brienne and to replace him with the liberal Jacques Necker. In a carnival spirit, "Rascality" took to the streets of Paris in celebration. After three days of this public tumult, an overreactive cavalry officer led a charge into the mob, leaving "a great many killed and wounded." For the time being at least, "Rascality is brushed back into its dim depths, and the streets are swept clear," providing a few months of quiet and a pause for reflection. "A Wonder and new Thing," Carlyle says of this mob: "as yet gamboling merely, in awkward Brobdingnag sport, not without quaintness; hardly in anger: yet in his huge half-vacant laugh lurks a shade of grimness,—which could unfold itself!" [55]

In fact, however, these prepolitical "gambolings" of the mob are hardly a "Wonder and new Thing" at all. Carlyle is here falling into the trap of reading history backward, of reading into the events of September 1788 the meaning which subsequently will "unfold itself" in the course of the Revolution. In phrases which anticipate the words he later will use to characterize the Chartist movement, he captures accurately enough the prepolitical quality of this popular demonstration: "as yet gamboling merely, in awkward

Brobdingnag sport" points to the unfocused energy of such a movement, exigent so far as it knows what it wants, but diffuse, easily denied, lacking the grimness that will come with the development of a deeper sense of what is needful. But if one does not look at September 1788 with the hindsight afforded by the subsequent development of just such a deeper political sense, one will see a scene which is in fact no novelty at all. The eighteenth century was far from unfamiliar with the urban mob, which, E. J. Hobsbawm writes, "may be defined as the movement of all classes of the urban poor for the achievement of economic or political changes by direct action—that is by riot and rebellion—but as a movement which was as yet inspired by no specific ideology. . . ." [56]

In seeing the mob as a "new Thing," Carlyle is measuring by the standards of the fully evolved, politically conscious street movement of a later phase of revolutionary history. His judgment, therefore, is accurate only insofar as it refers to the extent to which this mob foreshadows that into which it will "unfold itself." The problem with this view is that in seeing the mob's actions in terms of the political consciousness which is to come, one tends to ignore the long and distinguished pedigree of popular direct action in European history. Mob actions—generally in the form of food riots and price-fixing seizures of markets—punctuate the history of eighteenth-century England and France, but there is no sense of this in Carlyle, who seems to have subscribed, along with all other nineteenth-century British historians, to the erroneous belief that the French Revolution saw the first emergence of the *menu peuple* out of their homes and onto the historical stage. The enormity of the distortion created by this misinterpretation of the recent past becomes strikingly clear when one considers that the British historian's own side of the channel was even more used to mob actions than France, for England was, as Gwyn A. Williams has observed, "pre-eminently the country of the eighteenth-century mob. It is often difficult, in the ill-policed England of the squires, to find a year free from mob outbreaks." [57] George Rudé, who has made invaluable studies of mob action in France and Britain before the Revolution, claims to have found records of no fewer than 275 outbreaks of rioting in the last two thirds of the eighteenth century, and one is hardly inclined to doubt his figures when one observes that the *Annual Register* of 1766 lists forty separate outbreaks of food rioting in England for that one year alone, ranging from enforced sales to confiscations, destruction of mills, scattering of provisions, and even one case of "general insurrection" at Norwich.[58] George Orwell's Ministry of Truth hardly could have done a better job of rewriting history than was done by the generation of historians who turned an age of chronic disturbance into what Burke described as a "time of profound peace."

Thus, writing at a time when the eighteenth century had come to seem like an age of remarkable serenity, a pastoral age toward which those who were living through the industrial revolution could look back nostalgically, Carlyle seems totally ignorant of the extensive "prepolitical" activities of the lower classes throughout the eighteenth century in England and on the Continent.[59] What is more, he undoubtedly was aided in falling into this error by the fact that in doing so he was in perfect accord with the liberal and the Hegelian readings of history, both of which tended to imagine that before the French Revolution "the People" were much more docile than in fact they were.

One can readily see why the Hegelian and liberal versions of history, both of which define historical progress as the gradual dissemination downward of freedom and of political self-consciousness, should tend to give short shrift to the tradition of popular direct action. "The History of the world is none other than the progress of the consciousness of Freedom," Hegel proclaimed in the Introduction to the work in which he traced this progress from the freedom of one all-powerful individual through the freedom of a more numerous ruling class, to the freedom of all—the freedom of "man *as man.*"[60] Obviously, if man *as man*—that is, propertyless man— is to begin gesticulating about his rights before the bourgeoisie properly gets into the picture, the Hegelian scenario will not work; the riots of the poor throughout the eighteenth century, regardless of whether or not one terms them "prepolitical," are like the entrance of so many actors onstage before their cue, and of course they are an embarrassment to the playwright.

What is more, if the premature appearance of popular political action is an embarrassment to Hegelians, it is an even more profound shock to bourgeois liberals, for this tradition of food and market disturbances calls into question the entire liberal conception of freedom—not just who fought for it when, but what in fact it is. When liberal historians speak of freedom, they mean thereby the liberation of society from all the "irrational" accretions of use and wont which were handed down from the remote, medieval past. In the areas of religion, government, aesthetics, law, and morality, the

English liberal rationalists launched an all-out attack on the superstitions, prejudices, stupidities, and follies that kept mankind from using the rational accountancy of the principle of utility to realize its own desires. In the works of the rationalist writers, as Jeremy Bentham said of his own works, "men at large were invited to break loose from the trammels of authority and ancestor-wisdom. . . ."[61] Especially in the field of economics, the followers of Bentham worked toward realizing such a conception of freedom, and as a result the "free market" is the beginning and end of the liberal conception of freedom: a free market in labor for workers and employers, a free market in goods for merchants and customers, a free market in ideas for consumers and vendors of intellection.

Yet if this is what freedom meant, this is precisely what the lower classes wanted to have nothing to do with, from their first stirrings at eighteenth-century markets down into the twentieth century. As workers they fought not for freedom of contract, but for the traditional protections of laboring men. Far from seeking to "break loose from the trammels of authority," it was for enforcement of the "ancestor-wisdom" embodied in the Elizabethan apprenticeship statutes that they petitioned Parliament. An early nineteenth-century deposition from the handloom weavers, at the time the most numerous class of industrial workers, supplies the following testimony: "The Weavers, urged by the difficulties with which they were surrounded, took means of laying their case before the Legislature and humbly prayed for protection from the ruin which threatened to overwhelm them, they suggested the utility of fixing a minimum on the price of their Labour but their petitions were of no use to them and their application of no avail, the Weavers then imagined that if the apprentice Law was enforced it might be of some benefit to their trade by restraining the influx of hands, but as soon as they attempted to have recourse to this measure the apprentice Law was entirely abrogated."[62]

Moreover, just as it was not anything a liberal would recognize as freedom that the eighteenth- and nineteenth-century laborers sought in their capacity as workers, so it was not a so-called "free market" for which they struggled in their capacity as consumers. The majority of popular disturbances in the eighteenth century involved rioting in the local markets, followed by seizure of the stores of forestallers and enforced sale at customary prices. "Such 'riots' were popularly regarded as acts of justice, and their leaders held as heroes," E. P. Thompson writes. "In most cases they culminated in the enforced sale of provisions at the customary or popular price, analogous to the French 'taxation populaire', the proceeds being given to the owners." Such outbreaks grew in frequency and intensity through the eighteenth century, the final years of which saw the "last desperate effort by the people to reimpose the older moral economy as against the economy of the free market." [63] A fair market, not a free market, was what they demanded, just as their proletarian offspring were to spurn the offer of free trade in labor and call instead for a fair day's wages.

The fact of the matter is that the liberal-Hegelian myth of the broadening down of a consciousness of freedom from class to class has no basis in reality, if one understands the word "freedom" in the sense the liberals mean. That conception of freedom which could allow John Stuart Mill, who is certainly an authentic spokesman for the liberal creed, to defend the practices of forestallers in grain was exactly what the growing political consciousness of the working classes had to set itself against.[64] Indeed, in France the sansculottes pushed Robespierre and the Jacobins into establishing the notorious Maximum in order to *undo* the free trade which the bourgeois revolution had established and to reassert the price controls which had existed under the ancien régime.

Thus, it makes perfect sense for liberal historians to pass over the manifestations of social activism among the lower classes in the eighteenth century, for by doing so they can assimilate the ultimate mobilization of the sansculotterie to their own conception of historical evolution. But why does Carlyle, too, dwell on the newness of the mob as a political force? Certainly he had little interest in shoring up the myths of rationalist liberalism.

The answer, I believe, lies in Carlyle's conception of what and who the sansculottic classes were, and especially in his sense of their role in the Revolution. At the beginning of the Sixth Book of the first volume of his *History*, Carlyle pauses to define the Revolution, and the passage in which he does so will bear close attention:

Here perhaps is the place to fix, a little more precisely, what these two words, *French Revolution*, shall mean; for, strictly considered, they have as many meanings as there are speakers of them. All things are in revolution; in change from moment to moment, which becomes sensible from epoch to epoch: in this Time-World of ours there is properly nothing else but revolution and mutation, and even nothing else conceivable. Revolution, you answer, means *speedier* change. Whereupon one has still to ask: How speedy? At what degree of speed; in what particular points of this variable course, which varies in velocity, but can never stop till Time itself stops, does revolution begin and end; cease to be ordinary mutation, and again become such? It is a thing that will depend on definition more or less arbitrary.

For ourselves, we answer that French Revolution means here the open violent Rebellion, and Victory, of disimprisoned Anarchy against corrupt worn-out Authority: how Anarchy breaks prison; bursts-up from the infinite Deep, and rages uncontrollable, immeasurable, enveloping a world; in phasis after phasis of fever-frenzy;—till the frenzy burning itself out, and what elements of new Order it held (since all Force holds such) developing themselves, the Uncontrollable be got, if not reimprisoned, yet harnessed, and its mad forces made to work towards their object as sane regulated ones. For as Hierarchies and Dynasties of all kinds, Theocracies, Aristocracies, Autocracies, Strumpetocracies, have ruled over the world; so it was appointed, in the decrees of Providence, that this same Victorious Anarchy, Jacobinism, Sansculottism, French Revolution, Horrors of French Revolution, or what else mortals name it, should have its turn. The 'destructive wrath' of Sansculottism: this is what we speak, having unhappily no voice for singing.[65]

If one picks one's way through this passage carefully enough, the following account of the ontology of revolution emerges: an Order or Structure (Authority) is attacked by a Force (Anarchy, whose presence in Carlyle's writings is often signaled by images of fire). Revolution is the name of this process. One should note that the force is by definition anarchic and the structure is by definition ordered; this is not a matter of value judgment, for Carlyle never makes any claims about the moral worth of the order. The revolutionary process then leaves as a residue a new structure, in connection with which the important point to be noted is that this new structure was somehow implicit in the force which destroyed the old structure rather than in the old structure itself. This conception is strikingly unlike the conservative model of revolution, which maintains that one social structure can derive only from another, so that the principles of any new order must be derivable from the old. Hence Edmund Burke condemned the revolutionary process on the ground that, in thoroughly destroying the old order, it eliminated the possibility of a new; and hence the pains Tocqueville took to show that the achievements of the Revolution were all latent in the ancien régime. Carlyle, on the other hand, never imagines a social or political structure to be anything but a precipitate of force or energy—society being for him, as I have observed repeatedly, the pattern of the ways in which men act and interact with each other. Thus for Carlyle it is only through revolutionary force that a new order can emerge at all.

Yet, although the Revolution is to be seen as the process in which the old structure of authority is consumed by the fire-force of anarchy, and although the "elements of new Order" are implicit in that anarchic fire-force, nevertheless Carlyle insists that the revolutionary process is not identical with the new order. Only after the anarchic force of the Revolution has been dissipated can the residue of order it contained manifest itself as a new social structure. In other words, although the new social order is in some sense to be derived from the sansculottes, it is not to be a sansculottic order—that is to say, it is not to be a replacement of the governing committee of the first three estates with a governing committee of the fourth. Like Proudhon, who declared that "It is a contradiction in terms to say that a government can be revolutionary, for the simple reason that it is the government," Carlyle held that it was a paradox to erect the force of the Revolution into a principle of order.[66]

Using the "Clothes Philosophy" he had developed to such elaborate lengths in *Sartor Resartus*, Carlyle worked out an iconology in which clothes stand as the symbolic realization of the actual structure of society. In this extended metaphor the ancien régime, as an order which once in fact reflected social reality but now no longer does, is a worn out suit of clothes; similarly, the various bourgeois constitutionalist parties which attempt to regenerate French society by drafting a new constitution appear as men who offer merely the design for a suit of clothes, which they hope to pass off as the suit itself. And the sansculottes are, as their name implies, precisely the unclothed, the "Destitute-of-Breeches." Theirs is "a mournful Destitution; which however, if Twenty millions share it, may become more effective than most Possessions!"[67] But precisely because their effectiveness derives from the absence of the "Cloth-habits" which symbolize social organization, it cannot be the basis of a social order.

As a result of this inability to find in the anarchistic force of the sansculottes a possible model for the new ordering of society, Carlyle seems to be analyzing half of the Revolution in class terms while seeing the other half in some terms other than those of class. Thus he speaks of the Girondin deputies both as representatives of a social class (the bourgeoisie) and as promulgators of the political system of that class (bourgeois liberalism); in contrast, the Montagnards, insofar as they are the representatives of the sansculottes, are champions of "anarchy," by which Carlyle means that they have no political system to promulgate.

In this sense, Carlyle has accomplished a difficult feat of political insight and then balked at what is almost an inevitable corollary of it. On the one hand, he is never deluded by the law-and-order rhetoric of the Girondin ministers into imagining that they were talking about anything other than a class hegemony. When the bourgeoisie strives to contain the Revolution in the name of order, Carlyle makes perfectly clear that what they are talking about is really only a bourgeois order; when they talk of the "reign of Law and Liberty," he takes care to point out that they mean only law and liberty "according as the habits, persuasions and endeavours of the educated, moneyed, respectable class prescribe." [68] To recognize, as he does, that what passes for order in a bourgeois world is merely the order of a particular class is not a small achievement. But on the other hand, once he has perceived this fact Carlyle does not go on to see the actions of the sansculottes as tending toward anything that could be called a sansculottic order. His account of the Revolution recognizes the existence of a class government of the bourgeoisie; it recognizes—and is indeed openly partisan of—the class struggle of the sansculottes to overthrow such a government; but it categorically denies the possibility of a class government of the sansculottes.

There can be, Carlyle contends, no such thing as a sansculottic order—that is, a society organized in terms of the class hegemony of the sansculottes—because the sansculottes are, properly speaking, not a social class at all. In a society which divided itself into three estates, they were the fourth. Carlyle, who was both living in and writing about social orders which tended to see citizenship more as an attribute of property than as an attribute of personality, recognized that in a very real sense the propertyless are outside of such a society and that to describe them as though they were merely the "lower" class within the social structure would not adequately reflect their relationship to a social system whose operant principle is not so much one of hierarchy as it is one of exclusion.

But even while we acknowledge the realism of Carlyle's perception of the social position of the Fourth Estate, we also must admit that there is a significant failure here. A thinker of the first importance, it seems to me, in principle should not have been limited by the definitions of social reality that were given to him, and it goes without saying that Carlyle's work would have been far more satisfying if at this point he could have redefined the elements which constitute society in such a way as to circumvent such exclusivistic ideas. But at the same time we should recognize the magnitude of the task involved in such a redefinition; indeed, even Marx, who came closer to accomplishing this task than any other radical thinker of the nineteenth century, is not completely free of such exclusivism, as we can see from the fact that the Marxist definition of class primarily in terms of one's relation to the means of production, rather than in terms of property, tends to leave the considerable bulk of the Lumpenproletariat outside of the social structure in much the same way as the bourgeois definition excludes the sansculottes.

Furthermore, it must be said on Carlyle's behalf that his sense that sansculottism is categorically incapable of providing the principle upon which a new social order can be built is coupled with a vivid, almost visionary sense of the role the sansculottes must play in creating that order. They are, after all, the center of his history, and it is their strength as well as their fury that he celebrates; "these people," he wrote, in a remarkable turn of phrase, "are not without ferocity; they have sinews and indignation." [69] For Carlyle the relationship between the revolutionary force of the sansculottes and the new social order they are to help build can be expressed only in terms of paradoxes, just as his ontology of revolution is expressed in the paradoxical postulate that the postrevolutionary order must derive from the anarchic force that destroyed the old order while at the same time it must be—simply by virtue of the fact that it is an order at all—the very antithesis of that anarchic force.

Intimately acquainted with paradox as a result of his instinctive perception of the principle of the satanic-divine at work in the universe, Carlyle quite naturally came to see the goal of the Revolution as both a realization and a repudiation of sansculottic force. Indeed, it was the universal condition of man to be engaged in a perpetual struggle against the anarchic forces of nature—both the world's and his own—in which any too thorough victory was no less surely fatal than defeat. Were man to end this struggle once and for all by rooting out all remnants in him of "Nature's waste inorganic Deep, which men name Orcus, Chaos, primeval Night," [70] he would perish by Inanity—the name Carlyle gives to the fatal condition that results from the atrophy of our taproots into reality. Were he, on the other hand, to permit the triumph of untamed nature, he would perish in the explosion of the "powder-mines of bottomless guilt and criminality" that lie at the deepest level of his psyche.[71]

Using the resonant language of oxymoron to express this conception of the relationship between man and society and its application to the case of the sansculottes and the French Revolution, Carlyle defines the new order toward which the Revolution is tending as "Sansculottism Accoutred." [72] It is imperative that the fire-force of sansculottism be negated, he says, for it is "a thing *without* order, a thing proceeding from beyond and beneath the region of order." [73] Yet it is no less imperative that it be in some sense preserved, for it is "a genuine outburst of Nature; issuing from, or communicating with, the deepest deep of Nature. When so much goes grinning and grimacing as a lifeless Formality, and under the stiff buckram no heart can be felt beating, here once more, if nowhere else, is a Sincerity and Reality." [74]

4. The Reign of Terror

Carlyle discerns the first signs that sansculottism has begun its evolution toward "a new singular system of Culottism" in the birth of the Committee of Public Safety in March 1793.[75] "An insignificant-looking thing at first, this Committee, but with a principle of growth in it," he comments, for it is through this committee that sansculottism begins to reify itself as an institution and that the anarchic force of the Revolution begins to crystallize out as a structure of order.[76] "[T]he Anarchy, we may say, has *organised* itself," Carlyle observes, noting that it has done so without losing its connection with the elemental anarchy of nature—that is, without becoming estranged from the existential reality that gave it its strength.[77]

It is, Carlyle realizes, tragically inevitable that what he calls the organization of anarchy—that is, the institutionalization of the primal energies of man—will take shape as an institutionalized form of violence. Yet Carlyle boldly refuses to condemn the Reign of Terror: "We, for our part, find it more edifying to know, one good time, that this Republic and National Tigress *is* a New-Birth; a Fact of Nature among Formulas, in an Age of Formulas. . . . But the Fact, let all men observe, is a genuine and sincere one; the sincerest of Facts; terrible in its sincerity, as very Death. Whatsoever is equally sincere may front it, and beard it, but whatsoever is *not?*—" [78]

One cannot but be struck by the audacity of the way in which Carlyle deals with the Terror. Among English intellectuals and men of letters, the French Revolution had been virtually without defenders from the moment it passed beyond its bourgeois phase, and many who were friends of the Revolution in 1789 changed their tune in 1793. Even the radical political clubs, such as the Friends of Revolution, whose letter of congratulation to the French National Assembly in 1790 had stirred Burke to respond with his *Reflections*, withdrew their support when events in France escalated to regicide; thereafter respectable "radicals," who remained staunch in defense of their own prerogatives and militant in the struggle for their own rights, were very careful to distinguish between reform and revolution, and to dissociate themselves from the latter. Only among the working classes—indeed, only among the advanced and articulate sections of the working classes—did the French Revolution continue to serve as a talisman, guide, and hope, as it so notably did in the case of the Chartist-Marxist George Julian Harney, who styled himself the "Friend of the People" and strove to emulate Marat in all the details of his career, and in the case of Bronterre O'Brien, who claimed to have learned much from Saint-Just.[79]

Thus, when one considers the fact that the Revolution of 1793 was without literary apologists until the writing of Carlyle's history, one becomes aware of the courage Carlyle showed in taking the stand he did. Indeed, even his closest friends denounced him publicly for it. In an essay on Carlyle's writings which appeared in the *London and Westminster Review* in 1839, John Sterling called Carlyle's treatment of the Terror "wretchedly perverse" and declared that it was a symptom of Carlyle's "hatred for things as they are, showing itself in cool mockery at their destruction, and in joy at manifestations, however monstrous, of the will to destroy them. . . ."[80]

In his attempts to depict the Terror as other than the inexcusable monstrosity popular opinion held it to be, Carlyle takes many lines of approach. The most elementary of his arguments simply points out that those who condemn the Terror generally are people who do not recognize that over the course of history the balance of terror has been on the side of the ruling classes. The mob, he admits, is not innocent of atrocities: "Thus have there been, especially by vehement tempers reduced to a state of desperation, very miserable things done." But fairness demands that the other side of the ledger be kept always open: "Kings themselves, not in desperation, but only in difficulty, have sat hatching, for year and day, . . . their Bartholomew Business. . . . Nay the same black boulder-stones of these Paris Prisons have seen Prison-massacres before now. . . ."[81] In the same vein Carlyle bids us remember that the death toll of the Terror is a mere fraction of the number sent to die in a single meaningless war. "It is not far from the two-hundredth part of what perished in the entire Seven-Years War. By which Seven-Years War, did not the great Fritz wrench Silesia from the great Theresa . . . ?" [82]

Of course, Carlyle is well aware that this sort of moral arithmetic, which merely weighs atrocities on one side against those on the other, is ethically rather worthless, but it is, he maintains, clearly preferable to the hypocrisy of bourgeois historians who are moved to pity at executions of the *noblesse* while their chronicles scarcely record the far more numerous deaths of soldiers in time of war. Indeed, Carlyle repeatedly insists that it is merely class bias that leads respectable people into denouncing the horrors of the French Revolution, which took the lives of aristocrats and men of property, while accepting the morality of warfare, which takes the lives of the underclass from whom the soldiery is drawn. The Revolution is, Carlyle claims, simply a form of warfare—albeit a new form, class warfare. Morally it is no more defensible than warfare, but by the same token it is no less so. "Fell Slaughter, one of the most authentic products of the Pit you would say, once give it Customs, becomes War, with Laws of War; and is Customary and Moral enough; and red individuals carry the tools of it girt round their haunches, not without an air of pride,—which do thou nowise blame. While, see! so long as it is but dressed in hodden or russet; and Revolution, less frequent than War, has not yet got its Laws of Revolution, but the hodden or russet individuals are Uncustomary—O shrieking beloved brother blockheads of Mankind, let us close those wide mouths of ours; let us cease shrieking, and begin considering!" [83]

Although Carlyle vigorously defends the Terror from the narrow, class-based attacks of respectable horrified onlookers, he is not therefore willing simply to condone such carnage. Not being disposed to value the lives of the *noblesse* more highly than those of the poor, he will not judge the Terror in terms other than those used in judging warfare; but, not being a pacifist, he will not categorically denounce the destruction wrought by this terrible act of war, although he recognizes its hideous wastefulness. In sum, he deals with the Reign of Terror by insisting that humane moral judgments be separated from sociopolitical judgments, at least to the extent that the latter not be permitted to masquerade as the former. For the victims of Terror as living human beings he feels genuine pity; "at bottom," he writes, "it is not the King dying, but the man." For the man Carlyle expresses sincere though limited sympathy, but for the king his judgment is most harsh indeed: "It is ever so; and thou shouldst know it, O haughty tyrannous man: injustice breeds injustice; curses and falsehoods do verily return, 'always *home*,' wide as they may wander." [84] Even when he is disposed to be sympathetic, however, Carlyle cannot forget that the deserved or undeserved sufferings of the victims of the Terror must always be seen in relation to the wider context of human misery: "Unhappy Family!" he writes of the royal family on the eve of their execution, "Who would not weep for it, were there not a whole world to be wept for?" [85]

What is more, Carlyle's attitude toward the Terror is at all points informed by the beliefs expressed in his ontology of revolution, which analyzes the Revolution as a complex struggle between the satanic forces of chaotic reality and the human requirements for organization and order. Insofar as the Terror results from the dissolution of the social order, it is the expression of the deepest, most depraved levels of human nature, of the "powder-mines of bottomless guilt and criminality [upon which] the purest of us walk[s]." [86] But insofar as it is the deliberate policy of the Committee of Public Safety functioning in its capacity as an organ of the "new singular system of Culottism," it represents, rather, a grim decision as to what is strategically needful, a product of that grotesque rationality that has always come into play in states of war. Salut Publique is for Carlyle "Sansculottism Accoutred"—that is to say, on the one hand it is the organization of anarchic force and therefore a system of order, while on the other hand it is an order built on chaos. The emergence of Marat's committee of the Terror as the governing body of France is a fact which Carlyle sees as overloaded with contradictions, for it is an instance of history's most profound riddle: it is a revolutionary government. Salut Publique is thus an incarnate paradox: Insofar as it is a government it points toward the new order which will one day be born out of the Revolution—a radically equalitarian order, free of all the vestiges of privilege: "For the wise man may now everywhere discern that he must found on his manhood, not on the garnitures of his manhood." [87] But insofar as it is revolutionary it is doomed: "Sansculottism, Anarchy . . . , is to perish in a new singular system of Culottism and Arrangement. For Arrangement is indispensable to man. . . ." [88]

Because it occupies this crucial intersection between arrangement and anarchy, there is in the Reign of Terror an ineffable, inexpressible quality that puts it beyond the reach of the yes-no dichotomies with which human speech is wont to pass judgments. To Carlyle the Terror is a fact so real and yet so contradictory that any effort to judge it must be morally supererogatory. "To Marat and the Committee of Watchfulness," he concludes, "not praise;—not even blame, such as could be meted out in these insufficient dialects of ours; expressive silence rather!" [89]

Carlyle concludes his *History of the French Revolution* with the expulsion of the sansculottes from the National Convention on May 20, 1795. "The very windows need to be thrown up, that Sansculottism may escape fast enough. . . . Permanent-session ends at three in the morning. Sansculottism once more flung resupine, lies sprawling; sprawling its *last*." [90] Like the Revolution itself, Carlyle's *History* ends when the construction of the "new singular system of Culottism" had barely gotten under way. With the ninth of Thermidor, the promise held out of an order based on "manhood, not on the garnitures of manhood," was brutally withdrawn and the Revolution was left unfinished.

Yet in his *History of the French Revolution* Carlyle provided English readers with the very model of radical revolution, producing one of the finest codifications of the *ur*-revolution which still today stands at the fountainhead of modern revolutionary mythology. Carlyle's *History* marks a major turning point in English attitudes toward the French Revolution, for before Carlyle English middle-class radicals had applauded the French Revolution, if they did so at all, only because they saw in 1789 a French version of the English Revolution of 1688. [91] But Carlyle turned that all around, making unmistakably clear for the first time that the value of the French Revolution was not to be measured by the extent to which it was modeled on the English Revolution of the seventeenth century, but by the extent to which it would be the model for the English Revolution of the nineteenth.

We can now see why Carlyle told Froude that "I should not have known what to make of this world at all, if it had not been for the French Revolution," for this incomplete revolution is not only the paradigm of Carlyle's own thought, which has by this point in his career come to express itself invariably in books and essays that stop just short of consummation, but also the template from which the history of the nineteenth century will be cut. Carlyle had ended his "Signs of the Times" with a statement of his hopes that his generation would see the completion of the work left unfinished by the

Revolution; he had concluded *Sartor Resartus* by hinting that the Paris revolution of 1830 might prove to be the beginning of this longed-for last phase. Now, in the concluding pages of his *History of the French Revolution,* he still looks forward to the completion of the Revolution. Thermidor plunged France into the reign of the aristocracy of wealth, symbolized for Carlyle by the salon society which centered upon the fashionable, thrice-married Thérésa Cabarrús. The hegemony of the modern cash aristocracy is, he writes, "the course through which all European Societies are, at this hour, travelling. Apparently a still baser sort of Aristocracy? An infinitely baser; the basest yet known. In which, however, there is this advantage, that, like Anarchy itself, it cannot continue." [92] When a mob of dandies called the "jeunesse dorée," or Gilded Youth, breaks into the halls of the National Convention on the ninth of Thermidor and drives the sansculottes out, for the moment money has triumphed over manhood and sansculottism has fallen prey to dandyism, its absolute antithesis. But surely, Carlyle says, the Revolution was not fought for this: "Destroying of Bastilles, discomfiting of Brunswicks, fronting of Principalities and Powers, of Earth and Tophet, all that thou hast dared and endured,—it was for a Republic of the Cabarus Saloons? Patience; thou must have patience: the end is not yet." [93]

VI

Revolution and the State

We saw in Chapter V that Carlyle judged the various constitutionalist parties—principally the Lafayettists outside the Assembly
and the Gironde inside—to be political failures. They were
doomed because, above all else, they were unable to speak to or for
the forces which really held the balance of power in revolutionary
France, most notably the sansculottic underclass. Throughout his
French Revolution Carlyle speaks harshly and scornfully of these
parties, in part, no doubt, because they had been weighed in the
scales of history and found wanting. But beside such pragmatic considerations, Carlyle also was evaluating them in terms of his deep
and abiding antipathy to the very principle of government by constitution, which was the cornerstone of the Girondin system.

In this chapter I should like to examine the constitutionalist principle and Carlyle's position with regard to it from an ideological
rather than a pragmatically political point of view. In order to do
this, it will be necessary to put Carlyle to the side for a while and
focus instead on the doctrines of constitutionalist liberalism. In the
past Carlyle has suffered at the hands of critics who, as liberal heirs
of the Girondin tradition, could not but look askance at his antiliberalism. This being the case, there is nothing to be gained by an
analysis of Carlyle's critique of constitutionalism which is not preceded by a critique of constitutionalism itself, for until one is clear
in his own mind about the value of the system Carlyle attacked, one
cannot even begin to evaluate his position.

1. The Constitutional State

Although hints of constitutionalist or contractualist thought—
for the two are ultimately the same, inasmuch as the social contract

is the prototype of all political constitutions—can be traced back to the works of various medieval scholars and are to be found in the writings of Machiavelli, it is not until Hobbes and Locke put the social contract at the bases of their political theories that the contractualist tradition properly so called can be said to have begun, and it is especially Locke who stands at the headwaters of European constitutionalist liberalism. However, the idea of a social contract did not come to take on its full sloganistic importance until Jean-Jacques Rousseau published his *Contrat social* in 1762, and the contractualism relevant to my purposes, and to the French Revolution, need not be followed back any further than this.

Through the nineteenth century and into the twentieth, the contractual nature of the state was held to be the element which made possible a reconciliation of state power with personal freedom. In the past half century, however, this belief has come increasingly into question, so much so that it is scarcely tenable any longer. Indeed, it has been asserted that contractual theory and its practical application to political life lead, both logically and historically, to some form of totalitarian system. In their studies of totalitarianism, J. L. Talmon and Hannah Arendt single out different aspects of the theory of social contract to account for the drift from freedom, and because Talmon's argument is in a sense the more elementary of the two, it will serve as a convenient starting place.

In essence, Talmon says that in Rousseau's writings the "general will," which is the basic ingredient of the social contract and which must be clearly distinguished from the mere will of the majority, is gradually elevated to the status of an absolute which rules in the name of the people; hence the seeming paradox in the title of Talmon's book, *The Origins of Totalitarian Democracy*. "Ultimately," Talmon writes, "the general will is to Rousseau something like a mathematical truth or a Platonic idea. It has an objective existence of its own, whether perceived or not. It has nevertheless to be discovered by the human mind. But having discovered it, the human mind simply cannot honestly refuse to accept it." [1]

Further, Talmon traces the almost inevitable sequence by which this abstract political absolute of Rousseau's theory became, in the practice of Robespierre, the moral underpinning of a totalitarian system. Initially, "Robespierre was profoundly convinced that the people's will, if allowed free, genuine and complete expression, could not fail to prove identical with the true general will." But circumstances were to convince him that such was in fact not the case, and in the end "Robespierre came to admit to himself that the people could not be trusted to voice its real will. . . . From the point of view of real democracy and the true general will the task was therefore not just to let the people speak, freely and spontaneously, and then to accept their verdict as final and absolute. It was first to create the conditions for a true expression of the popular will." [2]

Whether one finds Robespierre's position admirable or deplorable is here beside the point, for if one takes seriously the powers of an oppressive regime to generate coerced consent, to socialize its victims to the very system that enslaves them—that is, if one recognizes the possibility of what Marxists call "false consciousness"—then Robespierre's conclusion seems solidly in accord with reality. This is why revolutionaries from Plato to Robert Owen have felt that they could not produce a new social order unless they were given charge of the children before they had been shaped by the old order. It is not necessarily patronizing to assume that people brought up under a system that stunts and maims them will be stunted and maimed; indeed, many revolutionaries who could not conceivably be accused of holding patronizing attitudes toward their clients have reached this conclusion, although, among *narodniki* and anarchists, for example, the choice as to what this conclusion indicated in the way of remedy was diametrically opposed to Robespierre's. But in either case—whether one goes to the people in an attempt to educate and teach them as the first step in creating "the conditions for a true expression of the popular will," or whether one presumes to speak for the general will and uses the people to fight for what they themselves may not recognize as needful for making possible their own expression of the general will—one is assuming that the expressed will of the people and the true general will are not identical. The fact that the people in whose names most revolutions have been fought rarely have been in the vanguards of the revolutionary movements indicates that the Robespierrist position is far from being an aberration.

Thus, according to Talmon, the state based upon the general will of its population cancels the liberties of the individual wills of its members and ignores their rights in favor of the abstract rights of the generality. This argument was anticipated by Rousseau himself, for in his *Discourse on the Origin and Foundations of Inequality among Men* he conducted a devastating investigation into the contractual state he later was to celebrate in *The Social Contract*. The invention of abstract justifications of the state came about, Rousseau says, when some possessor of historically sanctioned rights, privileges, powers, and advantages over his neighbors, feeling the pressure brought to bear by their attempts to challenge his position, "finally conceived the most deliberate project that ever entered the human mind. It was to use in his favor the very forces of those who attacked him, to make his defenders out of his adversaries, inspire them with other maxims, and give them other institutions which were as favorable to him as natural right was adverse." [3] Thus was born the legitimated state. As a result of its legitimation, there can be no solid ground on which an individual can stand if he wishes to launch counterclaims against the state, inasmuch as any of the rights on which he may wish to base his counterclaims are already definitionally included in the state, which is, as we have seen already, held to be identical with himself.

The end product of this process of legitimizing stands out clearly in Rousseau's *Contrat social*. "[B]efore considering the act by which a people submits to a king," Rousseau very reasonably observes, "we ought to scrutinize the act by which people become *a* people, for that act, being necessarily antecedent to the other, is the real foundation of society." [4] This act of original constitution involves no less than the total annihilation of the individuality of the state's members: "These articles of association, rightly understood, are reducible to a single one, namely the total alienation by each associate of himself and all his rights to the whole community." From this it follows that the "sovereign," whether this be a prince, a legislature, or a system of laws, can be defined as merely the active principle of the body politic as constituted by the aforementioned act of alienation. A sovereign so conceived can have no rights—this was the revolutionary content of Rousseau's message—over against the constituted body because he is merely an aspect of it: "there neither is, nor can be, any kind of fundamental law binding on the people as a body, not even the social contract itself." [5]

For the purposes of the present argument, however, the operative phrase here is "as a body," for although the sovereign can hold no sway over the people "as a body," the people-as-a-body (or what purports to be such) does of course hold sway over mere individuals and their private wills. If, as Rousseau wrote, the people are *citizens*, in so far as they share in the sovereign power, and *subjects*, in so far as they put themselves under the law of the state," then one should add that their subjection rises exactly in proportion to their sovereignty.[6] Thus any state actually constructed along Rousseau's lines, in which the sovereign is indeed the active principle of the general will, is by the tautology of definition absolute: "Now, as the sovereign is formed entirely of the individuals who compose it, it has not, nor could it have, any interest contrary to theirs. . . . The sovereign by the mere fact that it is, is always all that it ought to be." [7]

In *The Origins of Totalitarianism*, Hannah Arendt presents a significantly different version of Talmon's contention that in predicating the state upon the consent of the people in the form of the single, overriding abstraction of a general will, one inevitably sets that will in opposition to the concrete plurality of individual wills within the society. Arendt argues that the danger of the constitutionalist system lies not so much in its failure to guarantee the rights it is in principle supposed to secure, as in the very nature of human rights as it conceives them. According to Arendt, the use of an abstractly conceived system of "rights of man" as the foundation of the state is fraught with the same dangers as is the idea of the general will, for rights so conceived are contentless and nonobjective in much the same way as is the general will. Insofar as men are willing to base their claims to sovereignty on their rights as men, rather than on their rights as Englishmen, Frenchmen, or whatever, they come to conceive of themselves as men in general rather than as citizens. Their rights thus cease to be based on an authoritative writ from history, cease to be rights laboriously wrung by themselves and their ancestors from the historical setting in which they were placed, and become instead abstractions with little or no authority. To rely upon the generalized "rights of man" is, Arendt writes, to resign oneself to "the abstract nakedness of being human and nothing but human" and to renounce all one's claims upon one's historical community, which alone is in a position to guarantee one's rights.[8]

Rights conceived in this ahistorical way no longer mediate between the citizen and the state as a system for defining the individual both within and against the larger community because, as ideal, timeless abstractions, they have no point of contact with the historical community. Thus man as an individual and man as a citizen within the state merge into the undifferentiated entity known as the human being in general, and such a man's rights are regarded as merely a part of the definition of himself. They are unenforceable exactly in proportion as they are inalienable.

What is more, when the rights which we look to the state to enforce are dehistoricized and absolutized in the manner just described, the conception of the state too undergoes an analogous transformation. It ceases to be a system of historically sanctioned institutions and becomes instead an abstraction, the content of which is simply the product of the infinite multiplication of the generalized human beings who populate it. What happens to man's rights in such a situation should be immediately clear. Kenneth Burke has described a trick of the way the mind works which he calls the "paradox of purity." The conception of a "pure" substance, Burke maintains, is functionally the same thing as the negation of that substance; for example, the theological contention that god has not any particular substance or shape, but has, rather, "pure" substance and "pure" shape, comes down to saying that he has no substance and shape at all.[9] It is this paradox that is at work in the situation I have been describing: in claiming for man not the particular rights of an Englishman or Frenchman but the "pure" rights of man, one renders him pretty much devoid of rights. "The paradox involved in the loss of human rights," Arendt explains, "is that such loss coincides with the instant when a person becomes a human being in general. . . ."[10]

In short, Arendt argues that the consensual state—the state based on contract and consent—is overlegitimated in the sense that it bases itself not on the power it derives from the historical conditions which make its government possible, but rather on the absolute right which it claims to derive from the rights of its citizens and which make its power a matter of principle. Thus where Talmon saw the general will as the weak link in contractual theory, Arendt directs her attention to the general rights which that will is supposed to express.

At this point it should be clear that it is possible to go one step farther still and trace the danger of totalitarian absolutism back to the very idea of the "constituted" state itself. If we are to understand the term *constitution*, we must think of the American rather than the British usage, for in British political thought the "constitution" is merely a descriptive term, whereas in American thought (and in French, which took the American pattern as a model) a constitution is definitive, constitutive. The British constitution is, as is widely known, not a document or a legislative act, but rather the sum total of institutions, habits, and customs which govern social and political life in England: "Our Constitution," Edmund Burke said, "is a prescriptive constitution; it is a constitution whose sole authority is, that it has existed time out of mind." [11] In the usual dichotomy between a society predicated on a constitution and an organic society, the English constitution is clearly organic, nonconstitutional—that is, the government is based on evolutionary principles that rely heavily on precedent and wont.

In American political thought, on the other hand, there is a tendency to conceive of a constitution as a document which has been created by a constituent body, approved, codified, stored safely in the archives, which is susceptible of "strict" or "lax" construction, and which can be consulted by any literate person. A society which conceives of itself as established on such a constitution obviously is one which fully accepts the concept of a "social contract," for the constitution itself is that contract and its ratification is the clearly recognized acceptance of the terms of that contract. For the most part the European contractualist tradition has had to depend upon the fiction that at some time in the prehistoric past such a contract was implicitly or explicitly entered into, but Americans know that the acceptance of this contract is not a fiction, and they can even point to the desk at which it was signed.

More than three quarters of a century ago Woodrow Wilson called attention to the fact that even before the eighteenth century had ended Americans had lost all "serious disposition to quarrel with the Constitution itself. . . . It was recognized as no longer fashionable to say aught against the principles of the Constitution; but all men could not be of one mind, and political parties began to take form in antagonistic schools of constitutional construction. . . . [O]pposition to the Constitution as a constitution, and even hostile criticism of its provisions, ceased almost immediately upon its adoption; and not only ceased, but gave place to an undiscriminating and almost blind worship of its principles. . . ." [12]

The phenomenon Wilson is pointing to owes its existence to the fact that a constitution in the American sense is, so to speak, the ultimate turtle on the back of which the entire sociopolitical structure rests. As Kenneth Burke, who has made the study of constitutions one of the priority items in his miscellaneous career, observes, the American legal tradition has insisted that the Constitution itself is the fundamental criterion of legality; "it would abandon 'natural law' or 'divine law' as criteria, looking only to the Constitution itself and not to any scientific, metaphysical, or theological doctrines. . . ." [13] This is as it must be, Burke goes on to explain, because to have recourse to any such extraconstitutional criteria as natural or divine law would be immediately to declare a constitution behind the Constitution, and thereby explode at once the fiction of a social contract—for whatever governed the Constitution obviously would be something not contracted for.

In this sense, a constitution, conceived in the American way, is an ultimate, absolute entity, a self-legitimating principle. In this power of self-legitimation constitutions are like religious systems, for in both constitutional theory and theology the sacred texts can be known to be sacred only by the fact that they declare themselves to be so. It is at this point, when the state declares itself to be its own legitimating principle, that it takes on the impregnable powers which are the hallmark of the modern state—that it becomes, in short, the Leviathan first described by Thomas Hobbes. Talmon and Arendt are quite right in recognizing that these powers derive from the state's overlegitimation—that is, from its assertion that it has an absolute, ahistorical validity which is different in kind from and superior to its merely pragmatic and historical authority. But I think they are mistaken in identifying this overlegitimation as an aspect of the promotion of the general will or of general rights to the status of an absolute. On the contrary, the overlegitimation in question, with the totalitarian possibilities it involves, enters the picture the moment one speaks of a constitution or social contract at all. One does not have to erect some absolute general will to get this result: the contract or constitution itself, *regardless of its content*, will serve this purpose.[14]

2. Legitimacy and Force

Among the most potent sources of this overlegitimation is, it seems to me, the denial of force or power as a factor in political arrangements. Max Weber's definition of the state as "a human community that (successfully) claims the *monopoly of the legitimate use of physical force* within a given territory," if it is accepted by the liberal constitutionalist at all, is translated to mean that the state reserves the right to use force for peace-keeping purposes.[15] Thus R. M. MacIver, in *The Modern State*, defines the state in terms of law rather than in terms of force, adding that the state enjoys the right to use force only "to prevent the rule of force itself. That is why, in the last resort, force can be entrusted to the state, that it may be everywhere subjected to law." [16] Indeed, even in admitting that the state employs force in this way, the liberal mind does not conceive of these peace-keeping functions as uses of force, but as the suppression of force, for in the liberal conception of politics force is almost by definition something extraneous, abnormal, and invariably tainted with illegality. Hence the tendency to imagine that wars are discontinuous with normal political functioning, as expressed in the platitude that one has recourse to war only when the regular diplomatic machinery breaks down. Few people, I imagine, really believe that this is so, Clausewitz's famous aphorism to the contrary being so palpably correct; yet it persists as an article of piety because the liberal-constitutionalist tradition allows no other way to conceive of force.

Essentially, the liberal-constitutionalist theory of the state is idealistic and antipragmatic, fancying that its ideal-type of the state as a product of a mythical social contract is in fact a description of the state which actually functions as a going concern. This typical bit of self-delusion has a long history which culminated in the theories of the Political Economists, with their complete fusion of power and rights as factors in the political world. Political Economy's theory of the state—that is, the contemporary liberal theory—involves simultaneously the apotheosis and the denial of the role of force in history, and it is important for this analysis because it provided the context in which Carlyle worked and against which he was in reaction.

In James Mill's *Essay on Government*, a piece written in 1819 for the *Encyclopaedia Britannica* as the official pronouncement of Political Economy on the subject, private property appears as virtually the only basis of government. Because economic scarcity is one of the most fundamental facts of the human environment, Mill argues, labor is essential for the procurement of the objects of needs and desires. Because labor is inherently undesirable, his syllogism proceeds, it is necessary to attach inducements to it, and the most natural inducement to labor is to ensure "to every man the greatest possible quantity of the produce of his labor." And finally, because the produce of one's labor naturally comes to oneself unless some superior force intervenes to expropriate it, no positive system is needed to guarantee this result, but only a negative system to prevent the possibility of piracy. Thus men come together originally to form a community to protect their property. "The object, it is plain, can best be attained when a great number of men combine and delegate to a small number the power necessary for protecting them all. This is government." [17]

In Mill's analysis, then, private property is historically prior to civil society as well as to government, and is the source and cause simultaneously of both. The emphasis on property in Mill's account highlights how one-sided the conception of contract had become by the nineteenth century. Completely lacking here is any trace of the corrosive insight into the relationship between private property and the formation of civil society that had been a major part of the contractual tradition handed down by Hobbes and Rousseau. Hobbes had recognized that although personal possessions undoubtedly were to be found in the state of nature, private property per se cannot be said to have existed before the establishment of civil society, inasmuch as "Every man by nature hath right to all things, that is to say, to do whatsoever he listeth to whom he listeth, to possess, use, and enjoy all things he will and can." [18] In the Hobbesian war of each against all, the tenure of property can be nothing but a transitory accident until such time as a polity is developed to clarify and enforce the distinction between *meum* and *tuum:* "In this warre of every man against every man, this also is consequent; . . . that there can be no Propriety, no Dominion, no *Mine* and *Thine* distinct; but onely that to be every mans, that he can get; and for so long, as he can keep it." [19]

Rousseau, following up Hobbes's insight into the absence of "propriety" and "dominion" in the state of nature, concludes that the establishment of a pattern of personal possessions, which led in turn to the creation of distinctions between rich and poor, preceded the creation of civil society. Civil society itself does not begin until the rich, who are constantly subject to depradations by their less fortunate neighbors, succeed in inducing these neighbors to accept the idea of forming a civil society complete with laws of property. In this way the rich manage to turn "a clever usurpation into an irrevocable right." [20] Possessions thus become property as a result of a series of developments which is, one can readily see, precisely the reverse of that sketched by Mill. In Mill's reading the state comes into being to enforce the producer's natural right to the produce of his labor, whereas in Rousseau's interpretation civil society was created in order to give legitimacy to a "clever usurpation" to which "natural law was adverse." [21]

What is more, Mill's militantly bourgeois theory of the social contract not only rejects completely the radical ideas of Rousseau, but it also repudiates the far more moderate understanding of this issue which had been a part of the tradition of British economic thought since Adam Smith. Smith's famous description of the division of labor in the first chapter of his *Wealth of Nations* is an account of the coming together of individual producers, living more or less in a state of nature, for the purpose of cooperating in the distribution of economic goods.[22] The first form of civil society is, therefore, the communal market. Such a civil society might then choose to constitute itself as a political aggregate by designating a portion of its resources and personnel for the purpose of establishing organizations for mutual protection, as Mill describes, but the results would be quite different from those delineated in Mill's *Essay*. In Smith's reading personal possessions form the basis of the market community, and it is this community that is the basis of government, whereas in Mill's account the market disappears, as property is at once the cause of community and of government—which are in fact identical. In other words, Mill's fundamental definitions make it impossible to conceive of government as anything other than an institution in the service of property, whereas Smith admits just such a possibility—namely, government in the service of the community or market. It is this possibility that enabled Marx to develop his economics on the basis of classical economics, whereas he could make nothing of the writings of Mill and his group, and in fact denounced them for their conception of a state existing solely for the purpose of preserving private property.[23]

A society such as we see in Mill's *Essay*, a society without a market, is a purely political aggregate, for the people are related to one another not in terms of economic functioning but in terms of power. Although Mill, as a Political Economist, imagined he was establishing the principles of government on the basis of the laws of economics, he was in fact doing the opposite—that is, establishing the principles of economics on the basis of the laws of politics. The marketless polity we see in the *Essay on Government* provides a fairly accurate picture of the new order capitalist production was introducing into English social, political, and economic relations—an order in which the traditional set of market relationships was being replaced by a new set of relationships modeled on political or quasi-political lines. This point is generally obscured by the fact that this new set of relationships has been named the "laws of the marketplace," although in fact they are the very antithesis of the laws that have governed marketplaces for the greatest part of human history. A traditional market has customary laws of its own, as anyone knows who has ever found himself in a situation where he was expected to haggle with a merchant. These laws provide the traditional means of arranging social and economic relationships, and they are in marked contrast to the so-called rational laws of the modern equivalent of the market. In *The Making of the English Working Class*, E. P. Thompson contrasts the "older moral economy" to the "economy of the free market" and describes the struggles of the working class, toward the end of the eighteenth century, to preserve the few remaining vestiges of the former.[24] By the time Mill wrote his *Essay* in 1819 the "moral economy," it is safe to say, had been largely extirpated from England and replaced by a "political economy"—that is, a system in which the economic laws of the marketplace have given way to laws more appropriate to the political arena.

One can recognize what I have called the political or quasi-political model behind this new "free-market economy" in the fact that Political Economy analyzes wealth in terms appropriate to power. Power is necessarily a relative commodity; one cannot have power except with respect to people relatively less powerful. In this sense power is what Thorstein Veblen would have called an invidious concept. Wealth, on the other hand, was never treated as an invidious concept until the time of the Political Economists—after which time it hardly ever has been treated as anything else. When John Ruskin, later in the nineteenth century, pointed out that in the British economy as it then existed, "The force of the guinea you have in your pocket depends wholly on the default of a guinea in your neighbour's pocket," he was reflecting the vast change that had come over economic thinking (and economic reality) since the time of Adam Smith.[25] To Smith, who lived in a mercantile age when the crucial transaction of economic life was the buying and selling of goods, such a statement would have been incomprehensible, for the value of the goods on the merchant's shelves was absolutely dependent on the presence of a guinea in the consumer's pocket. Within a few decades of the publication of the *Wealth of Nations*, however, the crucial transaction of economic life had more and more come to be the buying and selling of labor, and in this transaction it is indeed the case that the poverty of one of the parties is incontestably to the benefit of the other. In such an economic system wealth becomes an invidious substance and can be described in terms appropriate to relationships of power.

Such description was—or should have been—the task of Political Economy. In fact, however, although Political Economy treated economic relations of wealth as though they were relationships of power, it could never bring itself to analyze the nature of power. "The elements out of which the power of coercing others is fabricated are obvious to all," James Mill says, but of course they are not.[26] Mill, like his bourgeois liberal descendants, argues as though he felt that by transforming economic relationships into quasi-political relationships and then describing these relationships of power in terms of the so-called laws of the marketplace, he could avoid meeting the need to attend to the nature of power. Indeed, as Ralf Dahrendorf has pointed out, modern liberal thinkers tend to imagine that relationships of power do not exist, except as aberrations, in their market-rational society. Belief in this "utopia of powerlessness, of which neither modern political theory nor modern political practice seems to tire," has been a hallmark of the liberal tradition from the time of Mill to the present.[27] Thus one contemporary liberal with solid New Deal credentials has written an 800-page book entitled *Power* in which he does not once stop to examine "the elements out of which the power of coercing others is fabricated," and another liberal theorist has announced that "Power is . . . neither the center nor the essence of politics." [28]

Beset with the fantasy that it has eliminated power from political life and replaced it with rational, legal relationships, liberalism, in the words of Franz Neumann, has become "in large measure an ideology tending (often unintentionally) to prevent the search for the locus of political power and to render more secure its actual holders." [29] As a result, the idea that the state is actually based on power—on historical arrangements that give it authority rather than on abstract concepts that give it legitimacy—sounds, to the liberal ear, like an invitation to all sorts of terroristic tyranny.

In fact it is nothing of the sort. The recognition of the role of force in politics is simply a pragmatic refusal to accept the idea of the consensual state as more than a legitimating myth, and the ideologues of force—of course I am referring to Carlyle, with his dictum that might and right are fundamentally identical—are simply saying that, all theory aside, the state is what it is. By reintroducing force as a category of political thought one refuses to legitimate the state at all, adopting instead a skeptical and cynical attitude toward government. The notion that theorists of force are abetting the cause of tyranny derives from an elementary misconception in which their theories are analyzed as though they were theories of legitimacy. Carlyle's hero theory, for example, does *not* say that power should be in the hands of the strong; on the contrary, it recognizes that such a statement would be an absurd tautology: power is by definition whatever is in the hands of the strong and the strong are by definition whoever hold power.

The charge that Carlyle and other political theorists who make great use of the idea of force are playing into the hands of the fascists, if indeed they are not the fascists themselves, is based on a total misapprehension of the relationship between politics and political thought, between history and the philosophy of history. No state ever attempts to legitimate itself by alluding to its power to rule; no dictator ever claims that the right behind his government is his ability to get away with whatever he wants. Even the imperious claim that such-and-such will be law because it is the king's will, haughty as it sounds, is not an appeal to the sanction of force, for it points to whatever legitimates the king's will as a governing principle. If, on the other hand, the king were to say that such-and-such will be law because he has the power to see to it that it becomes law, because his might makes it right, he would in fact be denying his absolute kingship and putting the issue on the most pragmatic grounds imaginable—in short, asking for trouble. An anecdote will illustrate. James Anthony Froude, Carlyle's disciple and biographer, fully accepted his master's dictum that might and right in the long run come down to the same thing. As a representative of the Colonial Secretary in Boer Africa, Froude made a speech to the African colonists in which he used this argument to justify England's right to govern the colony. The following day he was shocked to learn that his audience interpreted his words as an invitation to rebellion. He need not have been, for if he had learned Carlyle's lesson properly he would have known that the inevitable corollary of the idea that "no country had a right to more independence than it could defend by force of arms" is the idea that any country has a right to as much independence as it can gain by force of arms.[30]

In other words, the theory that politics is at bottom force, far from legitimating inhumane abuses of power, legitimates nothing. As Michael Walzer explains, the idea that political authority is erected on a foundation of force rather than of right "granted legitimacy to no particular sovereign—except to the one who actually held and exercised power. In fact, obedience was always imposed by force, since it was only by its forcefulness that it [authority] could be recognized." Thus Calvin, who is for Walzer the source of this conception of the role of force in government, "ignored the medieval distinction between legitimate rulers and usurpers; in fact, he condemned any effort to make lawful distinctions: 'It belongeth not to us to be inquisitive by what right and title a prince reigneth . . . and whether he have it by good and lawful inheritance . . .' 'To us it ought to suffice that they do rule. . . .' " [31]

As a support for tyrants this doctrine, it should be immediately apparent, is a redundancy, for it confers legitimacy only upon those rulers who do not need it, who have the naked power to enforce their wills. Conversely, it invites challenges to such despots insofar as it provides an argument which a priori justifies any successful attempt to overthrow them. As Rousseau pointed out, by recognizing that governmental authority is purely a matter of power, one abolishes the specious legitimacy the state claims to derive from the sociopolitical contract and permits "the despot [to be] master only as long as he is the strongest. . . ." [32] Thus the idea that force is the constituent ingredient of civil government can never be of assistance to the authoritarian state, whereas the idea that civil government transcends force by turning it into law unquestionably assists the state by idealizing it and putting it above secular struggle.

The power theory of the state will always serve on the side of resistance to a powerful state, never as its ideological support, for it is, as I have said, skeptical and cynical about authority. Quite obviously, a malevolent government which had the power to carry out its evil designs would never care to point to that power as its justification; it might not care to argue about legitimacy at all, for it would not need to, but if it wanted to lend an aura of legality to its proceedings it would do so by pointing to something other than its power as its source of legitimacy; for example, it might cite the race of the rulers or their divine right or even the general will of the governed.[33] Conversely, one can imagine no more corrosive doctrine to level against an authoritarian state than the simple declaration that they can't get away with this, for in saying this one denies authority completely and thereby permits the government and its enemies to fight the matter out as they can. Of course, one may object that the government probably has greater force at its disposal than do its enemies, so that putting the issue on this level means that the authorities are most likely to win. But such would be the case anyway, and merely denying that it is a question of force does not make it any less so.

For this reason, the liberal-contractual tradition, with its denial of the role of force in political life, tends to adopt a very unrealistic understanding of the state. The state rules in fact because it can, but claims to rule because it should, because it enjoys a hypothetical legitimacy. It uses force itself, but does not regard it as such, and adds to the burden of those who would resist the double task of inventing a principle of legitimation which can stand against the state's claim to speak for the general will, and of bearing the stigma of immorality and illegality if they, like the state, have recourse to force.

3. Revolutionary Organicism

In Carlyle's analysis of constitutionalist liberal thought, the self-legitimating state is held to be a menace not primarily because it monopolizes the principle of legitimacy and therefore makes criticism impossible, but because, in basing itself on a historical principles, it removes the political realm from the historical dimension in which human action occurs. In contrast to the organicist conception of the state, in which the state derives its writ of authority from the historical community in which it exists, the constitutionalist state need bear little or no relation to the community over which it holds sway. Although Carlyle shares with twentieth-century thinkers like Talmon and Arendt a distrust of liberalism's tendency to overlegitimate and absolutize the state, and although he counters this danger by emphasizing the role of force as a counterlegitimate principle, his attention to a large extent is directed to another quarter. It is not so much the absolutizing of the state as it is the undermining of society that Carlyle fears from the hands of the liberals.

In his attempt to combat this tendency Carlyle turned to the theories of organic society which, before they passed through his hands, had been the exclusive property of conservative ideology. According to constitutionalist thought, human history can be traced back to a presocial aggregate of isolated individuals living in what is commonly but unjustifiably called a "state of nature." Only when these individuals, through an act of contract, constitute themselves as a society can the history of civil society be said to begin. Given such a pedigree, the ontological status of society is decidedly second-rate, both in the sense that society is not "real" in the same way as the tangible, concrete individuals who compose it, and in the sense that it is a derivative product of these unfederated individuals. Thus society is held to be a highly artificial entity.

In contrast, for the organicist school of thought and Carlyle along with it, the logical (and even historical) priority given by liberalism to the individual over society seems to be thoroughly out of touch with reality. According to Carlyle, the idea of isolated individuals choosing at some point to *form* a society is a baseless fallacy, for people comprise a society by the mere fact of their being in such proximity as to cause them to interact. Indeed, as we have seen in Chapter III, society is nothing but the system of their interactions. Thus society is a historical, not a rational, entity, and as such it provides the scene for historical action. Running like an intermittently submerged river through the whole of Carlyle's *History of the French Revolution* is a discontinuous analysis of the nature of society which invariably begins with one form or another of the assertion that society can be correctly conceptualized only when it is recognized to be a way of acting, and, moreover, a way of acting that is grounded in history. Society, he tells us in a typical expression of this organicist creed, is a "System of Habits," a pattern of "*fixed ways* of acting and believing. . . . Herein too, in this its System of Habits, acquired, retained how you will, lies the true Law-Code and Constitution of a Society; the only Code, though an unwritten one, which it can nowise *dis*obey." [34]

In contrast to this "true Law-Code and Constitution" of civil society, the constituted law of a society—that is, the law that appears in the enactments of the state—is of secondary importance. Indeed, the state derives such validity as it has only from the closeness of its fit to the relationships actually to be found in social interaction and described in the unwritten "true Law-Code": "The Constitution, the set of Laws, or prescribed Habits of Acting, that men will live under, is the one which images their Convictions,—their Faith as to this wondrous Universe, and what rights, duties, capabilities they have there: which stands sanctioned, therefore, by Necessity itself. . . . Other Laws, whereof there are always enough *ready-made*, are usurpations; which men do not obey, but rebel against, and abolish at their earliest convenience." [35]

In these terms, the efforts of the Constituent Assembly—and especially of the Gironde, those "pedants of the Revolution, if not Jesuits of it!" [36]—to establish the new France upon a constitution are supererogatory to say the least, for their constitution is at best a naive redundancy and at worst an insupportable imposition. If the Assembly's constitution is binding, Carlyle is saying, then it is not necessary, for it can be binding only insofar as it reflects the convictions about social cooperation which already exist in the minds of men; if, on the other hand, men do not accept the model of cooperation formulated in the constitution, then it cannot be binding except by force, in which case it is meaningless to talk of a social contract at all.[37]

The constitution, then, as I have said repeatedly, must exist in the minds and actions of the people if it is to exist at all. "In every French head," Carlyle writes, "there hangs now, whether for terror or for hope, some prophetic picture of a New France: prophecy which brings, nay which almost *is*, its own fulfilment. . . ."[38] Proof of the fact that the Gironde's constitution does not reflect this inner constitution, this "true Law-Code," lies in the inability of the Girondin government to mobilize the French people. "A Constitution . . . will march," according to Carlyle, "when it images, if not the old Habits and Beliefs of the Constituted, then accurately their Rights, or better indeed their Mights. . . ."[39] This the Assembly's constitution fails to do, so that, let the Legislative Assembly go what way it will, "the History of France, one finds, is seldom or never there."[40]

Where is it, then? Carlyle's answer will come as a surprise to people who have been taught to see him as a Tory or a reactionary or to believe that the organicist conception of society invariably means what it meant to Edmund Burke or to Menenius. The organic constitution of France, Carlyle says, insofar as it can be located in any institutionalized body at all, is to be found in the Jacobin clubs, with their "mother society" in Paris and "daughter societies" spread throughout France. What is more, it is to be found there in proportion as the Jacobins have given over being the representatives of bourgeois respectability and have permitted their clubs to express the wishes and aspirations of the common people. Thus, even while the National Assembly is proving itself unable to generate a workable constitution, the Revolution, Carlyle tells us, is not without "her Constitution that *can* march; her *not* impotent Parliament; or call it, Ecumenic Council, and General-Assembly of the Jean-Jacques Churches: the MOTHER SOCIETY, namely! Mother Society with her three hundred full-grown Daughters; with what we can call little Grand-daughters trying to walk, in every village of France, numerable, as Burke thinks, by the hundred thousand. This is the true Constitution; made not by Twelve hundred august Senators, but by Nature herself; and has grown, unconsciously, out of the wants and the efforts of these Twenty-five Millions of men. . . . A Governing power must exist: your other powers here are simulacra; this power is *it*."[41]

In *Sartor Resartus* Carlyle had used the phrase "Organic Filaments" to denominate all that he saw as natural, spontaneous, and
vital in the "Fire-whirlwind" of historical process. "[E]ver as the
ashes of the Old are blown about," he had Professor Teufelsdröckh
say, "do organic filaments of the New mysteriously spin themselves:
and amid the rushing and the waving of the Whirlwind-element
come tones of a melodious Deathsong, which end not but in tones
of a more melodious Birthsong." [42] It was such speculations from
Teufelsdröckh that led Carlyle to discern in his hypothetical professor "a deep, silent, slow-burning, inextinguishable Radicalism, such
as fills us with shuddering admiration." [43] Now, in writing on the
French Revolution, he notes "how, under an old figure"—that is,
in the idiom borrowed from *Sartor*—"Jacobinism shoots forth
organic filaments to the utmost corners of confused dissolved
France; organising it anew. . . ." [44]

By attributing an organic nature to the Revolution, Carlyle has
appropriated the rhetorical arsenal of the British conservative tradition and has deployed it in the name of the Revolution. Working in
an intellectual milieu in which the competing definitions of man's
place in society were the atomistic individualism of constitutionalist
liberalism and the organicism of Burkean conservatism, Carlyle
worked out for himself, with so far as I can tell no important predecessors, a system of thought capable of attacking the assumptions of
bourgeois liberalism without lapsing into reaction. It consisted primarily of the starkly simple but effective strategy of reapplying the
terms of traditional conservatism. The evolutionary argument which
in Burke's hands is a diatribe against change and a defense of government becomes with Carlyle an ideology of change which is intensely skeptical about the legitimacy of government. When Burke
spoke of the evolution of the British sociopolitical system, his emphasis was on the *product*, so that the bias was for stability. When
Carlyle, writing forty years later, with the French Revolution behind him and the industrial revolution around him, speaks in the
same terms, he is focusing on the *process*, so that the result is a doctrine of permanent revolution: "in this Time-World of ours there is
properly nothing else but revolution and mutation, and even nothing else conceivable." [45] So long as he stayed true to these insights,
he was in a fair way toward becoming the foremost radical intellectual of nineteenth-century England.

Carlyle's attack on the liberal theories of contract and constitution, and his replacement of them with a sense of an organic society

in which organic growth develops out of revolutionary activism, make his *History of the French Revolution* an unambiguous affirmation of the creative force of revolution. "In bourgeois mythology," David Caute has written, "revolution is pure negation, purely destructive, the work of 'subversives,' 'foreign agents,' Taine's 'cosmopolitan rogues.' In fact the successful revolution is constructive and optimistic; it does not imagine that its cause can triumph on the streets alone; it begins to examine existing institutions rationally in terms of their future possibilities. It confines its destructive blows to those spheres where constructive work may follow." [46] Although not so naive as to believe, with Caute, that revolutionary violence "confines" its activities to areas where constructive work can follow, Carlyle unhesitatingly answers those who would see only destructive force in Jacobinism and its Terror by declaring that Jacobinism "is not death, but rather new organisation, and life out of death: destructive, indeed, of the remnants of the Old; but to the New important, indispensable." [47] If any aspect of the Revolution was purely destructive, it was the Girondin-constitutionalist phase, which, as I have noted already, saw in the people only a destructive force, "explosive material, for blowing down Bastilles with!" In contrast, the Jacobin societies make it possible for even the lowliest citizen to "walk to the nearest Town; and there, in the Daughter Society, make [his] ejaculation into an articulate oration, into an action, guided forward by the Mother of Patriotism herself." [48] Thus the search that began in *Sartor Resartus* for a way in which it would be possible to transcend feeling, thought, and speech, and to enter the realm of action has ended successfully in a community of "Twenty-five Millions of men" coming together in the taverns and meeting rooms of a revolutionary political club. "This properly is the grand fact of the Time." [49]

VII

The English Revolution

In November 1839 Carlyle published an extended essay on the Chartist movement. The work appeared as a pamphlet, "a little separate book," for Carlyle decided to have it printed at his own expense when he was unable to make satisfactory arrangements for its publication in the periodical press. Even while the manuscript was still in the hands of John Lockhart of the *Quarterly Review*, Carlyle looked forward to its being rejected. "Lockhart has it," he wrote to John Sterling in November, "for it was partly promised to him, at least the refusal of it was: and that I conjecture, will be all he will enjoy of it. Such an Article, equally astonishing to Girondin Radicals, Donothing Aristocrat Conservatives, and unbelieving Dilettante Whigs, can hope for no harbour in any Review." [1]

Carlyle, of course, was exaggerating; he liked to imagine that he was rather too hot an item for the English press to handle. In fact, John Stuart Mill, whose *London and Westminster Review* was in the process of foundering, had read the manuscript and offered to publish it. "It is a glorious piece of work," he wrote to Carlyle, "& will be a blessed gospel to many, if they read it & lay it to heart. . . . I should be very averse to disturb any other arrangement you may have made, or may wish to make—but it would delight me much to let this be the last dying speech of a Radical Review. I do not think a radical review *ought* to die without saying all this—& no one else could say it half as well. Any number of copies of it might be printed in pamphlet form from the same types." [2]

For reasons that are rather obscure, Carlyle found this generous offer unacceptable. To Mill he explained that "After a good deal of consulting and considering this way and that, I have found that on the whole it would be best to give Fraser the Paper, and let him send it out as a Pamphlet. . . ." [3] His friendship with Mill, whom he had once fancied to be a disciple of his, had grown rather cool by this time, and this may have played a part in his decision not to let Mill have the essay; besides, he seems to have felt that Mill had slighted him in rejecting the same essay some time earlier, and the present situation provided him with a chance to crow about their respective reverses of fortune: "I offered them this very thing two years ago, the blockheads, and they dared not let me write it then," Carlyle wrote to his mother. "If they had taken more of my counsel, they need not perhaps have been in a sinking state at present. But they went their own way, and now their Review is to cease. . . ." [4]

Carlyle was strangely attached to his *Chartism* essay, and he seemed unwilling to let it be associated with anyone else, as though publication in Lockhart's or Mill's magazines would make it less purely his own. But the fact that Mill was willing to publish it, and that Carlyle was only indulging his conceit of himself as a loner when he claimed it could have found no harbor in any review, does not make his *Chartism* less astonishing than he claimed it to be. It is a startling bold essay which not only undertakes a defense of the Chartist movement at a time when respectable opinion was hardly in a frame of mind to receive such, but also offers a critique of Chartism from a radical vantage point to the left of Chartism itself.

Carlyle's unsystematic analysis of the Chartist movement provides an invaluable index of his political thought as it stood three years after the publication of *The French Revolution* and three years before the publication of *Past and Present*. It would not be far from the mark to say that, in its political ideas, *Chartism* is a radical manifesto unmatched in scope among the products of indigenous English radicalism. In its program, however, in Carlyle's specific proposals for restoring England to sociopolitical health, Carlyle once again runs into the cul de sac which by now we should have come to expect with him. In the final analysis, *Chartism* is a fiery missile hurled at the "British heathen," only to shiver into splinters as it crashed against the invisible but immovable wall Carlyle always seems to have kept between himself and his target.

1. The Condition of England

The Chartist movement formally began on May 8, 1838, with the publication of the People's Charter, with its famous six points— manhood suffrage, vote by ballot, annual parliaments, pay for members of Parliament, abolition of the property qualification for members, and equal electoral districts. Through 1838 the movement grew electrically, its followers soon coming to number in the millions. Although the celebrated petition its leaders presented to Parliament in the summer of 1839 contained well over a million signatures, the House of Commons ridiculed it and then voted, 237 to 48, against taking it into consideration. The defeat of the petition left the movement, which from the start had been poorly led and subject to intense factional strife, with its most illustrious banner in tatters. Unable to decide on a unified response to the parliamentary rebuff, Chartism collapsed, and the government, seeing its chance, began rounding up and jailing Chartist leaders.

That the movement revived after the debacle of 1839, flourished in the forties, and even staggered into the fifties is beside the point here. What is not beside the point is the fact that even in the winter of 1839, when Chartism was at the lowest point in its history up to that time—William Lovett, Feargus O'Connor, and most of the major Chartist leaders were in prison even as Carlyle was writing —Carlyle was convinced that England had not yet heard the last of Chartism. "We are aware that, according to the newspapers, Chartism is extinct; that a Reform Ministry has 'put down the chimera of Chartism' in the most felicitous effectual manner," he wrote, and then added: "The distracted incoherent embodiment of Chartism, whereby in late months it took shape and became visible, this has been put down; . . . but the living essence of Chartism has not been put down." [5]

Thus in the last months of 1839 Carlyle foresaw that Chartism would rally. Indeed, this prediction is the essential point of his *Chartism*, for Carlyle is not concerned with examining the history of the movement or its status as he writes, but with its history to come. "The matter of Chartism is weighty, deep-rooted, far-extending; did not begin yesterday; will by no means end this day or tomorrow. Reform Ministry, constabulary rural police, new levy of soldiers, grants of money to Birmingham; all this is well, or is not well; all this will put down only the embodiment or 'chimera' of Chartism. The essence continuing, new and ever new embodiments, chimeras madder or less mad, have to continue. The melancholy fact remains, that this thing known at present by the name of Chartism does exist; has existed; and, either 'put down,' into secret treason, with rusty pistols, vitriol bottle and match-box, or openly brandishing pike and torch (one knows not in which case *more* fatal-looking), is like to exist till quite other methods have been tried with it." [6]

Chartism, Carlyle maintains, will remain a potent force in English social and political life so long as the conditions which gave rise to it remain uncorrected. What is more, there is little hope that they will be corrected because they have not even been accurately perceived. As early as 1830 Carlyle had been troubled by what he was to call the "Condition-of-England Question": "Our Political Economists," he wrote in his Journal in June of that year, "should collect statistical *facts:* such as, What is the lowest sum a man can live on in various countries; what is the highest he gets to live on; How many people work with their hands, How many with their heads, How many not at all;—and innumerable such. What all want to know is the condition of our fellow men, and strange to say, it is the thing least of all understood, or to be understood as matters go." [7] Ten years later, in *Chartism*, he was still complaining that "The condition of the working-man in this country, what it is and has been, whether it is improving or retrograding,—is a question to which from statistics hitherto no solution can be got." [8]

Because the Condition-of-England question is, as Carlyle says, "the alpha and omega of all" questions that confront the body politic, and because Political Economists have been lamentably short of believable answers, he is willing to spend what was for him an unusual amount of systematic effort in spelling out specifically the types of information that will be needed if a true assessment of the economic facts of life is to be had.

In the first place, one would need to have reliable information about daily wage rates, an area so intensely fought over that even parliamentary inquiries could never get to the bottom of the matter, and were forced merely to put on the record the contradictory claims of masters and workers, which differed often by as much as fifty percent. "And then," Carlyle writes, "given the average of wages, what is the constancy of employment; what is the difficulty of finding employment; the fluctuation from season to season, from year to year? Is it constant, calculable wages; or fluctuating, incalculable, more or less of the nature of gambling? This second circumstance, of quality in wages, is perhaps even more important than the primary one of quantity." Third, one would want to know the sociological nature of labor relations in industry: does the laborer enjoy the prospect of upward mobility, of becoming himself a master manufacturer or at least self-employed? Is his relationship to his employer a cooperative or a coercive one? "In a word, what degree of contentment can a human creature be supposed to enjoy in that position?" Fourth, one would want statistics that point to the psychological welfare of the working people. If figures were available on the savings habits of the workingman they would go a long way toward providing answers here, for by "laying up money, he proves that his condition, painful as it may be without and within, is not yet desperate. . . ." The fondness of the Political Economists for invoking thriftiness as a plan of salvation for the lower class, Carlyle recognized, was based on ignorance of the psychology of the poor; one does not become hopeful because one saves, but saves because one is hopeful. As Cobbett had observed, the root of *thrift* is *thriving*.[9]

Finally, having ascertained the quality and quantity of wages, the social conditions of labor, and the attitude of the working class, one would want to know, above all, whether work was available. "The simple fundamental question, Can the labouring man in this England of ours, who is willing to labour, find work, and subsistence by his work? is a matter of mere conjecture and assertion hitherto. . . ."[10]

Were clear and unambiguous information to be obtained in these five categories, Carlyle points out, it would be possible to begin taking steps to ameliorate problems in a realistic manner. As matters stand, however, the economic experts in Parliament tacitly acknowledge the validity of the Chartists' grievances by the priority they accord to amendment of the poor laws, yet, by their ignorance of the true state of affairs, they succeed only in exacerbating the situation. Thus in the Poor Law Amendment Act of 1834[11] the Reformed Parliament attempted to deal with the problem of poverty by means of vigorous application of the Malthusian principle that rendering the condition of paupers more ghastly—"less eligible" was the euphemism of the day—would discourage paupers from breeding. Toward this end large workhouses, or Bastilles, as they soon came to be called, were to be constructed throughout England. They were to be administered from a central authority in London, and the only way in which indigents could secure relief would be by entering the workhouse. Thus both the system of outdoor relief, which had existed in parts of England uninterruptedly from Elizabethan times, and the Speenhamland system, an innovation dating from the late eighteenth century which worked on the principle of augmenting wages when they fell below what the authorities considered a subsistence level, were to be replaced by a uniform system of workhouses in which the sexes were segregated, hard labor was demanded, and diet and living conditions were rendered as unpleasant as the ingenuity and cupidity of the overseers could make them.

Few major pieces of legislation have ever enjoyed such unremitting odium as this one, of which perhaps the only good that can be said is that it inspired Dickens to write *Oliver Twist*.[12] "That this Poor-Law Amendment Act . . . should be, as we sometimes hear it named, the 'chief glory' of a Reform Cabinet, betokens, one would imagine, rather a scarcity of glory there," Carlyle wrote with undisguised scorn. "To say to the poor, Ye shall eat the bread of affliction and drink the water of affliction, and be very miserable while here, required not so much a stretch of heroic faculty in any sense, as due toughness of bowels. If paupers are made miserable, paupers will needs decline in multitude. It is a secret known to all rat-catchers. . . ."[13]

In addition to being appalled by the inhumanity of the system, Carlyle was especially angered by the fact that the New Poor Law had been passed by a Parliament operating out of almost total ignorance of the condition of the working class. Although Edwin Chadwick, the moving spirit behind the New Poor Law, boasted that it was "the first great piece of legislation based upon scientific or economical principles," in fact, as Carlyle points out, Parliament had decreed that he who did not work must suffer the consequences without bothering to ascertain whether work was actually available.[14] "[T]he Legislature," he writes, "satisfied to legislate in the dark, has not yet sought any evidence [on the question of the availability of work]. They pass their New Poor-Law Bill, without evidence as to all this. Perhaps their New Poor-Law Bill is itself only intended as an *experimentum crucis* to ascertain all this?"[15]

The fact that Chartist workers resented the New Poor Law almost as intensely as they resented their poverty is as good an index as any of the utter bankruptcy of liberal economic theory. The New Poor Law was, after all, an attempt to apply systematically to the problem of poverty the same laissez-faire principles that were held to be responsible for England's economic growth; just as Political Economists argued that the unfettered operation of "natural" economic processes had led and would continue to lead to prosperity, so they argued that the extension of this hands-off attitude toward the poor would result in the amelioration of their condition.

To be sure, there is room for considerable debate as to whether clamping the indigent in Poor-Law Bastilles genuinely qualifies as "leaving them alone." Imprisonment, it would seem, is scarcely compatible with the principles of laissez-faire. Yet to the defenders of the New Poor Law, the "less eligibility" principle applied within the workhouses amounted to turning the poor over to the laws of nature, and in this sense the New Poor Law was a bona fide application of laissez-faire doctrine to the poor. Indeed, life in the workhouses did approximate conditions in a state of nature: it was solitary, poor, nasty, brutish, and short.

Carlyle instinctively recognized that this sort of Malthusian severity would not work, not only because it was morally depraved, but because the very same economic laws that worked toward increasing what was crassly called prosperity also worked to produce the increasing immiserization of the working class. As Carlyle analyzes it, the same law of competition in the open marketplace, which all economists agreed was necessary for driving up prices and productivity, worked just as inexorably to drive wages down, so "that the condition of the lower multitude of English labourers approximates more and more to that of the Irish [immigrants] competing with them in all markets. . . ." As a result, unskilled labor will tend to be done "not at the English price, but at an approximation to the Irish price: at a price superior as yet to the Irish, that is, superior to scarcity of third-rate potatoes for thirty weeks yearly; superior, yet hourly, with the arrival of every new steamboat, sinking nearer to an equality with that." [16]

This is a startling insight, for it means that the poverty of the English working class is not merely an unfortunate failure of the economic system, but is rather an inherent part of that system. Of course, Malthus and the Political Economists had recognized as much; the fact that wages must permanently remain at subsistence level for the lowest-paid section of the working class was one of the principal tenets of their system, and its corollary, as Andrew Ure explained in his *Philosophy of Manufactures*, was that "It is . . . the constant aim and tendency of every improvement in machinery" to "equalise" all labor at or near the price of the lowest-paid segment of the labor market.[17] But where the Political Economists assumed that they closed the book on this ugly matter by demonstrating that the laws which produced both prosperity and poverty were laws of nature, Carlyle refused to accept the laissez-faire axiom that "Whatever goes on, ought . . . to go on." [18] Nature provided man, he had been saying for years, with chaos and disorder, and the purpose of human action—especially political action—always had been to introduce order into this natural chaos. In such a context, for Parliament to operate on the principles of laissez-faire is "as good as an *abdication* on the part of governors; an admission that they are henceforth incompetent to govern, that they are not there to govern at all, but to do—one knows not what!" [19]

In the last analysis Carlyle well knew that the governing classes of England had not chosen to abdicate. Rather, they had chosen not to meddle with natural laws because it was to their advantage not to meddle with them, at least in the short-sighted sense that for the time being the laws of nature were operating in such a way as to make things quite comfortable for the manufacturing interest. Carlyle had no answers for them on this score; he begged only to remind them that if it was natural for a competitive economy to produce poverty as well as prosperity, and "If it is in the natural order of things that there must be discontent," then it also follows that "Chartism is one of the most natural phenomena in England." [20] It is natural, he points out in one of the scarcely veiled threats with which he studded the pages of *Chartism*, in exactly the same sense as the French Revolution was natural. " 'Laissez-faire, Leave them to do?' " he apostrophizes. "The thing they will *do,* if so left, is too frightful to think of! It has been done once, in sight of the whole earth, in these generations: can it need to be done a second time?" [21]

2. Political Reform, Social Reform, and the "Reform of the Heart"

Carlyle and the Chartists were in fundamental agreement on the fact that a reform in the social institutions of England would be needed if a repetition of the French Revolution were to be avoided. In calling for such a reform the Chartists put primary emphasis on the democratization of political institutions as the way of achieving these salutary changes, whereas Carlyle tended to be quite suspicious about what democracy could accomplish in this field, sensing that the connection between access to ballot boxes and the ability to change oppressive social institutions was not nearly so obvious as the democrats felt it to be. I shall be examining Carlyle's antidemocratic arguments in detail in Chapter IX, where I can place them in the context of his fully developed political thought; here, however, it should be noted that when he criticized Chartism for its commitment to democracy, it was, in an important sense, because he stood to the left of the Chartist movement rather than to its right, as most of his critics have contended. He has nothing in common with those who denounced democracy because they feared the "vast spoliation" that Macaulay predicted would follow if Parliament acceded to the Chartists' demands.[22] Unlike such critics of democracy as Matthew Arnold, John Ruskin, or even John Stuart Mill, Carlyle was never uneasy about what the workingmen would do with the vote when they got it. On the contrary, he had grave apprehensions about what they would not be able to do with their votes, for as Carlyle saw it, democracy was merely an extension into political form of the economic principles of laissez-faire which had gotten the workers into the predicament in which they found themselves in 1839.

For Carlyle, the feature of Chartist democracy which doomed it beforehand could be discerned in the fact that none of the Chartist leaders desired democracy as an instrument for securing a government run on behalf of the proletarian masses. On the contrary, almost all of their attacks on the Reformed Parliament and on the unreformed Parliament that had preceded it were directed against Parliament as an organ of what they called "class government." For the most part, the Chartists were democrats because they felt that the present Parliament favored the landed and manufacturing interests, just as the parliaments before reform had favored the landed interest alone. The purpose of further extension of the franchise was, therefore, to eliminate this class bias in the legislative body, rather than to create a legislative body which represented primarily the interests of the most numerous class in England. With the single exception of James Bronterre O'Brien, who astounded the Chartist Convention of 1839 by suggesting that the Chartists forget about reforming the House of Commons and instead elect their own representative body to serve as a revolutionary government, Chartism was a movement aimed at using democracy to secure classless government.

Even if this attempt to eliminate "class government" were to succeed in producing a classless government, Carlyle warned, this would prove to be a condition far from ideal for people who were not living in a classless society. Given existing property relationships, a government which merely purged itself of class favoritism would be committed to avoiding partisan interference in the natural functioning of the economy, and the result could only be a self-regulating economy absolutely identical to the state of affairs desired by the manufacturing interests in Manchester. In effect, a classless government would still be a bourgeois government and, as he wrote in 1850, would still sanction "Slopshirts attainable three-halfpence cheaper, by the ruin of living bodies and immortal souls." [23] This result was inevitable because, as the Political Economists recognized, in a capitalist system such as that found in England, the unchecked operation of natural economic laws tends to favor the possessors of property. Of course, Political Economy used this argument to justify as a natural phenomenon the pleasant position in which property owners found themselves, but Carlyle was quite capable of turning this perception around and concluding that the very fact that nature tended to favor the propertied classes meant that it must be the primary duty of government to redress this balance by favoring the naturally disadvantaged class. Indeed, if this were not the case, then what would be the purpose of government? "Whatsoever great British interest can the least speak for itself, for that beyond all they [the members of the government] are called to speak," he wrote in *Chartism*. "They are either speakers for that great dumb toiling class which cannot speak, or they are nothing that one can well specify." [24]

Thus Carlyle argued, in his attack on democracy, that franchise reform could not possibly succeed in reforming the manifestly unjust social and economic structures of his country. In line with a long tradition which extends from Karl Marx through Gaetano Mosca to Herbert Marcuse, Carlyle based his dislike of parliamentary democracy on the contention that it inevitably would be a sham, useless for the task of changing the condition of the people. The democratic movement, he felt, served only to divert attention from social and economic problems that should be attacked directly. In many ways this seems like sound advice. The various strains that made up English radicalism in the 1830s were palpably going nowhere. The Radical party in Parliament, or what purported to be such, had subsided, as J. S. Mill quickly observed, into being "a mere *côté gauche* of the Whig party"; Carlyle, who was less kindly disposed toward them, dubbed them the "Paralytic Radicals." [25] And the Chartists, from whom one might have hoped for more, went on petitioning Parliament with a persistency that must have made them seem somewhat ineducable; indeed, even after the movement had collapsed in the fifties, William Lovett, the author of the Charter, could still be found sending up to Parliament petitions that amounted to little more than private memoranda on specific abuses—a parody of this once potent movement that surely must be one of the more lugubrious phenomena of nineteenth-century working-class radicalism. Our hindsight confirms Carlyle's insight into the fruitlessness of the course the radical movement had embarked upon.

On the other hand, one gets the unmistakable sense that Carlyle was bluffing when he called for more direct action aimed toward social change. What action? Carlyle himself does not seem to have known: "To the practical man, therefore, we will repeat that he has, as the first thing he can 'do,' to gird himself up for actual doing; to know well that he is either there to do, or not there at all. Once rightly girded up, how many things will present themselves as doable which now are not attemptable!" [26] This is the prose of a man treading water, hoping that if he can stay afloat long enough some ship is bound to come over the horizon. Carlyle never tired of repeating the advice he had given as early as *Sartor Resartus*—"*Do the Duty which lies nearest thee*"—and in this recommendation he showed both the strength and the weakness of his activist ideology.[27]

For Carlyle, who conceived of ideas as derivative products of action—in the sense that idea systems have no primary content of their own but are, rather, codifications of interactive patterns—action necessarily precedes faith or conviction. "Faith," he often observed, "is properly the one thing needful," but he was well aware that faith is not to be had for the asking.[28] One cannot *have faith* unless it is possible to *act out faithfulness* in the context in which one finds oneself. Just as legality and morality cannot be said to exist in the Hobbesian state of nature, which does not contain any political system from which they could derive, so social ideas have no reality for Carlyle until they are concretized in social life.

In this way Carlyle's contemplative maxim that "Faith is properly the one thing needful" is counterbalanced by his activist maxim that "Doubt of any sort cannot be removed except by Action." [29] In his essay on Chartism he makes clear that there was no hyperbole involved in his use of the phrase "of any sort": the maxim is fully intended to cover politics as well as religion, for at a time when doubts have arisen as to what men's rights are, the only way of settling these doubts is to test them in the crucible of political struggle. For this reason Carlyle maintained that "All men are justified in demanding and searching for their rights; moreover, justified or not, they will do it: by Chartisms, Radicalisms, French Revolutions, or whatsoever methods they have." [30]

This pragmatic test of rights is one we can easily recognize as appropriate to revolutionary situations, in which "Force is not yet distinguished into Bidden and Forbidden"—in which, that is, success is identical to justification.[31] But it is not a test we are used to applying to "normal" political situations, and the fact that Carlyle so applied it indicates, at the very least, that he, like many other Englishmen of the period, regarded nineteenth-century England as a proto-revolutionary scene. Furthermore, because England was in a potentially revolutionary situation, Carlyle knew that it would not be possible to predict the nature of the postrevolutionary order, for there is no way of knowing in advance what system of rights and obligations will correspond to whatever arrangement of forces succeeds in stabilizing itself in the end.

In a certain sense one might say that the virtue of Carlyle's activist ideology lies precisely in this ability to call for revolutionary struggle in order to determine "what portion of his rights [man] has any chance of being able to make good," while at the same time remaining remarkably free of dogmatism about the outcome of that struggle.[32] On the other hand, this same freedom from dogmatism renders Carlyle's activism almost contentless. Here the flaw in the idea that doubt cannot be removed except by action becomes apparent, for one can never know what action to take until one has taken it. Thus, even while calling for direct action to ameliorate social and economic conditions, Carlyle refuses to offer a program for such regeneration. Instead, when he does get down to making practical suggestions at the end of the *Chartism* essay, he confines himself to promoting what he himself recognizes to be stopgap measures which can be instituted even within the present social and economic system: an emigration program for reducing the workers' sufferings insofar as they are attributable to surplus population, and an extensive program of education for eliminating illiteracy among the lower classes.

Aware that both emigration and literacy are obviously trivial solutions to profound problems, and that he has nothing more substantial to offer, Carlyle directs his attention to the task of convincing the ruling classes to reform their own consciousnesses, to reform themselves. After all of his revolutionary rhetoric, Carlyle ends up calling for a reform of the human heart, a reform in the sensibilities of the men who direct society. "[T]he cure, if it is to be a cure, must begin at the heart," he writes: "not in his condition only but in himself must the Patient be all changed." [33] In his study of Ruskin, John D. Rosenberg calls "this desire to revolutionize not institutions but the human heart" the "ultimate radicalism." [34] Unfortunately, if there is anything ultimate about this mode of thought, it is only in the sense that social thinkers who arrive at this point generally have gone as far as they are going to go. I do not mean to imply that the task of making proselytes among the upper classes is necessarily not a legitimate function of molders of revolutionary sensibility. On the contrary, the extent to which revolutions come from above has often been remarked. In his *Social Origins of Dictatorship and Democracy* Barrington Moore observes how the commercial, industrial, and agricultural revolutions that transformed England in the seventeenth and eighteenth centuries moved down rather than up the social scale; "under the impact of commerce and some industry," he writes, "English society was breaking apart from the top downward. . . ." [35] Similarly, the extent to which radical initiative in the French Revolution came from the ranks of the nobility and the bourgeoisie has been pointed out already on these pages. Using examples such as these, Peter Kropotkin once observed that "no revolution, whether peaceful or violent, has ever taken place without the new ideals having deeply penetrated into the very class whose economic and political privileges were to be assailed." [36]

Despite the historical examples, however, such reasoning is, it seems to me, based largely on an error in drawing historical analogies. In the English case, for example, far from being "the very class whose economic and political privileges were to be assailed," those landlords who engaged in the transformation of the countryside from a household to a capitalized economy were the very class who stood most to gain from the transformation. In the French case, the radical element in the nobility was drawn from those portions of the titled classes who were often in extremely bad shape financially and who were politically frustrated by the fact that their privileges increasingly were being siphoned off to the growing bourgeois-dominated bureaucracy. In Russia it may have been true, as Kropotkin observes, that the emancipation of the serfs in 1861 would never have been accomplished "if a consciousness of the injustice of their privileges had not spread widely within the serf-owners' class itself," but this consciousness spread only when, as in the case of Kropotkin's own father, the serf-owners found the economic burdens of maintaining an increasingly outmoded system of servile labor to be more expensive than their diminishing revenues could comfortably support.[37]

In all of these situations the presence of radical ideas among the upper classes can be linked to their own deep and serious political grievances and/or economic dissatisfactions. It may be that potentially the most volatile elements in a revolutionary situation are the propertied classes—when they have reasons of their own to be so —for they have not only the indignation of the exploited group but also the means for turning their indignation to account. But none of this applied to mid-nineteenth-century England, where the level of prosperity and the intensity of self-congratulation among the middle and upper classes were unexampled in previous history. There is, in short, no reason to believe that England had within it the material for making British Mirabeaus. Any attempts to sow seeds of radicalism in these quarters were bound to bring in very scanty harvests.

Marxists commonly scorn efforts to reform the upper classes on the grounds that they bespeak an unrealistic faith in the power of reasonable ideas to shape society and history, and indeed there may be some justification for labeling men like Fourier, Owen, and St. Simon utopians in this sense. But by no stretch of the powers of polemical indignation can Ruskin, Morris, Dickens, or Carlyle be accused of entertaining too lofty a faith in the efficacy of ideas. Among them, therefore, the call for a reform of the human heart must be recognized to be not so much an expression of faith in humanity as an expression of their failure to have anything more substantial to offer. No one had a keener sense than John Ruskin of the power of social environment to shape a man's mind—to stunt and maim him if he were a machine worker, to make him narrow and egotistical if he were the owner of the machine. Indeed, Ruskin would not have found the modern industrial system so intolerable if it were not for its power to warp the men who took part in it. Yet to know this and still to call for a self-initiated spiritual reform is simply to ignore the fact that the capitalist-industrial system has the very power over men which one is indicting it for having. Similarly with Dickens, who certainly knew better, one can find traces of the notion that men are capable of molding their own consciousnesses at will. Although Dickens, in his character Bounderby, revealed more clearly than any other imaginative writer of the nineteenth century that the idea of the self-made man is a shameless hoax, he was still capable of giving his assent to the typically bourgeois concept of the self-made man as embodied in the Brothers Cheeryble, his models of social regeneration through self-initiated personal reform; and in "The Christmas Carol" he told the fable of how this revolution could come about. Thus, both Dickens and Ruskin spoke in terms of a reform of the heart despite the fact that all their better insights militated against faith in reform from this direction.

It is with Carlyle as it is with these two men, upon both of whom he had a profound influence. When one finds him arguing that the change to the new social order "must begin at the heart," one should recognize that, far from expressing his deepest convictions, he is moving against them. Carlyle's sense that it was his calling to serve as a "missionary . . . to the British heathen" is blatantly atavistic.[38] In this phrase—and in the role which it all too accurately describes—one can see clearly the last traces of the religious duties his parents had always intended he should take up. No one could criticize a clergyman for calling upon his flock to change their minds and hearts; that is his job. But Carlyle had given up the clergy precisely because he found that the real problems which beset him were not amenable to spiritual correction, inasmuch as historical change, he had seen as early as "Signs of the Times," must be achieved through action rather than through idea.

Carlyle was, quite consistently, a historical determinist in his sense of how historical—especially social—forces shape the minds of men and in his sense of how, as we have observed repeatedly, the specific patterns of action within a particular society give shape to and indeed are identical with the ideas that seem to govern that society. Just as it would have been meaningless to urge the people of France, on the eve of the Revolution, to have faith in the hierarchical principles of the ancien régime, which no longer corresponded to reality, so it would be meaningless to urge the propertied classes of England in 1839 to act toward their social inferiors as though real bonds of mutual feeling and responsibility existed between them. In his theory of the "cash nexus," which I shall examine in the next chapter, Carlyle unambiguously acknowledged that the root problem of English society was not merely the fact that the upper classes no longer felt themselves obligated to the lower; more important, the problem lay in the fact that modern society was structured in such a way that these traditional bonds had ceased to exist. Asking people to act as though they existed could accomplish nothing.[39] If it took the "sinews and indignation" of the armed sansculottes to accomplish a revolution in France and overthrow a political order which was not grounded in social reality, what reason was there to believe that Marley's ghost could do the job in England?

Carlyle's sense of the hopelessness of regenerating England by reforming the hearts of the respectable classes throws some light on the purpose of the blatant threats which litter the pages of his *Chartism*. These threats remind us that Carlyle does not want to imply that reform of the heart is the only way to social regeneration. It is the only way *for the bourgeoisie*, which is not the same thing at all. Thus his call for a reform of the heart means that unless the higher orders figure out some method of mending their ways, the proletariat will do it for them, "and in a fashion that will please nobody." [40] To be sure, in certain moods Carlyle entertained utopian hopes about what the upper classes could accomplish, but he did not let these hopes replace his sense of revolutionary urgency. He called for a reform of the heart as an ultimatum, not a proposal, for he was too much of a realist to believe that the English upper classes could perform a feat of moral self-levitation and too little of a crank to suggest how they might go about it. But he was desperate enough to feel that unless they did, their world would blow up in their faces. It may be, as I have argued, a delusion to imagine that the ruling classes can build a new social order merely by willing it, but if so, so much the worse for the ruling classes.

In the final analysis, there is a quixotic quality, not unmixed with irony, in Carlyle's position. On the one hand, he addressed his call for inner reforms to the property-owning and ruling classes; his idea in writing *Chartism*, he said, was to "send it out as a Pamphlet for the *Tories* to read." [41] Yet his point in doing so was to urge upon them changes which he did not think them capable of making. On the other hand, he recognized that, in light of the failure of the upper classes, the task of remaking England will fall to the proletariat; yet he did not speak to them and had no hand to give them in the work he assigned to them. In this sense, then, Carlyle's exhortations toward spiritual reform indicate that in 1839 his radical activism was coming up empty. Using the terms of my earlier analysis, one might say that he was now paying the price for having chosen the idea of action over action itself.

3. A Note on the "New Mythus"

Despite Carlyle's awareness that preaching in Babylon would be for him as fruitless as it had been for the Old Testament prophets to whom he is so often compared, he never attempted to work directly with and to write for the working classes. In *Sartor Resartus* he had announced that English society was desperately in need of a "new Mythus" to replace the worn-out creeds handed down from the eighteenth century, but, for largely personal reasons which I examined in Chapter III, he had been unable to supply it. Yet it does not seem that Carlyle's personal difficulty in being unable to move from faith in action to action itself would have been an insuperable problem if there had not been factors in the society around him which contributed to his problem. Just as I observed in Chapter II that the political options open to Carlyle were limited by the low saliency of political movements to the left of Westminster Radicalism,[42] so here I should note that his entire development as a political thinker was stunted by the absence from England of either a living radical tradition or a community of radical intellectuals to which he could turn.

The importance of this missing element in Carlyle's cultural environment should not be underestimated, for if we want to conjecture on how Carlyle might have resolved his dilemma, we would have to imagine him generating by himself a new social vision. I do not mean to imply that it was in principle impossible that Carlyle should have done this, for it simply is not the case that all thinkers must operate exclusively within the framework given to them by their predecessors and contemporaries. Undoubtedly there have been thinkers capable of forming fundamentally new outlooks, of generating totally new givens with which others can then work. But Carlyle simply was not one of these. Who such men are is in fact a rather deep question. Even Marx, who one might think came closer than anyone else to doing it in the nineteenth century, had the benefit of a milieu which was unavailable to Carlyle. He began his work in the context of the alienated intelligentsia of the German universities and could draw strength until he was well on his way from the Young Hegelian movement. What is more, one cannot stand Hegel on his feet unless one has a Hegel. In England there was no analogous intellectual class, no analogous movement, and no Hegel.

This background, to be sure, did not create Marx, and if there had been anything like it in England it would not have made a Karl Marx out of a Thomas Carlyle. But one should not underestimate the importance to a thinker of an intelligentsia of somewhat like-minded souls for shaping, correcting, and molding his thought in the alembic of controversy. Intellectual isolation is a costly proposition, as much because it can let one wander down out of the way paths as because it forecloses possibilities. Despite his carefully cultivated reputation as a solitary thinker, it is not altogether clear that Carlyle wanted to or was willing to pay this price, as we can see from the delusive eagerness with which he jumped to the conclusion that John Stuart Mill was a "mystic" like himself and that in Mill and a few others he could discern "the rudiments of a mystic school" beginning to form around him.[43] Perhaps if there had been a community of radical intellectuals in England Carlyle could have gained much from it and contributed much to it. But there was not, and Carlyle and England, too, suffered for it.

VIII

Wealth and Power

Even before he had finished work on his *French Revolution*, Carlyle had begun to consider using Oliver Cromwell as the subject for his next major historical work. In the late 1830s his commitment to writing on the Commonwealth period grew and he was soon into the massive reading regimen that always preceded his historical works. In 1840 he included a lecture on Cromwell in the series of lectures published as *On Heroes and Hero-Worship*, but before he even started writing his study of the Puritan Revolution he was moved to reassess his sense of priorities, to put Cromwell aside, and to direct his attention to the work which was published in 1843 as *Past and Present*.

The legend that surrounds this book has it that a trip to Huntingdonshire in 1842, for the purpose of inspecting some of the sites where Cromwell acted, brought Carlyle for the first time face to face with the condition of England in a way that shocked and angered him. Whereas in his earlier writings what had struck him as the central problem of the age had been a sort of spiritual, moral, and generally cultural malaise, he now saw, so the story goes, that hard, grinding poverty was the inescapable fact to be dealt with, and that the condition of England could not be understood unless one could come to grips with this brutal state of affairs. In a matter of seven or ten weeks, working with a passionate speed that contrasted strikingly with his usual slow and agonizing method of composition, he produced the manuscript of *Past and Present*.

Certainly this is an appealing story, and it goes some way to account for the intensity as well as the disorganization of the book. Unfortunately, it does not square with the facts. We know that *Past and Present* was not written as rapidly as the legend would have it;

although the exact dates of composition are unknown, at least six months went into its production.[1] The two-months' composition of *Past and Present*, like so many of the mistaken ideas circulated about Carlyle, is in a sense traceable to Carlyle himself. To be sure, he never deliberately misinformed anyone about the history of this work, but for some reason or other—even his wife confessed that she could not guess what it was—he kept the fact that he was working on it secret: "he lets everybody go on questioning him of his Cromwell," she wrote, "and answers so as to leave them in the persuasion that he is very busy with that and nothing else." Only by looking over his shoulder as he wrote and noting the absence of Cromwell's name from page after page of manuscript did Jane Welsh Carlyle come to realize that something other than a book on Cromwell was in the works, "and . . . that Cromwell was not begun—that probably half a dozen other volumes will be published before that." [2] It was of course to be expected that those who believed Carlyle to be working on Cromwell until January 1843 would imagine that *Past and Present* had been written in the short space between that date and its appearance in March.

If the fact that *Past and Present* was written in a few weeks turns out to be legendary, so too does the notion that its motive force was the sudden inspiration brought about by the 1842 tour. As early as October 1841 Carlyle had made note in his Journal of his serious misgivings about the propriety of writing on Cromwell when problems of more immediate concern seemed to call for his attention. "Ought I to write now of Oliver Cromwell?" he asked himself, and answered, "*Gott weiss;* I cannot yet see clearly. . . . What a need of some speaker to the practical world at present! They would hear *me* if, alas! I had anything to say. Again and again of late I ask myself in whispers, Is it the duty of a citizen to be silent, to paint mere Heroisms, Cromwells, &c.?" [3]

These whispers were to become louder and louder as time passed, although occasionally he was able to still them by positing a connection between Cromwell and the contemporary situation, as in this comment to Ralph Waldo Emerson from August 1842: "For my heart is sick and sore in behalf of my own poor generation; nay I feel withal as if the one hope of help for it consisted in the possibility of new Cromwells and new Puritans: thus do the two centuries stand related to me, the seventeenth *worthless* except precisely in so far as it could be made the *nineteenth;* and yet let anybody *try* that enterprise! Heaven help me." [4]

Nevertheless, the doubts remained, and as the condition of England worsened Carlyle became increasingly convinced that he was too deeply involved in the nineteenth century to be able to afford the luxury of working on a literary evocation of the seventeenth. Thus he wrote to his wife during the great strikes of 1842, which had started in Manchester and spread into Lancashire, Yorkshire, and beyond: "The Manchester insurrection continues—the tenth day of it now. . . . A country in a lamentabler state, to my eyes, than ours even now, has rarely shown itself under the sun." He went on to add, most significantly, "We seem to be near anarchies, things nameless, and a secret voice whispers now and then to me, 'Thou, behold thou too art of it—thou must be of it!' " [5]

In this way the same "secret voice" which had told him in 1841 that it was not "the duty of a citizen to be silent" spoke again in 1842 to remind him that, in the political turmoil that characterized the "Hungry Forties," he must inevitably take part—that indeed he was a part of it whether he willed it so or not. Here we have an index of how far Carlyle had come from that point in 1829 when he had tried to convince himself that "the true duty of man [was] to stand utterly aloof from politics," for he was now wrestling with the realization that "the duty of a citizen" pointed in precisely the opposite direction.[6] The struggle which Carlyle waged with himself over this question was not without its costs in terms of spiritual ease, yet it must have been with a feeling almost of relief, when *Past and Present* was completed, that he wrote to John Sterling, who had foreseen that it was to work of this sort that Carlyle would have to devote himself: "It was John Sterling, I think, that first told me my nature was Political; it is strange enough how, beyond expectation, that oracle is verifying itself." [7]

1. Medievalism

Past and Present has earned a very mixed reputation in the century and a quarter since it appeared. Emery Neff, a distinguished Carlyle scholar of a few decades back, summed up the majority view when he wrote that in *Past and Present* Carlyle showed the first clear signs of "turning toward the Conservatives." [8] This view has been more or less echoed by all those who see in Carlyle's career a drift from some sort of angry radicalism toward outright reaction. In the minority is Emerson, who wrote at the time of the book's appearance that it was a work "as full of treason as a nut is full of meat." [9] With Emerson is Friedrich Engels, who praised *Past and Present* in his *Condition of the Working Class in England in 1844*, a work which owes a considerable debt to Carlyle, and who singled it out, in a review written for the *Deutsch-Französische Jahrbücher*, as the only recent book from England worth reading. "Look where you will [in contemporary English literature]," he wrote, "Carlyle's book is the only one that strikes a human chord, that sets forth the human condition, and that develops a human point of view." [10] Despite his complaint that Carlyle's political thought was altogether too speculative, too far removed from political action, the depth of Carlyle's radicalism was apparent to him, and he noted that the British socialist movement could profit greatly from such a radical theorist. On the same side are Thomas Cooper, the Chartist poet who dedicated his *Purgatory of Suicides* to Carlyle, and John Ruskin and William Morris, who were both to claim that they had learned their socialist principles from the pages of *Past and Present*. There is, in short, an extremely wide divergence of opinion on how one is to take Carlyle, and especially *Past and Present*, although the conservative interpretation has prevailed of late to such an extent that no challenger has arisen to argue with the contention, put forth around the time of the Second World War, that Carlyle had turned so far to the right that he could plausibly be ranked as an ideologue of fascism.[11]

The case for Carlyle's conservatism, insofar as this tendency is to be found in *Past and Present*, cites as evidence two factors in his thought: his medievalism and his authoritarianism. Deferring consideration of the second count until later, I shall begin by noting that the first rests primarily on what is taken to be the reactionary import of the medievalist notions contained in the large middle section of the book. In this section Carlyle examines the authority structure and the economic system of a medieval monastery for the purpose of contrasting these arrangements with those of contemporary English society in the heyday of industrial expansion.

Because almost all of the denunciatory literature on Carlyle operates on the assumption that there is something inherently reactionary in turning to the past for one's social models, one would do well to begin by observing that this assumption has absolutely no validity. I already have had occasion to note that the use of the past as a model is quite common among revolutionary thinkers; [12] indeed, an orientation to the past is part of the basic equipment of political realists of all stamps, irrespective of whether they are radical or reactionary. Only the liberal tradition among important political movements has considered the historical past to be irrelevant, for liberalism is committed to an idealistic vision of the state and society which, as noted in the discussion of legitimacy and force in Chapter VI, does not depend upon historical authenticity. Since Plato wrote his *Republic*, utopian thinkers have been designing ideal societies which they located either in the future, in an out of the way corner of the world, or, as in Plato's case, in the mind itself. But for almost as long, realistic thinkers have been planning to build or alter real societies, and as infallibly as the instincts of the utopians have drawn them toward the future, the instincts of the realists have drawn them toward the past, for nothing could be more natural than that men engaged in making history should turn to history in search of heuristic models. Indeed, it is only when one can recognize the lineaments of one's own aims embodied in some piece of actual history that one can know that one is working toward something authentically possible.

To be sure, those who attempt to recreate the past in the present can never really succeed; if they are able to change society at all it will be because they have made something new rather than because they have recreated something old. As Marx observed, it is generally a mistake to identify "new historical creations" with "older and even defunct forms of social life, to which they may bear a certain likeness." [13] But the fact that any new social form is not equatable with older models does not mean that the models were not necessary for making it. In this respect it is interesting to note that Marx made the observation quoted here in connection with the Paris Commune of 1871, which, he insisted, was not to be seen as a recreation of medieval communes. Yet this point was important to Marx precisely because the medieval communes did play an important role in the tradition of cooperative anarchism which informed the thinking of the builders of the Commune. In other words, if the Commune of 1871 was not a twelfth-century commune, neither, one must admit, could it have been built without the historical ideal of the twelfth century guiding the hands of its builders.

A political thinker's use of an ancient model to make his polemical points in no way constitutes even a prima facie case that his thought is reactionary. Of course, if Carlyle had rented land on which he built a genuinely medieval community, complete with dungeons, spade agriculture, and cholera, the matter would be quite different and one could say that his medievalism was reactionary.

On this score, however, one should note that (with the single exception of John Ruskin) the only innovators who ever actually build those Disneylands of the social conscience known as model communities are on the rationalist-idealist side of the political spectrum; indeed, it is reasonable to assume that utopian thinkers engage in such enterprises precisely because, lacking genuine historical models, they must construct models of their own. New Harmony was built to provide Owen with what Bury St. Edmunds gave to Carlyle, and the important difference between these models lies not in the fact that Carlyle's, drawn from the past, is reactionary, whereas Owen's is up-to-date and progressive, but in the fact that the former can serve to generate what Georges Sorel was to call myth whereas the latter cannot.[14] It is precisely this myth-generating potential of the past that led socialists like Engels to study the primitive communism of the Iroquois nation and anarchists like Proudhon and Kropotkin to study the Middle Ages. In all of these cases the models are used to provide historically validated nuclei around which to organize thought and action. Our judgment as to whether a thinker is reactionary or progressive must be based on the content of the model, not on the mere fact that a model from the past, even from a particular epoch of the past, exists.[15]

In the remainder of this chapter and in the following one I shall examine the uses to which Carlyle put his medieval model, and it should become apparent that the simple and reactionary desire to return to the past played little role in his thinking. Far from being, as Eric Bentley claims, "a succession of sentimental regressive fantasies [in which Carlyle] wish[es] himself back at St. Edmundsbury being bossed around by Abbot Samson," *Past and Present* never cuts the past off from the present in the way that a regressive fantasy would.[16] On the contrary, the past is at all points used for heuristic purposes because Carlyle believed that the regeneration of England could in important respects be forwarded by recreating some of the features of the economic, social, and political systems of the Middle Ages in the context of modern, industrial England. Indeed, the idea that the past should limit the present was so foreign to his intention that he could insist, when occasion demanded, on a radically innovative approach to contemporary problems. "The hour having struck, let us not say 'impossible':—it will have to be possible!" he wrote, adding, with what must have struck many of his readers as a frighteningly bold willingness to discard tradition and precedent: " 'Contrary to the habits of Parliament, the habits of Government?'

Yes: but did any Parliament or Government ever sit in a Year For-ty-three before?" [17]

G. K. Chesterton seems closer to the truth than Bentley when he says that Carlyle's problem on this score, far from being a too thor-ough retreat into the past, was a too willing acceptance of the pres-ent. Carlyle, he wrote, compromised his radicalism by coming to terms with industrialism; he "never contradicted the whole trend of the age as Cobbett did," Chesterton complained.[18] A more balanced account than either Chesterton or Bentley provides should, I be-lieve, take cognizance both of Carlyle's fascination with the past of Bury St. Edmunds and of his celebration of the present age of in-dustrial production. It is true that a great deal of nineteenth-century medievalism follows the line set down in Augustus Welby Pugin's *Contrasts* and asks us to choose between the abbey and the factory. But this is not the case with Carlyle, who sees that the problem with the dark satanic mills of Victorian industry lies in the fact that they are dark and satanic, not in the fact that they are mills. He asks, therefore, whether it would be possible to isolate the features that made the abbey an appropriate setting for manly endeavor and to reproduce them in an appropriate form in the modern world.

This question can be answered only in the context of Carlyle's analysis of the problems of contemporary England. One cannot know what he intended the twelfth century to provide unless one is clear about what he thought the nineteenth century lacked. For this reason my examination of *Past and Present* will focus, in the remain-der of this chapter, on Carlyle's diagnosis of the economic and social problems which beset his own epoch. Then, in Chapter IX, I shall turn to the political conclusions that follow from Carlyle's analysis.

2. Carlyle's Critique of Political Economy

Past and Present contains a carelessly assorted mixture of passages announcing the principles which could lead England to economic well-being and passages denouncing the principles of Political Econ-omy, which were in fact leading her toward ruin and revolution. In the following pages I shall sort these out, providing what amounts to a synthetic recreation of a critique of Political Economy which is latent in the pages of *Past and Present*. Considering the early date of this work and Carlyle's temperamental disinclination to systematic analysis, one can hardly be surprised at the way he scattered his economic observations about. For this reason only the synthetic procedure used here, putting together an observation from here and another from there, can reveal that Carlyle's critique of Political Economy, though neither so thorough nor so subtle as Marx's, is as surprisingly comprehensive as it is unsystematic.

The cardinal principles of classical Political Economy are, first, the principle of the division of labor, which was adumbrated on the opening pages of *The Wealth of Nations;* second, the principle of the self-adjusting nature of an economic system based on the laws of supply and demand as found in the so-called free market, with its corollary proclaiming the inutility of governmental or social interference with the functioning of the free market; and third, overriding the whole system, the principle of private property. Working in no systematic fashion, Carlyle focused his critique of Political Economy on these three principles.

I shall start with the division of labor because Political Economy starts there, in the sense that it is only with the historical appearance of a division of labor that the subject matter of Political Economy comes into existence. In the earliest stages of human development each man produced whatever was necessary to supply his own wants. During this prehistoric period there is nothing that can properly be called an economic system, for there is no economy and no system. As a result of what Adam Smith describes as a "very slow and gradual" process, however, the rudiments of economic organization were introduced into human behavior. Because of "a certain propensity in human nature"—specifically, "the propensity to truck, barter, and exchange one thing for another"—men began to develop cooperative methods for satisfying their individual wants and needs. "[I]t is this same trucking disposition which originally gives occasion to the division of labour," Smith tells us.[19] As men begin to exchange the goods they have appropriated, a rudimentary economy comes into being, and as each man realizes that it is to his benefit to concentrate his work efforts on one particular form of production, satisfying his other needs by trading the goods so produced with other men who specialize in other lines of production, a simple form of socioeconomic system is born. Such a system, to be sure, is social in a highly limited sense, for it consists of only one institution—the market. Nevertheless, this primitive economy is an analogue of fully developed social and political systems inasmuch as it serves to unite the interests of one man to those of another. Smith insists that the principle of division of labor is a principle of social cooperation, and insofar as this is the case the division of labor eliminates even before it arises the problem which Hobbes's political philosophy was designed to solve. The warfare of each against all, which according to the Hobbesian tradition is the condition of primitive man, plays no part in the anthropological theories of classical economics, and no social contract is necessary here inasmuch as social and economic relationships of a cooperative nature are spontaneously entered into by men who previously had wandered through their forests in sublimely individualistic indifference to one another's existence. Smith's division of labor is important to Political Economy because from it derives the traditional liberal hostility to social and political interference with economic relationships, which are held to be quite capable of taking care of themselves.

That the system which results from the division of labor is a cooperative one is the unshakable faith of all of its students from Smith down to Emile Durkheim, whose *Division of Labor in Society* stands as the summation of almost a century and a half of thinking on this subject. According to Durkheim, the division of labor arises from the "need of happiness" which urges "the individual to specialize more and more. To be sure, as all specialization supposes the simultaneous presence of several individuals and their co-operation, it is not possible without a society. But in place of being its determinate cause, society would only be the means through which it is realized, the necessary material in the organization of the divided work. It would even be an effect of the phenomenon rather than its cause. Is it not endlessly repeated that the need for co-operation has given birth to societies? They would then be formed so that work could be divided, rather than work being divided for social reasons." [20]

Carlyle stands in total opposition to this view of the division of labor, which he sees as the very antithesis of a principle of social organization. Where Smith and Durkheim postulate that society comes together so that work can be divided, Carlyle insists that such division shatters social organization. "We call it a Society; and go about professing openly the totalest separation, isolation. Our life is not a mutual helpfulness; but rather, cloaked under due laws-of-war, named 'fair competition' and so forth, it is a mutual hostility." [21] One need not be surprised that Carlyle, who was working without the benefit of any thoroughly conducted economic analysis, should differ so extremely from what was in his day and still largely remains orthodox economic opinion on the division of labor, for he was starting from diametrically opposite principles.

Political Economy begins from the assumption of complete atomism: primitive man works in isolation from his fellow men until such time as he leaves off private production and comes to meet them in the marketplace for the purpose of dividing the products of labor. The market generated by this coming together for exchange is the only form of society which classical Political Economy recognizes, from which it follows that if the society envisaged by Political Economy is to have any coherence at all, it must perforce be the coherence which derives from the division of labor and from the market which is its institutionalized expression. But because Carlyle does not accept the atomistic premises of Political Economy, he is free to question the role of the division of labor and the market as sources of social cohesion.

By assuming that the existence of society is logically and historically prior to that of the individual, Carlyle was able to see that the division of labor and the market could not possibly be socially unifying forces. The difference between Carlyle and the Political Economists on this point is almost exclusively one of perspective, for as Marx explained, the division of labor, looked at from the vantage point of factory gates, obviously will appear as the factor which brings formerly unrelated individuals into cooperative contact with each other; conversely, looked at from the point of view of society as a whole, the division of labor will be seen to produce an "anarchy" which surprisingly duplicates the Hobbesian jungle. "The division of labour within the society brings into contact independent commodity-producers, who acknowledge no other authority but that of competition, of the coercion exerted by the pressure of their mutual interests; just as in the animal kingdom, the *bellum omnium contra omnes* more or less preserves the conditions of existence of every species." [22]

Both Carlyle and Marx insist, for much the same reasons, that a distinction must be drawn between the division of labor as a social principle and the division of labor as an industrial principle. In the factory the division of labor serves as an organizing device, despite the fact that it is brutally exploited by those in command; only when the division of labor extends beyond the factory walls does it become a principle of "anarchy" (Marx), of "mutual hostility" (Carlyle). Both therefore conclude that the task of social regeneration can be advanced by ending the reign of the division of labor as a social principle without necessarily abandoning its legitimate uses in industry. It is precisely this feature in the systems of both Carlyle and Marx which explains why they were able, almost alone among nineteenth-century radicals, to attack industrial capitalism without lapsing into the machine-breaking attitudes which mar so much of Victorian anticapitalist writings. Perhaps Ruskin was right in maintaining that no amount of social or political amelioration could ever improve the lot of a man set to making pinheads for ten hours a day, but if so, he was right in so thoroughly anachronistic a way that his efforts were foredoomed to futility. In contrast, Carlyle and Marx accepted the industrial organization of work as their starting points and directed their attention to the task of altering social arrangements which spring from a given technological base while preserving that industrial base more or less intact.

Carlyle's code term for this social transformation, which he borrowed from the St. Simonians, is the "Organisation of Labour": "Alas, what a business will this be, which our Continental friends, groping this long while somewhat absurdly about it and about it, call 'Organisation of Labour';—which must be taken out of the hands of absurd windy persons, and put into the hands of wise, laborious, modest and valiant men, to begin with it straightway; to proceed with it, and succeed in it more and more, if Europe, at any rate if England, is to continue habitable much longer." [23]

Unfortunately, it is not very easy to tell precisely what sort of transformation Carlyle had in mind when he spoke of the organization of labor. As usual, he is long on generalizations and rather short on recommendations, with the result that *Past and Present* contains only one formulation which can be used to characterize the organization of labor as he envisions it. Rather elliptically to be sure, Carlyle describes a quasi-syndicalist system, the first principle of which is to remove the laborer from the vagaries of the labor market by guaranteeing him permanence of employment. "This once secured, the basis of all good results were laid," Carlyle predicted, and the foremost of these results will be the recognition that the worker cannot be considered a mere "hand" hired into an industry which is imagined to be a going concern operating independently of his presence.[24] Thus the worker's physical relationship to the means of production will remain unchanged while his social relationship to them will undergo a revolution.

At this point in the development of what Carlyle occasionally calls the "Chivalry of Labour," the laborer will come to be recognized as what essentially he always has been—a creative partner in the concern. Carlyle, of course, deals with these matters tentatively, as though he were leery of being too explicit. "A question arises here," he writes: "Whether, in some ulterior, perhaps some not far-distant stage of this 'Chivalry of Labour,' your Master-Worker may not find it possible, and needful, to grant his Workers permanent *interest* in his enterprise and theirs? So that it become, in practical result, what in essential fact and justice it ever is, a joint enterprise; all men, from the Chief Master down to the lowest Overseer and Operative, economically as well as loyally concerned for it?—Which question I do not answer. The answer, near or else far, is perhaps, Yes;—and yet one knows the difficulties." [25] Leaving aside the doubts and hesitancies which surround Carlyle's expression of this idea, one can see that the organization of labor as a "joint enterprise" of all strata within the industrial system amounts to the abrogation of the division of labor as a social force, for it abolishes at once the most insidious form taken by that division—namely, the separation of owner-entrepreneurs from wage laborers.

Carlyle is, fortunately, more explicit in expressing his disagreement with the second of the fundamental principles of Political Economy—the belief in a free-market system which makes the economy a self-regulating machine. In the first place, working on the level of assertion rather than argument, Carlyle insists that the free-market economy is an ethical monstrosity: "Verily Mammon-worship is a melancholy creed. When Cain, for his own behoof, had killed Abel, and was questioned, 'Where is thy brother?' he too made answer, 'Am I my brother's keeper?' Did I not pay my brother *his* wages, the thing he had merited from me?" [26] It goes without saying that such a line of attack will not take one very far against the close reasonings of Ricardo and Company, and I quote this passage simply to make the point that Carlyle's antipathy to the free-market system is fundamentally moral before it is anything else.

Carlyle begins his attack on the principle of the free market by accepting Political Economy's definition of it. Again he may be likened to Marx in that he finds no reason to deny that the relationships which characterize the capitalist market are indeed free, and thus he raises no factual objection to the capitalist's claim that he did in fact "pay my brother *his* wages, the thing he had merited from me." [27] Yet if the workingman is formally free, both in the sense that he is able to sell his labor power as he chooses and in the sense that equivalent for equivalent is exchanged in this transaction, it is nevertheless the case that this formal freedom is, as both Carlyle and Marx realize, not at all to be confused with substantive freedom:

"This liberty," Carlyle writes, "turns out, before it have long continued in action, with all men flinging up their caps round it, to be, for the Working Millions a liberty to die by want of food. . . ." [28] The fact that the Political Economists are unmistakably right in saying that the free-market system provides its members with liberty and unmistakably wrong in assuming that such liberty is of benefit to its possessors leads Carlyle to conclude that "Liberty requires new definitions." [29] In attempting to provide these new definitions Carlyle was once again brought to consider the problem of work and the worker's relation to his product.[30] We already have seen that in *Sartor Resartus* he developed his "Gospel of Work" in an attempt to find an instrument that could free him from the self-involvement he so much feared. There he had written of the spiritual crisis which culminated in his intense feeling that "To me the Universe was all void of Life, of Purpose, of Volition, even of Hostility: it was one huge, dead, immeasurable Steam-engine, rolling on, in its dead indifference, to grind me limb from limb." [31] By the time he wrote *Past and Present*, however, Carlyle had learned to project this perception outward, recognizing that it is the general condition of a citizenry faced with a dissolving social structure.[32] With this recognition Carlyle transcends the limitations which had vitiated his earlier reflections on work, for when his problem appeared as a purely personal spiritual problem it was inevitable that the conception of work with which he attempted to counter it would be of a purely personal nature also; when, however, he could recognize in his own symptoms the lineaments of a more general infection, it was no longer possible to overlook the social dimension of work. Indeed, he could now see that what he formerly had proposed as the goal of work, alienation of the self, was precisely the problem which modern conditions of work raised most imperatively, the problem most in need of solution.

It is no coincidence that the economic transaction which characterizes the labor market—the alienation by the laborer of his own labor—has provided the term most commonly used to describe the predicament of modern man. In the *Economic and Philosophic Manuscripts*, written within a year or two of *Past and Present* but unpublished during Marx's lifetime, Marx has given us a classic discussion of the connection between the economic act of self-alienation and the spiritual phenomenon known by the same name. Much the same point is made by Carlyle when he argues that the freedom of the free market in labor produces a form of "liberty . . .

which has to purchase itself by social isolation, and each man standing separate from the other, having 'no business with him' but a cash-account: this is such a liberty as the Earth seldom saw. . . ." [33] The direct result of this isolation, which the bourgeois world calls "liberty" and "freedom," is, Carlyle concludes, the anomic sense of living in "a world alien, not your world." [34] Only when the Political Economist's sense of liberty based on "social isolation" has been supplanted by a "new definition" of liberty which takes into account the social interconnectedness necessary for healthy communal organization can the organization of labor which Carlyle called for to replace the economists' division of labor begin to be realizable.

Just as Carlyle denounces Political Economy's conception of a free-market economy, so he dismisses the principle which the Political Economists claimed to derive from the free market. Orthodox economics held, with a serenity which surpasses understanding, that the mechanism of the free market was naturally self-correcting. No argument was needed to refute this claim: one had only to look around at the poverty which beset England in the late 1830s to know that this self-correcting machinery was a delusion. Nor would Carlyle permit the economists to beg off by claiming that the poverty he saw was a temporary aberration which it was necessary to tolerate until the supply-and-demand machine could right itself. On the contrary, Carlyle insists, citing Dr. William Alison, "these things are not of this year, or of last year, have no reference to our present state of commercial stagnation, but only to the common state." [35]

What is more, even if the pervasive poverty of England in the Hungry Forties were the result of a temporary accident of overproduction, as the economists argue, this fact would not help their case, for the very notion of overproduction indicts the entire economic system. As far as Carlyle is concerned, the concept of overproduction is a product of depraved thinking. The primary purpose of industry, after all, is to produce goods; only by providing this service can industry fulfill its secondary purpose of providing a livelihood for the entrepreneurs who run it. Yet to say that an industry is guilty of overproducing is to say that it is guilty of fulfilling its purpose. Like Thorstein Veblen, who also launched a withering attack on this absurd paradox of economic logic, Carlyle recognized that the manufacturers and economists who talk about overproduction have put the business functions of industry above its industrial functions.

Unfortunately, Carlyle does not exploit this insight as Veblen does, by insisting that the direction of industry according to business principles is an antisocial activity and a form of sabotage; [36] instead, Carlyle, who tended to be altogether too patient with the "Captains of Industry," finds in the idea of overproduction another stick with which to beat the government. By any standard it is a legitimate function of government, he reasons, to see to it that workers are paid for their labor; even the Benthamite night-watchman's state insists that debts and wages be truly paid. This being the case, Carlyle addresses the "Governing Class" with unanswerable logic: "My lords and gentlemen,—why, it was *you* that were appointed, by the fact and by the theory of your position on the Earth, to 'make and administer Laws,'—that is to say, in a world such as ours, to guard against 'gluts'; against honest operatives, who have done their work, remaining unfed! I say, *you* were appointed to preside over the Distribution and Apportionment of the Wáges of Work done. . . . These poor shirt-spinners . . . were set to make shirts. The Community with all its voices commanded them, saying, 'Make shirts';—and there the shirts are! Too many shirts? Well, that is a novelty, in this intemperate Earth, with its nine-hundred millions of bare backs! But the Community commanded you, saying, 'See that the shirts are well apportioned, that our Human Laws be emblem of God's Laws';—and where is the apportionment?" [37]

If, then, the social division of labor is an anarchic system which must be replaced by an organization of labor in which the workman will be recognized as having a "permanent interest" in the "joint enterprise" of which he forms an essential part, and if the free market is a hoax which must be replaced by a governmental system which will assure the just "Distribution and Apportionment of the Wages of Work done," then what, one may well wonder, is left of the third principle of Political Economy—the principle of private property, which undergirds the entire structure Carlyle was busy demolishing? The answer, obviously, is that nothing is left.

Carlyle discusses this matter specifically only with regard to landed property, as is natural at a time when the landed interest's virtual monopoly over governmental functions had not yet been dismantled. Writing three years before Corn Law Repeal exploded the political hegemony of the landed connection, Carlyle found it convenient to repeat an argument Cobbett had used in his *Legacy to Labourers*. An examination of English history, Carlyle says, teaches us that the landed Norman nobility holds its lands from the king in return for certain services provided to the crown. The chief of these services is the orderly government of the territory to which the noble lays claim: "I say, you did *not* make the Land of England; and, by the possession of it, you *are* bound to furnish guidance and government to England! That is the law of your position on this God's-Earth. . . ." [38] By this argument Carlyle inverts the traditional conservative line of reasoning, which sees the right of government as a right deriving from the ownership of real property. On the contrary, he argues, government is not a right but a responsibility which falls to the landed aristocracy as their means of paying for the fruits which they reap from lands which they possess but do not rightly own. Cobbett had pushed this argument as far as it would go, frankly declaring that the people would be within their rights if they were to confiscate lands which the aristocracy was unable to govern. "Well, then, what is the conclusion to which we come at last?" he asked in his final work. "Why, that the labourers have a right to subsistence out of the land, in all cases of inability to labour; that all those who are able to labour have a right to subsistence out of the land, in exchange for their labour; and that, if the holders of the land will not give them subsistence, in exchange for their labour, they have a right to the land itself." [39]

Carlyle, who was generally less bold than Cobbett, is less explicit about confiscation, and he therefore tends to put his thoughts on the subject into the mouths of a hypothetical rabble, where they serve as threats rather than as declarations of principle. "Do you count what treasuries of bitter indignation [the Corn Laws] are laying up for you in every just English heart?" he asks the aristocracy. "Do you know what questions, not as to Corn-prices and Sliding-scales alone, they are *forcing* every reflective Englishman to ask himself?" [40] The landed aristocracy, in short, no longer meets the obligations which entitle it to its lands, and is therefore not entitled to them. "Aristocracy has become Phantasm-Aristocracy, no longer able to *do* its work, not in the least conscious that it has any work longer to do. Unable, totally careless to *do* its work; careful only to clamour for the *wages* of doing its work. . . ." [41]

There is no denying that Carlyle would like to see this situation reversed; indeed, his reputation for Toryish leanings stems largely from the fact that he would seem to have had no principled reason for objecting if the aristocracy were to take control of England and govern it in such a way as to enhance the welfare of the masses. As far as he was concerned, it was an either-or proposition: either the aristocracy must provide a salubrious government or it must renounce its title to land and its pretensions of authority. At times he even seems keenly eager to see the nobility reassert itself,[42] but this is neither here nor there, for Carlyle never deluded himself into believing that the aristocracy was any more likely to rise from its torpor than the dead to rise from their graves. He could see clearly, by comparing the "Idle Aristocracy" of landowners to the "Working Aristocracy" of industrialists, that the future of the former was well-nigh hopeless: "Alas, alas, the Working Aristocracy, admonished by Trades-unions, Chartist conflagrations, above all by their own shrewd sense kept in perpetual communion with the fact of things, will assuredly reform themselves, and a working world will still be possible:—but the fate of the Idle Aristocracy, as one reads its horoscope hitherto in Corn-Laws and suchlike, is an abyss that fills one with despair." [43] Carlyle was fond of telling the landed aristocracy that they should abandon their dilettantish ways and reclaim their traditional prerogatives as governors, but I find nothing to indicate that he ever took their chances seriously. Even in his notorious essay of 1867, "Shooting Niagara: And After?" he tells the game-preserving class to do some useful work and then is at a loss to imagine what sort of useful work they might do. As a result, he is forced to conclude, rather dolefully, that "Few Noble Lords, I may believe, will think of taking this course; indeed not many, as Noble Lords now are, could do much good in it." [44] Those critics who imagine that Carlyle was a conservative or a reactionary in his attitude toward the aristocracy have missed the point: he only wanted to be one.

His thinking about the institution of private property in land, then, can be summed up by saying that, although he never explicitly advocated confiscation, he put his moral authority behind threats of confiscation, which he attributed to "every just English heart," and, what is more, he developed a line of reasoning which pointed to confiscation as its inevitable conclusion. Indeed, in *Past and Present* he speaks to the aristocracy in words that sound very much like a farewell: "We advise thee," he told them, "to put up thy parchments [i.e., title deeds]; to go home to thy place, and make no needless noise whatever." [45]

With respect to capitalist, industrial property, Carlyle's thinking seems to have been less carefully worked out and less rigorously developed. With industrial property as with landed property he held to a functional criterion of proprietorship which led him to envision the parceling out of ownership between the head-workers directing industry and the hand-workers in the shop itself. But, despite the fact that he speaks in quasi-syndicalist terms of establishing industry on the basis of joint ownership by erstwhile wage laborers and entrepreneurs, such ideas come in for very scant attention in his works, and for the most part his position seems to be more St. Simonian than syndicalist.

For a number of years Carlyle followed with keen interest the development of St. Simonianism in France, and, as I have noted already, he borrowed the concept of the "organization of labor" from that source. This St. Simonian influence is largely responsible for Carlyle's thoroughly misplaced faith in the ability of the so-called Captains of Industry to lead England to a new social order. Whenever he spoke about industry he tended, like his French counterparts, to feel that industrial entrepreneurs held the key to the future and that one of the most important steps his country could take toward a future of plenty and prosperity involved dismantling the remnants of feudal irrationality which continued to shackle this titanic class. When he was in this St. Simonian vein Carlyle was staunchly convinced that the failure to properly order English society to date had been the fault of the governing—especially the landed—classes and that the productive classes, when given their turn, would not fail in this way: "My firm belief is, that, finding himself now enchanted, hand-shackled, foot-shackled, in Poor-Law Bastilles and elsewhere, he [i.e., British industrialism] will retire three days to his bed, and *arrive* at a conclusion or two!" [46]

In Carlyle's arguments about Captains of Industry we can see one of the first signs that he was beginning to slow down and fall behind the times in his observations of contemporary socioeconomic conditions. Carlyle had been introduced to St. Simonianism in the 1820s, at a time when such ideas were far more appropriate to the British situation than they would be in 1843. As Marx observes, the postulation of common interests between workers and industrial entrepreneurs, and of irreconcilable conflict between both of them and the landed classes, was put forward as radical doctrine "at a time when the proletariat still had interests in common with the industrial and petty bourgeoisie. Compare, for example, the writings of Cobbett and P. L. Courrier or Saint-Simon, who originally numbered the industrial capitalists among his 'workers' as opposed to his 'idlers,' the rentiers." [47]

For the rest of his life Carlyle was to number the Captains of Industry among his workers and to insist that they are "England's hope at present." [48] The persistence with which he repeated these outdated St. Simonian doctrines may be an early indication of the drying up of his creative powers, which was to make his work after *Past and Present* an increasingly arid desert containing fewer and fewer new growths. For the time being, though, Carlyle was perceptive enough to see that there was much in the conduct of the Captains of Industry that made it virtually impossible for them to play the role in which he had cast them. Indeed, as soon as he begins to characterize the features that hedge the nobility of his "Working Aristocracy," he leaves St. Simon—and such of his own followers as Ruskin and Morris—far behind, for he recognizes that what is wrong with capitalist industry is precisely the capitalist principles upon which it is conducted. Where St. Simon drew no distinction between business and industry, so that bankers, for example, held some very prominent seats on the committee through which St. Simonianism would rule the world, Carlyle drew such a distinction and drew it sharply. For industrialism as a system of production he has nothing but praise: "noble LABOUR . . . ," he writes, "is yet to be the King of this Earth, and sit on the highest throne. . . ." [49] But for capitalism as the system of conducting industry on the basis of profit-and-loss business principles he has nothing but condemnation. He severely ridicules the notion that England's industrial superiority depended upon competitively underselling the other nations of Europe: "The saddest news is, that we should find our National Existence, as I sometimes hear it said, depend upon selling manufactured cotton at a farthing an ell cheaper than any other People. A most narrow stand for a great Nation to base itself upon! . . . Farthing cheaper per yard? No great Nation can stand on the apex of such a pyramid; screwing itself higher and higher; balancing on its great-toe!" he proclaimed.[50] The voice of industry is, he writes, "the one God's Voice we have heard in these two atheistic centuries," but it has been perverted by the principles of "Supply-and-demand, Cash-payment . . . , Free-trade, Competition, and Devil take the hindmost" until "we hear it not to be the Voice of God to us, but regard it merely as a Voice of earthly Profit-and-Loss." [51]

Writing at a time when the industrial management and the business management of manufacturing enterprises were invariably in the same hands, Carlyle separated them conceptually and called for the purging of business principles from industry. On every possible occasion he denounced developments in the field of advertising, or

"Puffery," as symptoms of the increasing power business was coming to exercise over industry. As early as 1831 he wryly commented that Political Economy should include a subdiscipline to be called the *"Statistics of Imposture"* for the purpose of discovering "How far . . . man's Want is supplied by true Ware; how far by the mere Appearance of true Ware. . . ." [52] Similarly, in *Past and Present* he asks us to "Consider . . . that great Hat seven-feet high, which now perambulates London Streets. . . . The Hatter in the Strand of London, instead of making better felt-hats than another, mounts a huge lath-and-plaster Hat, seven-feet high, upon wheels; sends a man to drive it through the streets; hoping to be saved *thereby*. He has not attempted to *make* better hats, as he was appointed by the Universe to do, and as with this ingenuity of his he could very probably have done; but his whole industry is turned to *persuade* us that he has made such! He too knows that the Quack has become God." [53]

The quack to whom Carlyle is referring is of course the businessman, for, as Thorstein Veblen pointed out eighty years after Carlyle wrote those words, "[The] decay of the old-fashioned competitive system has consisted in a substitution of competitive selling in the place of that competitive production of goods that is always presumed to be the chief and most serviceable feature of the competitive system. That is to say, it has been a substitution of salesmanship in the place of workmanship; as would be due to happen so soon as business came to take precedence of industry, salesmanship being a matter of business, not of industry; and business being a matter of salesmanship, not of workmanship." [54]

Ironically, history was to perform in fact the same disaggregation of industrial and business management that Carlyle called for, but it was to do so in precisely the way that Carlyle most feared. By the end of the nineteenth century it was apparent, preeminently to Veblen, that industrial management and business management were in the hands of two distinct sets of personnel, and that it was the latter who held sway. Carlyle had looked forward to the day when the Captains of Industry would no longer debase their "instinct of workmanship" [55] by considerations of salesmanship, and in a manner of speaking this situation has come to pass—but it has done so precisely because the Captains of Industry surrendered the salesmanly function to the business managers, from whom they willingly took their orders. "Before this turn in human affairs," Veblen writes, summing up the difference between Carlyle's day and his own, "thoughtful men were asking if business is good for industry, since then the engrossing question is whether industry is good for business." [56]

In 1843 Carlyle had indeed asked whether business was good for industry, and his answer was an unequivocal no. Yet, having given this answer, Carlyle persisted in the delusion that Plugson of Undershot, his prototypical manufacturer, would miraculously free himself from the snare of "Cheap and Nasty" production and reassert the primacy of honest workmanship. In 1867, in the infamous "Shooting Niagara: And After?" Carlyle finally acknowledged that his Captain of Industry, far from providing moral leadership for the working class, was in fact misleading it.[57] Yet even at this point he continued to believe that urging Plugson to mend his ways might help to improve the situation.

This stubborn persistence in a hopelessly inadequate prescription stems, as most such strategic blunders do, from a misconception of the nature of the problem to be dealt with. In Carlyle's case the mistake lay in thinking that the industrial and business aspects of capitalist manufacture were connected only accidentally, and that, therefore, it would be possible in principle to separate them without a root-and-branch reorganization of industry.[58] This mistake in turn derives from a striking inadequacy in Carlyle's critique of Political Economy. As we have seen, in the economic analyses of *Past and Present* Carlyle repudiated the notion that the division of labor was a means of social cooperation, insisted that the free market, especially the free market in labor, was a shameless hoax, and indicated a willingness to entertain alternatives to the institution of private property—certainly an impressive polemical achievement. Nevertheless, despite the fact that Carlyle was, one is inclined to say, temperamentally equipped with a naturally dialectical mind and an untaught tendency to perceive the universe in dialectical terms, he seems never to have applied dialectics in his economic analyses. As a result his critique of Political Economy is unnecessarily absolutistic, forcing him to substitute stridency and ringing moral imperatives for a genuine historical analysis of the economic institutions with which he is concerned. Unlike Marx, who used the Hegelian dialectic to turn Political Economy against itself, Carlyle was able to level against the Ricardian status quo only a flat repudiation, which left him with no conception of how one would get from the discredited system to a new social, economic, and moral order. Marx's economic analysis always kept itself within the categories established by bourgeois economics, in the sense that it took the economists' *homo economicus* and raised him to the level of a historical principle—namely, the principle of economic determinism. By doing this Marx was able to project Political Economy into history, to show the contradictions inherent in the classical economic system, and to combine this awareness of history with this awareness of contradiction in such a way as to demonstrate, at least logically, the inevitability of the collapse of industrial capitalism. For Marx, contradiction projected over time equals disintegration.

Carlyle, however, did not see Political Economy as contradicting itself; on the contrary, it was he who was doing the contradicting. The upshot of this missed opportunity was that Carlyle's sense of the unacceptability of the principles of Political Economy and his sense of history never fused. The former exists in a timeless space that too often resembles the realm of ethical and religious imperatives, and the latter relates to it only in the most blatantly apocalyptical fashion. Despite Carlyle's elaborate analogies between the past and the present, his analysis of the desperate situation produced by the prevailing economic system is carried on in ethically absolute and ahistorical terms. Because he does not see the system as self-contradicting, he does not see it as self-destroying, for it does not contain an internal principle of corruption. Therefore it can be destroyed only in two ways: by an act of will or conversion—that is, a reform of the heart—or by a violent, apocalyptical explosion. The former he often recognizes to be so unlikely as to make hoping for it nothing less than delusional, and he was therefore left to face, in one form or another, the prospect of revolutionary explosion.

What is more, even with respect to this more or less inevitable revolution, Carlyle's thinking suffers from his failure to historicize his critique of Political Economy. Here too the failure to see the capitalist system as self-contradictory turns out to be a costly mistake, for it means that Carlyle must assign to the revolution the task of exploding an economic system which would remain structurally sound up until the very end. Unlike Marx, for whom the revolution would be the last pitched battle of what later radicals were to stigmatize as a "dying culture," Carlyle could see revolution only as a final judgment passed by god and the proletariat against a system which refused to grow weaker on its own. There is nothing in Carlyle to correspond with Marx's sense of the inevitable inward collapse of capitalism, nothing to correspond with Marx's awareness that the indignation of the proletariat could only be half of the picture, the other half of which must be completed with the declining rate of profits and the ever-narrowing circumference of the business cycle. Without these factors to rot the system from within, Marx recognized, there was nothing to prevent the coming revolution from going the way of all peasant and artisan uprisings from the fifteenth century to the nineteenth. With them, however, one had every reason to be sanguine about the results of a proletarian revolution. In contrast, Carlyle, to whom a popular revolution appeared as an attack on a vicious but nonetheless hearty system, could face this prospect only with despair. Thus, while he yearned for revolutionary change, revolution itself was a prospect he contemplated with horror. This paradox Carlyle expressed in his desire to see the completion of the French Revolution without the repetition of it.

3. The Cash Nexus

The fear that the upper social classes are being infiltrated by outsiders who have no qualifications for deference except the possession of money is an old fear. The nouveaux riches, it seems, have been subjects of satires for as long as satires have been written, and the arriviste is invariably seen as a threat to the status values of traditional society. The difference between the social sphere of existence, which is organized in terms of status, and the economic sphere, organized in terms of wealth, was sensed instinctively by both the entrenched gentility and the moneyed gate-crashers, so that, generally speaking, it was the latter who were on the defensive. They took one of two courses, either adopting protective coloration by pretending to gentility, as in the case of Thackeray's John Pendennis, who bought an estate, a collection of newly minted family portraits, and a fabricated lineage with the money he got for his apothecary's shop; or launching a preemptive strike by impudently proclaiming that the self-made man was inherently superior to the man who had been made by his father.

Yet even while the arrivistes were engaged in these essentially defensive measures, the social gatekeepers themselves were already surrendering. Just when the possessors of social status began to recognize that status was unable to compete with money, even for their own loyalties, is not clear, but even in the seventeenth century we can find Lord Clarendon complaining that "a vile and sordid Love of Money" had grown to be the mortar which held society together. Similarly, David Lloyd contrasted the post-Commonwealth society in which he lived with an earlier age by pointing out that

"Noblemen in those days esteemed the love of their neighbours more than their fear, and the service and fealty of their tenants more than their money. Now the landlord hath the sweat of the tenant's brow in his coffers: then he had the best blood in his veins at his command." [59]

About a hundred years after Lloyd wrote these words and seventy years before Carlyle turned his attention to the "cash nexus," Adam Smith, in a passage which by any standard must rank as one of the high points of eighteenth-century prose, observed much the same phenomenon. Smith describes the process by which the great landed proprietors bartered their social status (which he terms "authority") and their political power for economic wealth, thereby becoming "as insignificant as any substantial burgher or tradesman in a city." He recounts how the English nobility, which successfully had resisted the efforts of the crown to subordinate their power to its own, was finally humbled by

the silent and insensible operation of foreign commerce and manufactures. . . . These gradually furnished the great proprietors with something for which they could exchange the whole surplus produce of their lands, and which they could consume themselves without sharing it either with tenants or retainers. All for ourselves, and nothing for other people, seems, in every age of the world, to have been the vile maxim of the masters of mankind. As soon, therefore, as they could find a method of consuming the whole value of their rents themselves, they had no disposition to share them with any other persons. For a pair of diamond buckles perhaps, or for something as frivolous and useless, they exchanged the maintenance, or what is the same thing, the price of the maintenance of a thousand men for a year, and with it the whole weight and authority which it could give them. The buckles, however, were to be all their own, and no other human creature was to have any share of them; whereas in the more ancient method of expence they must have shared with at least a thousand people. With the judges that were to determine the preference, this difference was perfectly decisive; and thus, for the gratification of the most childish, the meanest and the most sordid of all vanities, they gradually bartered their whole power and authority.

In a country where there is no foreign commerce, nor any of the finer manufactures, a man of ten thousand a year cannot well employ his revenue in any other way than in maintaining, perhaps, a thousand families, who are all of them necessarily at his command. In the present state of Europe, a man of ten thousand a year can spend his whole revenue, and he generally does so, without directly maintaining twenty people, or being able to command more than ten footmen not worth the commanding. [60]

In this brilliant piece of analysis Smith acutely diagnoses what is to be the overriding concern of his heirs in the nineteenth century

—the subversion of the social realm of status by the importation into it of the values appropriate to the economic sphere of wealth.[61] Half a century later Dickens was to begin generating a series of novels almost obsessed with this theme; from *Oliver Twist*, which he endlessly rewrote in all its possible permutations, to *Great Expectations*, which is a sort of diabolical parody of this original prototype, he returned again and again to this issue. In the earlier form of the story little Oliver, actually the scion of a respectable house, is kidnapped by criminals and doomed to wander England until he can find (or be discovered by) his true status group; in the later form Pip, truly a child of the lower classes, is as it were kidnapped by a robber who attempts to move him up in status just as Fagin had tried to pull Oliver down. What remains constant in both versions is the insistence that certain bloodlines of status and respectability remain unchanged by vicissitudes of wealth: charity boy or schoolboy, Oliver is still Oliver and Pip is still Pip.

In Thackeray too we see the same fascinated observation of the interplay between the status conferred by gentle birth and the pseudo-status conferred by money. And in Trollope's *The Way We Live Now* we find, especially in the figure of Melmotte, an insight into just how far the process had gone; for Melmotte proclaims again and again that wealth has so far appropriated the nature of status that it has come to take on the quality of intangibility which had always characterized status distinctions but never before had been an attribute of wealth. Wealth and status have become so indistinguishable that Melmotte is quite right when he insists that it does not matter that his railroad in America is a hoax and that his money is fictitious, for he will in fact be rich as long as the illusion is unbroken and people take him to be rich. In Melmotte's world, that is, wealth has become so entirely a status attribute that it exists exclusively as a function of social recognition.[62]

Trollope's Melmotte is an example in the social sphere of a phenomenon which, in the examination of James Mill's *Essay on Government* in Chapter VI, we already have seen at work in the political sphere.[63] Trollope and Mill each recognize one half of the same fact: that the forms of power and status have been filled by the content of wealth, and that, as a result, economic functioning has taken on attributes traditionally pertaining to the worlds of politics and society. So important was this fact that the nineteenth century developed two major ideologies for dealing with it. One of them, Political Economy, stood as its champion, while the other, Marxism, seemed to be denouncing it; but they both share the assumption that the springs that move men and history are of an economic nature. Marxism, no less than Political Economy, assumes that wealth, power, and status are or have become merely alternative forms of the same economic substance.

Whether in novels, economic theory, political analysis, or general culture criticism, perception of the fact that economic modes of functioning were replacing the categories of social and political life stands as one of the characteristic features of nineteenth-century consciousness. In the middle of the century Marx, Mill, Thackeray, Dickens, and Trollope all dealt with this phenomenon in one way or another, and at the end of the century a series of brilliant socio-logical formulations continued to show that in the identification of the social and economic spheres one could find the key to what had gone wrong with the modern world. Emile Durkheim's *anomie*, Ferdinand Tönnies' *Gesellschaft*, Thorstein Veblen's business ethic, and Max Weber's formal rationality stand against, respectively, the ideals of solidarity, *Gemeinschaft*, workmanship, and substantive ra-tionality. In each of these cases what is being observed is the disinte-gration of the normative, value-giving community and its replace-ment by "value-neutral" modes of behavior modeled on or derived from economic activity. As Tönnies observed, borrowing a phrase from Smith, in the Gesellschaft "Every man . . . becomes in some measure a merchant. . . ."[64]

In any survey of the literature dealing with the interpenetration of society by the economy the name of Thomas Carlyle must rank prominently, for it was Carlyle who set the terms for such discus-sions in nineteenth-century England. With his reiterated assertions that a "Cash Nexus" had come to replace traditional bonds of social solidarity, Carlyle codified in a most memorable way one of the main concerns of cultural criticism both in his century and in ours. There is, one must admit, nothing particularly distinctive in the content of Carlyle's analysis of the cash nexus. As an interpretation of the observable facts of modern society it is neither subtle nor complex. But, precisely because the idea of the cash nexus is both so simple and so fundamental, there is considerable danger of underesti-mating its importance and of misconceiving the conclusions to which it leads.

To a large extent the significance of the cash nexus critique has gone unnoticed heretofore because commentators on Carlyle have failed to notice that the critique is fundamentally sociological rather than ethical. Without a single exception, the literature on Carlyle has interpreted his ideas about the cash nexus as expressions of his dissatisfaction with the values of capitalistic society and as complaints about the disproportionate attention modern society has given to money relationships. Interpreted in this way, Carlyle's arguments are reduced to debates dealing with the quantitative question of the amount of emphasis a society should place on economic and noneconomic matters. The theory of the cash nexus thus becomes, descriptively, a claim that too much attention is given to money relationships, and, prescriptively, an insistent demand that more attention be paid to noneconomic forms of social interaction. Undoubtedly the most unfortunate result of this reduction of Carlyle's thought to an ethical principle lies in just this tendency to make its descriptive and its prescriptive dimensions identical, for in ethical discourse the postulation of values involves automatically the recommendation that those values be respected and the establishment of norms in terms of which actions are to be described and measured.

In other words, if the cash nexus critique is fundamentally ethical, then there never can be any doubt about what should be done about the situation; if the problem were simply one of a population's having forgotten certain values, then in principle reminding them of those values would be the way to correction. Yet, as we have seen already, Carlyle was for the most part quite well aware that the chances of ethical correction—what I have been calling a reform of the heart—were dim indeed. "Certainly it were a fond imagination to expect that any preaching of mine could abate Mammonism . . . ," he wrote in *Past and Present*, less because he doubted his own powers of argument or suspected that the public was irredeemable than because he recognized that preaching was an inappropriate approach to the problem.[65]

To understand why this should be so, we must acknowledge the fundamentally sociological nature of the cash nexus critique. Again and again Carlyle insists in his indictment of the modern order that the problem he is concerned with involves no less than the complete atrophy of the social world. As early as *Sartor Resartus* Carlyle had noted "that Teufelsdröckh is one of those who consider Society, properly so called, to be as good as extinct. . . ."[66] This change is qualitative, not merely quantitative; "all human dues and reciprocities have been fully changed into one great due of *cash payment*," he laments, making clear that the situation to be faced derives from the absence of socially derived norms.[67] What is more, such norms are absent from British culture because the social world, which is the only source from which they can be derived, has ceased to function.

In line with the thinking of modern structural sociology, Carlyle recognizes that the values whose loss he is lamenting have their roots in the institutional structures which channel and organize social interaction. As Talcott Parsons explains, the "self-interested motives" of individuals—that is, the motives that hold sway in what I have been calling the economic world—must be organized by social institutions if society is to have any normative system at all. These self-interested motives, Parsons writes, "cannot, as economic theory has tended to do, be treated at random relative to the *social* structure. . . . For it is precisely around social institutions that, to a very large extent, the content of self-interest is organized. Indeed, this organization of what are the otherwise, within broad limits, almost random potentialities of the self-interested tendencies of human action into a coherent system, may be said, in broad terms, to be one of the most important functions of institutions. Without it, society could scarcely be an order, in the sense in which we know it, at all." [68]

Using Parsons' terms, one may say that Carlyle's contention was no less than that society had become scarcely an order, in the sense in which we used to know it, at all. Insofar as the nonnormative, rational mode of functioning—that is, the economic world—has supplanted the normative, value-giving social world, it has destroyed not merely values, but the source of values as well. What is commonly described as the atomistic society of capitalistic relationships is, Carlyle explicitly insists, no society at all: "We call it a Society," he complains, but we "go about openly professing the totalest separation, isolation." [69] In other words, Carlyle recognized, as Parsons was to do, that "it is precisely around social institutions" that the economic world must be organized if there is to be a viable social order, but he did not think it therefore followed that British culture was so organized. As a thinker who took idea systems very seriously, seeing in them reflections of the arrangements actually operant in the societies from which they derived, Carlyle was not likely to conclude that economic theory was wrong in claiming that social relationships were derived from the self-interested actions of the economic world. The problem with Political Economy was not that it was mistaken but that it was tragically correct: Homo Economicus was not an economist's delusion, for he walked abroad in England as though he were a citizen.[70]

Two important conclusions are derivable from the foregoing analysis, and they define and give shape to the final stages in the development of Carlyle's thought. The first, which I have hinted at already, is the negative finding that the way out of the mid-nineteenth-century predicament can be found in neither the economic nor the social realm. Trying to cure England by applications of enlightened economic policy is, according to Carlyle's analysis, like dosing a patient with the virus that caused the disease from which he is dying. The poverty and wasted lives Carlyle saw around him resulted from the hegemony which the economic principles of self-interested calculation already maintained. Enlightened economic policy at best could shore up the system for a short while, postponing complete collapse for a decade or so; but this could not alter the fact that the competitive system based solely on a cash nexus was doomed, if for no other reason than that the judgment of god was pronounced against it.[71] Carlyle's Old Testament god, however, was a deity as notorious for his patience with the intolerable as he was celebrated for his ultimate firmness in dealing with it. Timely intercession was scarcely to be looked for from this quarter, so that unless one could find some principle of change that did not have its roots in the Greatest Happiness Principle, England was doomed to suffer either more or less quietly until the not very distant day when she would erupt into cataclysmic revolution.

Furthermore, given the fact that the problem to be solved results from the subversion of the social world of status relationships by the economic world of wealth relationships, it follows not only that one ought not turn to the economic world for answers but also that one cannot turn to the social world. Indeed, to believe that the problem can be cured in this way is to deny that it exists, for capitalist society at this stage in its historical career suffers precisely from the inability of institutionalized social values to play their customary role of domesticating and organizing self-interested motives.

From this point Carlyle was inescapably drawn to the second conclusion deducible from the cash nexus analysis. If his observation of the situation is correct, and if he is justified in concluding that neither the economic nor the social modalities of societal interaction are capable of generating a way out of the dilemma, then it follows that the answer, if there is to be one, must lie in the political modality. If the world of wealth is already too powerful, and if the world of status is moribund, then it must be to the world of power that we should turn.

This is of course precisely what Carlyle did, and it is for his theory of power politics that he is most widely known. This theory will provide the subject matter of my concluding chapter, but before turning to it I should like to observe that if the foregoing analysis has succeeded in its aims, it should enable us to recognize that Carlyle's principles of power politics are directly derivable from what certainly appears to be a lucid and insightful account of the problems that beset nineteenth-century England. It is important to emphasize this point because in the past the hero theory and the various political ideas that go along with it have been treated almost exclusively as products of psychopathological elements in Carlyle's personality. I hope it should be clear by now that considerations of psychopathology are irrelevant here; whether they exist or not is quite beside the point. The ascription of an "authoritarian personality" to Carlyle may be of some use to those who are curious about what sort of man Carlyle was, but such psychological insights are being blatantly misused when scholars exploit them to explain away a body of thought. If we were to imagine a Carlyle without these "pathological" attributes, a Carlyle blessed with the decent liberal's antipathy to political authoritarianism, we would still have a Carlyle who saw Victorian England as a jungle in which the values of rampant economic egoism had destroyed all the social nexes and all hopes of their spontaneous regeneration, and in which, therefore, the only hope of avoiding violent and undoubtedly futile revolution lay in the realm of power politics. The only difference would be that such a psychologically "healthy" Carlyle would have been likely to have repudiated this conclusion or to have closed his eyes to it, whereas the Carlyle we have before us accepted it and even welcomed it.

It is and has been my contention that Carlyle's theories of power politics are based on a hard core of observation and analysis. If we are to debunk these theories we must do so not by pointing to the real or imaginary pathological factors which may or may not have led Carlyle to observe what he observed and to reason as he reasoned, but by showing that the observations were erroneous or that the analysis was unsound.

IX

A Whole World of Heroes

Looking at Carlyle's career in retrospect, from the vantage point afforded by *Past and Present,* one becomes aware that his recognition that the solution to England's problems could be found only through the exercise of power had been in the cards for quite some time. Indeed, Carlyle had adopted a power political model of social change considerably before the date of *Past and Present.* In *Sartor Resartus* he had announced his conviction that in "Hero-worship . . . mayest thou discern the corner-stone of living-rock, whereon all Polities for the remotest time may stand secure," and after he had published his lectures *On Heroes and Hero-Worship and the Heroic in History* he wrote to John Stuart Mill that all the doctrines contained therein "lay most legible" in his earlier works.[1]

Yet it is only with *Past and Present,* and as a result of the developmental process I have traced through the first eight chapters of this study, that Carlyle's ideology of power finally falls into place as the completion of his system of thought. In a very real sense his conception of the place of the hero in history, as it appears in *Sartor* and *On Heroes,* is an idea that has come before its time, but with *Past and Present* it is transformed from an intuition into a master idea truly earned through a process of intellectual struggle. Carlyle's development as a thinker is, then, a gradual and at times painfully slow process of validating something which he believed himself to have known all along.

Trained by his family and his church to see the world in the absolutistic frame of reference provided by a sure knowledge of the presence of god as the intelligible center of the universe, Carlyle found himself, as early as his Edinburgh University days, faced with the cultural fact that the traditional cosmic order was dissolving, unable to resist the corrosive force of skeptical, egoistic, and relativistic modes of thought. Fighting a rearguard action for a time, he dealt with the modern world in his early essays as though it could be willed out of existence. Before long, however, it became inescapably clear that skepticism could not be argued away and that the values that had been lost with the loss of god could be regained, if at all, only on a new battlefield.

If the disappearance of god entailed for Carlyle an acute sense of the meaninglessness of life, he could, he discovered, work his way out of this "Centre of Indifference" by building for himself a new center of meaningfulness. By the logic of the situation such a center would have to begin with the self and yet would have to transcend self and relate it to the universe outside. If, in other words, god's world had collapsed into the self, it would be necessary to project that self back upon the world. Only through acting on the world would it be possible to live without the meaningfulness formerly derived from one's relationship to one's maker, for through such secular action one could replace this traditional relationship with one's relationship to what one had made.

For a long time Carlyle's awareness of the crucial significance of action was marred by an inadequate conceptualization of action itself. He was for many years willing to come to rest in what Hannah Arendt has described as the self-alienating world of "work" and to settle for what Karl Mannheim calls the "reproductive" mode of functioning; only gradually did he become aware that it would be necessary for him to move onward into Arendt's self-realizing world of action and Mannheim's creative, "political" mode.

Turning to the world of political action, Carlyle sought to get his bearings in it by means of an ambitious exploration of that world in its single most striking manifestation—the French Revolution. He learned therefrom the fallacy of regarding the political world as an arrangement of theoretically legitimated structures and the necessity of recognizing that, as a realm of pure action, it consisted essentially of authoritative arrangements based on force. Applying this lesson to domestic politics, he measured Chartism, the incipient revolutionary movement of England, by the standards of the French Revolution and concluded that it was impotent to complete the work that its parent revolution in France had begun.

Analyzing the contemporary situation in an attempt to find the type of action that could serve to complete the revolution, Carlyle realized that the master problem of the age was the atrophy of the traditional social structure and the disappearance of the substantively rational modes of action that derived from it. Thus his earliest intuition that the place of the self in the universe was being undermined by the rationalist spirit now became clearly a social rather than purely a personal or spiritual insight, for the hollow formalism of skeptical thought was now recognizable as merely the intellectual manifestation of a social order of which the elemental unit was the cash nexus.

Almost fifteen years before the writing of *Past and Present* Carlyle had been aware that the personal result of surrender to the skeptical spirit was the loss of the power to engage in meaningful action; "we have argued away all force from ourselves," he wrote in "Signs of the Times."[2] By 1840 it had become clear to him that precisely the same fate befell a social order which had taken formal rationality as its organizing principle. Obviously, the only way out of this "utopia of powerlessness," to use Ralf Dahrendorf's illuminating terminology, was to search for power, and the search for power begins and ends in the political world.

My discussion of Carlyle's reflections on power will be divided into two parts. It goes without saying that Carlyle was not alone in recognizing political power as the sovereign remedy for the ills of the day, for he lived at a time when the excluded and disfranchised majority of the population was clamoring for precisely this. Yet, as is widely known, Carlyle was utterly without sympathy for the democratic movement. In the following section, therefore, I shall examine Carlyle's critique of democracy in order to understand why he rejected the major form in which the search for power manifested itself in his own day. Then, in the final three sections of this chapter, I shall examine Carlyle's theories of power and political action in their fully developed form.

1. Radical and Bourgeois Democracy

Insofar as the popular democratic movement expressed working-class dissatisfaction with the British economic system and with the Reformed Parliament which tended to represent it, Carlyle welcomed and applauded it. That such dissatisfaction should take the form of a demand for democracy was, he felt, inevitable, and he never underestimated the value of democratic movements as protest movements. "Democracy, take it where you will in our Europe, is found but as a regulated method of rebellion and abrogation; it abrogates the old arrangement of things; and leaves, as we say, *zero* and vacuity for the institution of a new arrangement." [3] When the old order was as patently incapable of serving the needs of the people as the English government of the late 1830s and early 1840s appeared to be, then a clearing of the decks such as democracy offered was much to be desired.

When Carlyle comes to assess the value of democracy as a system of government rather than as a protest movement, however, his attitude is marked by the hostility and suspicion that have earned him his reputation as a major nineteenth-century antidemocrat. In many ways, though, this reputation is undeserved, as one can see if one examines his thoughts on democracy while keeping in mind a clear sense of what he and what the democrats meant by democracy. Democracy, it seems to me, means primarily one of two things: either it is a political system in which the mass of the population shares directly in policy decisions through actual participation at policy-making meetings or through the use of instructed delegates; or it is a political system in which the mass of the population participates in policy decisions only indirectly, through the election of responsible representatives.

The first of these definitions has little relevance to nineteenth-century discussions of democracy. Certainly the radical egalitarianism implied in the idea of the people directly participating in the political process plays, after Bentham, little or no role in the thinking of the bourgeois democratic movement. There can be no question but that in Jeremy Bentham England produced a bona fide democrat. His principle of "every man to count for one and no man for more than one" is based on an uncompromisingly radical democratic faith, and the implementation of that principle was among the leading causes to which he devoted his career. But I think there can be no question either that the difference between Bentham and the Westminster Radicals, the group most responsible for the struggle to apply Benthamite principles to English politics, lay in the fact that the latter devoted themselves to the systematic watering down of the potent liquors of Bentham's democracy.

In the first place, the Westminster Radicals did not look forward to a democratic system which would open the world of political action to all comers; on the contrary, for them democracy was a system in which the lower orders were to be given a voice in choosing political leaders from among the political classes but emphatically were not to be given entrée to the political arena themselves. Thus

Francis Place, the political lieutenant of the Westminster Radicals, candidly wrote that when he spoke of government by the people, "I mean those among them who take part in public affairs, by whom the rest *must* be governed." "The truth is," Place explained, "that the vulgarity will not choose men from among themselves; they never do so when left perfectly free to choose. In all such cases they invariably choose men of property, in whom they expect to find the requisite appropriate talent, honesty, and business-like habit. . . ." [4]

For bourgeois radicals like those of the Westminster group, it was important that the democratic movement be confined to the franchise question because it was their intention that democracy remain exclusively an electoral phenomenon. The political process was to be opened to all citizens—at least all male citizens, for their demands varied between manhood suffrage and universal suffrage—insofar as the political process was taken to mean merely the right to participate in choosing those who make political decisions; but by no means did they ever intend or imply that they wanted or even would permit this equality of enfranchisement to be used for securing social or economic equality. Indeed, even political equality itself, in other than the sense of equal enfranchisement, was not included in their designs; as John Stuart Mill wrote, by "representative government" the Benthamites meant a system in which "the people would be sufficiently under the guidance of educated intelligence, to make in general a good choice of persons to represent them, and having done so, to leave to those whom they had chosen a liberal discretion." [5]

The Westminster Radicals stressed the fact that "the vulgarity . . . invariably choose men of property" because only if this were the case could they be sure that control of the political process would remain in respectable hands which would not use it to undermine present social and economic arrangements. They denounced above all the hegemony which the landed interest still maintained over English political life, and they struggled to bring the political machinery of the country into harmony with the new social and economic order that had grown up in a commercial and industrial age. A Parliament that was still largely in the hands of the landed gentry, they felt, could not reflect the socioeconomic realities of nineteenth-century life, and it was toward changing this state of affairs that they aimed in their demand for a radical alteration in the membership of Parliament; but a Parliament in the hands of the proletariat might want to change the socioeconomic realities themselves, and this they had no intention of tolerating. "[W]hen directing and organising the Radical agitation," Elie Halévy explains, the Philosophical Radicals did not "doubt that in the equalitarian democracy to which they were tending the rich must remain the natural representatives of the poor. . . ." [6]

With attitudes such as these, the Philosophical Radicals could be democrats only insofar as democracy did not pose a threat either to wealth and the deference it could expect from the "vulgarity," or to the exclusive occupancy of the political sphere by the traditional governing classes, expanded to include the upper bourgeoisie. After the publication of Tocqueville's *Democracy in America*, however, it became increasingly difficult, if not impossible, to count on the democratic movement's willingness to confine itself to electoral matters, as the younger Mill was quick to recognize. The overriding point of Tocqueville's study is that social egalitarianism is the unavoidable concomitant of political democracy, for a system of political equality cannot be in existence long without developing into a system of social equality. With this discovery John Stuart Mill took over the leadership of English middle-class radicalism, focusing his attention on ways of preserving the cultural and social position of the better classes within an increasingly democratic context. Bentham had refused to make qualitative distinctions between the various pleasures to which people of various social orders were susceptible; "if the lower orders have been called the dregs of the population," he wrote, "the higher may, by a much clearer title, be termed the scum of it." [7] But Mill, to the delight of the soi-disant "cultivated" then and since, declared that Bentham had erred in imagining that all pleasures are equal: the demands of culture call upon us to recognize that pushpin is not equal to poetry. With this "correction" of Bentham, which amounts to saying that some pleasures are more equal than others, the radical basis of Bentham's democracy was once and for all destroyed. Mill's achievement as a theorist of democracy lay in his formulation of democratic principles which would not make it necessary for every man to count for one and no man for more than one.

In "What Utilitarianism Is," Mill explains "what I mean by difference of quality in pleasures, or what makes one pleasure more valuable than another, merely as a pleasure. . . ." "Of two pleasures," he writes, "if there be one to which all or almost all who have experience of both give a decided preference, irrespective of any feeling of moral obligation to prefer it, that is the more desirable pleasure. If one of the two is, by those who are completely acquainted with both, placed so far above the other that they prefer it, even though knowing it to be attended with a greater amount of discontent, and would not resign it for any quantity of the other pleasure which their nature is capable of, we are justified in ascribing to the preferred enjoyment a superiority in quality, so far outweighing quantity as to render it, in comparison, of small account." [8]

The elitist implications of this blow struck for culture become apparent in the next paragraph, when Mill goes on to make comparisons between "A being of higher faculties" and "one of an inferior type," between "the superior being" and "the inferior." Immediately there follows his famous aphorism: "It is better to be a human being dissatisfied, than a pig satisfied; better to be Socrates dissatisfied, than a fool satisfied." It does not take a keen ear for literary echoes to recognize that Mill's "pig satisfied" comes from the same barnyard as Burke's "swinish multitude." With the appearance of this essay in 1861, the Benthamite tradition can be said to have completed the process by which it transformed itself from a radically egalitarian to an elitist ideology. Except insofar as it was willing to enter into competition with Disraeli for a share of the deference of the "vulgarity," it had nothing further to offer the democratic movement.

If one turns from the bourgeois to the popular democratic movement one finds much the same indifference to the idea that democracy entails direct popular participation in political decision making. For a time the industrial workers of the north held democratic principles of the type described in my first definition with respect to their industrial relations. As Sidney and Beatrice Webb have shown, early trade unionism was staunchly committed to a program of delegational democracy, and toward this end union offices were held on a rotating basis and heavy use was made of referenda and rank-and-file initiatives. This ideal of delegational democracy was, however, confined to internal trade union matters and never extended into the political ideology of the workers.[9] On the contrary, we find in their political attitudes an unshakable faith in the powers of political leadership and a cult of personality centered on Feargus O'Connor.

Indeed, not only did the industrial working class not insist that it should participate directly in the making of political decisions, but it even tended, in selecting the representatives who would make the decisions on its behalf, to choose them from among the higher social classes, as Place had predicted it would. It was no Tory fantasy that

Walter Bagehot was expressing when he claimed that the English constitution was held together by the deference of the lower classes toward their social betters—as election returns after the 1867 franchise extension confirmed.[10] To be sure, two of the Chartists' points—the abolition of the property qualification for members of Parliament and the institution of payment to members—were aimed at making it possible for the workers to choose MPs from among themselves, but against this must be set the fact that no major Chartist leader was drawn from the industrial working class. Not until the rise of the Labour Party toward the end of the century did the industrial workers of England show any disposition to choose their political leaders from their own ranks, and it took almost thirty years of working-class enfranchisement for the first son of a worker to make his way to the British cabinet.[11]

If participatory or delegational forms of democracy were not what the factory operatives of the north meant by democracy, they were still less what the skilled artisans of the London Working Men's Association meant. Of course the LWMA rigorously purged the idea of leadership from its own ranks, for its members saw themselves as a fraternity of equals; as William Lovett explained, the LWMA had been formed precisely because he and his fellow founders were dissatisfied with the way "the masses, in their political organizations, were taught to look up to '*great men*' (or to men *professing greatness*) rather than to great principles." [12] But equality within its own ranks did not imply a thoroughgoing commitment to complete political equality, for the LWMA frankly saw itself as an avant-garde faction which had taken upon itself the role of directing and controlling the working-class political movement as a whole. For the LWMA, therefore, national democracy meant giving the working class the vote so that it could choose its governors from among the "honest, sober and reflecting portion" of its ranks—that is, the labor aristocracy.

Thus, neither among the bourgeois radicals, the factory operatives, nor the skilled artisans of the labor aristocracy did democracy mean participatory or delegational democracy. In one way or another all of the important nineteenth-century British democratic movements envisioned democracy as a governmental system in which the overwhelming bulk of the population would participate only in the electoral aspect of the political process. In this context, then, it is little wonder that Carlyle kept insisting that the extension of the franchise to the working class was neither here nor there as far as meaningful changes in the social conditions of England were concerned. The nation as a whole, he recognized, had lost the ability to act meaningfully in the political sphere, and democracy as the democrats of the time conceived it offered no solution to this problem inasmuch as occasional exercise of a voting privilege cannot by any stretch of the imagination be made to be the equivalent of action. "The notion that a man's liberty consists in giving his vote at election-hustings, and saying, 'Behold, now I too have my twenty-thousandth part of a Talker in our National Palaver; will not all the gods be good to me?'—is one of the pleasantest!" he wrote scornfully.[13]

I have noted already that Carlyle believed that the economic policy of a democratically elected legislature inevitably would be a continuation of the laissez-faire program of liberal governments, for a democratic legislature, committed to the removal of class bias in its enactments, would tend automatically to permit the unhindered operation of the "natural" laws which favored the owners of property.[14] When to this argument is added the purely political critique of democracy as an inadequate substitute for political action on the part of the masses, the product is an antidemocratic argument of considerable cogency, which is at the same time untainted with anti-popular sentiments.

In addition to these two arguments—that, politically, democracy is meaningless inasmuch as it does not provide an opportunity for the population as a whole to engage in decisive political action, and that, economically, its policy results would be a disastrous continuation of the policies of Manchester liberalism—Carlyle took a third approach to the issue that does indeed give a small measure of credibility to the charge that his antidemocratic sentiments derive from a reactionary attitude toward the people and their role in government. In this third argument—which does not figure prominently in Carlyle's writings until very late in his career, but which is virtually the only aspect of his campaign against democracy mentioned in the literature on him—Carlyle contends that the electoral process in no way assures that the decision reached by the electorate will be the right one. In this context Carlyle compares the state to a ship and its decisions to the captain's decision as to the course to be taken; if sailors mutiny and take upon themselves the task of determining their course by popular vote, he very reasonably points out, they do not increase the likelihood of their reaching port safely.

The weakness of this argument lies, as should be immediately apparent, in the inappositeness of the analogy, for it is not only the case that there does not exist in political life anything comparable to the "true" course that can be determined in navigation simply by consulting a map, but it is also the case that there is not even anything in politics to compare to the port at which sailors and captain alike are aiming. In political contexts one is more likely to find that the captain may want to go to Liverpool while the crew wants to go to New York. Given such a state of affairs, the notion that the crew cannot increase the likelihood of reaching its desired destination by itself taking over control of the ship is immediately recognizable as nonsense.

There is no denying that the line of reasoning adopted by Carlyle in his third argument against democracy is potentially dangerous insofar as it assumes, first, that there is a single universally acknowledged goal of state action, and, second, that there is an objectively correct way to reach it. From such thinking it may be only a short step to a defense of tyranny and totalitarianism, for this argument makes democracy appear to be supererogatory insofar as the important consideration, even from the point of view of the people themselves, is getting onto the right course.

There are, however, a number of considerations that should go a long way toward mitigating criticisms of Carlyle for having used this absolutist line of argument. In the first place, Carlyle never shows the slightest disposition to believe that the ruling classes of England are a jot more likely to know the right course than are the people themselves. Sailors are not likely to reach port safely by pooling their collective ignorance in order to decide on a course, but neither are they likely to do better by deferring to the single ignorance of the captain. Insofar as this is the case, Carlyle's argument is reactionary only in principle, for it is not accompanied by an attempt to argue that turning England into a democracy will take government out of the hands of a competent ruling class.

Moreover, far more important than the fact that Carlyle never used his sea-captain argument to defend the ruling classes is the fact that, to put it bluntly, belief in a unitary political goal and a correct path for reaching it did not seem very important to Carlyle. Indeed, these ideas are very foreign to the whole drift of his thought, for there were few men in nineteenth-century England who had a keener sense than Carlyle of the dynamic nature of the political world. His *French Revolution* is, as we have seen, informed at all points by a very lively awareness of the multiform nature of historical movement and the way in which combat and contention weave the web of historical reality. Far from being, as Neff, Cassirer, Bentley, and even Froude contend, the lynchpin of his right-wing ideology, Carlyle's third antidemocratic argument depends upon a type of rationalist absolutism which is completely alien to ⹁e spirit of all his historical works.[15]

That Carlyle should have lapsed into absolutist patterns of thought when he attempted to deal with the problem of parliamentary democracy is, I believe, a natural result of the fact that the only model of the parliamentary system of government current in English political thought at the time was such as would make absolutism an unavoidable adjunct of any discussion of the role of Parliament. For centuries English political theorists of both the left and the right have seen the legislative process in exactly the absolutist terms Carlyle uses. From Sir Edward Coke through Walter Bagehot, Parliament was described as a forum for the discussion of public issues by public-spirited legislators, rather than as an arena in which various interest groups do battle. "Parliament," Edmund Burke had declared to his constituents in Bristol, "is not a *congress* of ambassadors from different and hostile interests, which interests each must maintain, as an agent and advocate, against other agents and advocates; but Parliament is a *deliberative* assembly of *one* nation, with *one* interest, that of the whole—where not local purposes, not local prejudices, ought to guide, but the general good, resulting from the general reason of the whole. You choose a member, indeed; but when you have chosen him, he is not member of Bristol, but he is a member of *Parliament*." [16]

According to this conception of the legislative process, the worthy parliamentarian should sift the arguments of the distinct and often hostile interests of which society is composed, and from these conflicting claims distill out the best policy for all concerned. Such a model of the parliamentary process depends entirely upon the assumption that a "best policy" exists and that it is discernible by a sufficiently capacious intelligence. Make Parliament the closest possible approximation to the "Collective Wisdom" of the nation, and you virtually ensure its choosing the best course and arriving safely at port. Thinkers as diverse as Edmund Burke, Jeremy Bentham, William Cobbett, Matthew Arnold, John Stuart Mill—and Thomas Carlyle—all employed a model of the legislative process in which the individual legislator was expected to perform the task which twentieth-century political theory tends to assign to the legislative process as a whole. Today we are, in principle at least, less likely to be taken in by the fiction that the political process is merely man's tumultuous way of attempting to discover what it is objectively and absolutely best for the state to do, for the political process, it now seems clear, is not aimed at discovering the best decision that can be reached but at creating such decision as it can.[17]

It is significant in this context that Carlyle has recourse to rationalist-absolutist arguments only in connection with the question of the best way of securing an able legislature. There is, however, no justification for concluding that his use of this argument, with its assumption of the existence of timeless, absolute, rationally knowable political truths, reveals the presence in Carlyle of antipopular sentiments, inasmuch as it is based on well-nigh universal assumptions about the nature of parliamentary government. When he deals with politics in any context other than the purely legislative one, scarcely a trace of this absolutism is to be found—and the point to be borne in mind here is that he almost always deals with politics in other than legislative terms, for he did not believe that a deliberative assembly was capable of engaging in political action.

To Carlyle, for whom history is the constantly changing and multiform pattern of man's struggling movements through time, the ratiocinations of a deliberative body were totally irrelevant, for politics is a historical process rather than a rational one, a matter of strength rather than of wisdom. Political "truths" are not discovered by discussion: they are created by acting them out; they become true only insofar as one has the power to realize them in action, and action was precisely what a parliament was incapable of. Indeed, Walter Bagehot was to praise the British system of government specifically for its dampening effect on action, claiming that government by discussion provides "the greatest hindrance to the inherited mistake of human nature, to the desire to act promptly. . . ."[18] Carlyle detested it for much the same reason: "A Parliament, any conceivable Parliament," he wrote in 1850, "continuing to attempt the function of Governor, can lead us only into No-Government which is called Anarchy. . . ."[19] He had said of the Legislative Assembly in revolutionary France that "The history of the Revolution, one finds, is seldom or never there," and he found no reason to believe that the case would be any different with the English Houses of Parliament.

In sum, then, Carlyle's thoroughgoing critique of democracy is based on his conviction that a democratic government will inevitably be a bourgeois government committed to laissez-faire economic policies; that the right to exercise the privilege of choosing one twenty-thousandth part of one six-hundredth part of a deliberative body does not give the members of a community adequate scope for action in the political sphere; and, finally, that democracy is not an appropriate means for choosing a deliberative assembly—a fact which Carlyle finds more or less trivial inasmuch as he has no use whatsoever for deliberative assemblies.

What England needs, then, is a form of government capable of defending the interests of the classes least favored in the natural course of things, capable of decisive action itself, and allowing ample scope for action on the part of the people as a whole. In his hero theory Carlyle believed he had found the principles upon which such a type of government could be built.

2. The Hero in Carlylean History

Behind Carlyle's critique of democracy as an inadequate way of meeting the needs of the people—that is, as an inadequate method of organizing England for political and social regeneration—lay a positive sense of the direction English political life must take. The so-called hero theory served Carlyle as a focal point around which he could arrange all that he wanted to affirm about contemporary political reality. For him the hero theory was both a historical and a moral principle, and his claim that it "lay most legible" in all that he had written is not far from the truth.

There is nothing in the least complex or intricate about Carlyle's conception of heroes, their role in history, and the role he would have them play in society as he wants it to be, although the amount of polemical ink spilled on the subject can lead one to imagine that Carlyle's thinking about heroes and the heroic is a mass of subtleties which requires considerable critical unraveling. The hero theory is neither more nor less than the claim that, in the final analysis, the process we call history is a web of individual actions.

Carlyle begins his one book devoted specifically to the subject of heroes with the statement that "Universal History, the history of what man has accomplished in this world, is at bottom the History of the Great Men who have worked here." [20] It is an unfortunate opening, in that it has provided so convenient—though inaccurate—an encapsulation of his hero theory that practically all of the critical literature on the subject has amounted to little more than an extended gloss on this single text. For example, in Sidney Hook's *The Hero in History* we find that scornful attention is directed at "the Carlylean fantasy that the great man was responsible for the very conditions of his emergence and effectiveness," a conclusion which Hook apparently derives from Carlyle's statement that great men are at the "bottom" of the historical process. Hook then goes on to contrast Carlyle's excesses in this department with the more reasonable ideas of other thinkers who limited the latitude of history's great men to the area marked out by routinely present possibilities: "The reaction to the exaggerated 'heroism' of Carlyle in the nineteenth century did not deny the existence, and even the necessity, of the hero and heroic action in history. What it maintained was that the events to which such action led were determined by historical laws or by the needs of the period in which the hero appeared. . . . These social forces would summon up when necessary from the deeps of mankind some hero whose 'mission' it was to fulfill the historic tasks of the moment. The measure of his greatness consisted in his degree of awareness of what he was called upon to do." [21]

Surely Hook is right to call the idea of an omnipotent hero capable of turning the course of history an excess, but the fantasy is Hook's rather than Carlyle's. Indeed, one does not even know where to begin refuting such an interpretation—and it has been so influential, so commonly received as true, that its pernicious effects on Carlyle's reputation are beyond computation—for it is so totally unrelated to anything Carlyle wrote as to be beyond contradiction. Were it not for the fact that this sort of mangling of Carlyle by Hook and others has been so influential, one would of course ignore these parodies of Carlyle's thought. As it is, one must deal with them, and perhaps one may even be thankful to these distortions for providing an occasion for clarifying just how much Carlyle's hero theory means to imply about the role of the hero in history.

If one begins by applying a little common sense to the matter, one recognizes at once that the statement that history is fundamentally the history of great men makes no outlandish claims at all. It is, on the contrary, almost a truism. By opening any history book at random one can see immediately that there are far more capital letters than the number of sentences in the book might lead one to expect. Indexes are compiled for history books on the basis of the perception that the most salient moving forces of history are entities with proper names. Great men are, obviously, what most historical writing is concerned with, and it is therefore reasonable to assume that they are crucial to history itself.

Nowhere does Carlyle imply that these great men have an absolute power over the historical milieu in which they work. On the contrary, he was acutely aware of the importance of the character of an age in determining the range of achievement possible in that age; before one could determine what actions were possible at a given moment it was necessary to read the "signs of the times," as Carlyle indicated by inaugurating his career as a social commentator with an essay under that title. Thus Carlyle would not have written, as Albert Mathiez did in describing the political situation on the eve of the French Revolution, that "What was wanted at the head of the monarchy, to dominate the crisis which threatened, was a king. But there was nobody but Louis XVI." [22] Carlyle never permitted himself to forget that forces far larger than those which any man could have at his disposal already had dictated that "the French Kingship had not, by course of Nature, long to live." In such a context, Louis' incompetence could only "accelerate Nature," and, conversely, a heroic king could have done no more than retard it.[23] Although Carlyle does, indeed, exhort the king to take bold and forthright action, he generally does so with an ironic awareness that such action could be no more than a dignified, lovely, but nonetheless vain gesture. Thus Louis' attempt to flee in June 1791, which resulted in his ignominious capture at the Varennes archway by a grocer and a handful of villagers, earns from Carlyle this apostrophe: "Phlegmatic Louis, art thou but lazy, semi-animate phlegm, then, to the centre of thee? King, Captain-General, Sovereign Frank! if thy heart ever formed, since it began beating under the name of heart, any resolution at all, be it now then, or never in this world. . . . Alas, it was not *in* the poor phlegmatic man. Had it been in him, French History had never come under this Varennes Archway to decide itself," Carlyle concludes, offering the tantalizing suggestion that a hero in Louis' place indeed could have turned the course of history.[24]

Yet if one looks beyond this single sentence, offered at a moment of intense crisis as a way of characterizing the pusillanimous king, one cannot fail to observe that Carlyle knew that action of even the most heroic stamp could have done nothing to stop the course of the Revolution. Even as the king first contemplates flight, Carlyle asks, "Grant that poor Louis were safe with [General] Bouillé, what, on the whole, could he look for there? Exasperated Tickets of Entry [i.e., émigrés] answer: Much, all. But cold Reason answers: Little, almost nothing." [25] The frequent apostrophes in his *History of the French Revolution* should not be taken to mean that Carlyle imagined that bold and heroic action could deflect the larger forces of history; it was, rather, a question of meeting those forces with dignity. Thus Carlyle often calls upon a hero or would-be hero to act, to give some existential gesture asserting defiance of an unacceptable and unalterable state of affairs. Even after Louis is sentenced to death, Carlyle continues to urge him to action, not because he believes any possible action could stay his execution, but precisely because it cannot. "The silliest hunted deer dies not so," Carlyle reminds the king.[26]

So far is Carlyle from holding the doctrines of historical indeterminacy that Hook attributes to him that he is at great pains to point out, in connection with each of the heroes he discusses, the extent to which the hero's actions were shaped and conditioned by the world around him. The hero must be, he insists time and time again, in touch with "reality": "A man is right and invincible, virtuous and on the road towards sure conquest," Carlyle announces, "precisely while he joins himself to the great deep Law of the World, in spite of all superficial laws, temporary appearances, profit-and-loss calculations; he is victorious while he coöperates with that great central Law, not victorious otherwise. . . ." [27] Just as Hegel writes that "World-historical men—the Heroes of an epoch—must . . . be recognized as its clear-sighted ones," so Carlyle expresses his awareness of the historical limits within which the hero must operate by placing a high valuation on insight and clarity of vision as the most important qualities in a heroic actor.[28] Muhammad is a hero to Carlyle because "The great Fact of Existence is great to him," because "He has actually an eye for the world," because reality "glared-in upon him"; great poets are Carlylean heroes because of their "sincerity and depth of vision," and Shakespeare is held to be the supreme poet because there is not to be found "such a power of vision . . . in any other man"; Luther is placed in Carlyle's pantheon because of his unrelenting awareness of "the awful realities of things": "It is the property of every Hero, in every time, in every place and situation, that he come back to reality; that he stand upon things, and not shows of things"; John Knox, Carlyle says, is a man who "cannot live but by fact: he clings to reality as the shipwrecked sailor to the cliff." [29] Mirabeau, Carlyle claims, "has become a world-compeller, and ruler over men," not because he controls historical forces and can direct them at his will, but because he sees and understands the historical forces with which he must work: "the characteristic of Mirabeau . . . is veracity and sense, power of true *insight*, superiority of vision." [30] In the same way Danton, the "Mirabeau of Sansculottes," derives his power from his ability to comprehend the true state of things: "it is on the Earth and on Realities that he rests"; "like Mirabeau, [he] has a natural *eye*. . . ." [31] Even "Cassandra" Marat, with his infallibly accurate diagnoses of the situation around him, and Robespierre, "his feline eyes excellent in the twilight," take on heroic dimensions in proportion as they are able to "control" the Revolution by guiding it over a course whose direction is dictated by forces which they do not control.[32]

In all of these cases the greatness of the hero derives from his ability to recognize an as yet unrealized truth and to assist as midwife at its birth. Luther, Carlyle points out, did not bring the Reformation, for "the Reformation simply could not help coming." [33] The Carlylean hero is never a man who fashions history out of his own will, but is at all points a man willing, Carlyle says, to submit to the "great deep Law of the World," just as Hegel says that his world-historical man is one "whose own particular aims involve those large issues which are the will of the World-Spirit." [34] Thus a hero like Cromwell is impotent to act until historical developments have prepared the way for his mission: "Long years he had looked upon it [the godlessness of the king's government], in silence, in prayer; seeing no remedy on Earth; trusting well that a remedy in Heaven's goodness would come,—that such a course was false, unjust, and could not last for ever. And now behold the dawn of it; after twelve years silent waiting, all England stirs itself; there is to be once more a Parliament, the Right will get a voice for itself: inexpressible well-grounded hope has come again into the Earth. Was not such a Parliament worth being a member of? Cromwell threw down his ploughs, and hastened thither." [35]

Just as Cromwell is, Carlyle makes clear, in an important sense a product of the movement he led, so it is true of all of Carlyle's heroes that they act in response to the social needs of the cultures which produced them. "Before the Prophet can arise who, seeing through it [the false idol worshipped by the people], knows it to be mere wood, many men must have begun dimly to doubt that it was little more." [36] In this fact lies the open secret of Carlyle's theory of heroes and hero-worship, for on page after page Carlyle tirelessly reiterates that the hero is the virtual delegate of his followers, led on and incited by them, reflecting their desires back to them in the form of leadership. As Luther approached the Diet of Worms in 1521, "The people . . . crowded the windows and housetops, some of them calling out to him, in solemn words, not to recant: 'Whosoever denieth me before men!' they cried to him,—as in a kind of solemn petition and adjuration. Was it not in reality our petition too, the petition of the whole world . . . : 'Free us; it rests with thee; desert us not!' " [37]

It is always the case with the hero, Carlyle writes, that "What he says, all men were not far from saying, were longing to say." [38] Because this is the inevitable condition of herohood, it follows that the necessary preconditions for heroism lie in the people themselves: "Not a Hero only is needed, but a world fit for him; a world not of *Valets;*—the Hero comes almost in vain to it otherwise!" [39]

In thus acknowledging that the hero's career is shaped by the society in which he finds himself, Carlyle made sure that his hero theory was at all points compatible with his awareness of the role the masses of anonymous men play in history. "Social Life is the aggregate of all the individual men's Lives who constitute society; History is the essence of innumerable Biographies," he had written years earlier, and there is no contradiction between this statement and the one with which he opens *On Heroes and Hero-Worship.*[40] For Carlyle the idea that history should be the biography of great men and the idea that it should be the essence of the biographies "of all the individual men . . . who constitute society" were alternative forms of the same truth. A hero was a great man precisely because he was able to speak articulately "what all men were longing to say."

3. *"But I Say Unto You . . ."*

Carlyle's hero theory is Hegelian and Weberian rather than Nietzschean. For Nietzsche the context in which the hero can realize himself is a society of mass men, of "herd animals": "Whoever has preserved, and bred in himself, a strong will, together with an ample spirit, has more favorable opportunities than ever," Nietzsche wrote. "For the trainability of men has become very great in this democratic Europe; men who learn easily and adapt themselves easily are the rule: the herd animal, even highly intelligent, has been prepared. Whoever can command finds those who *must* obey. . . ."[41] The willfulness of the hero and the will-lessness—that is, the willing submission—of his followers are the key variables in the etiology of power as Nietzsche traces it.

Carlyle, however, speaks of submission in connection with the hero theory only rarely, and when he does it is significantly the hero rather than the hero-worshipper who must submit. The hero's role in "this great God's-World," Carlyle writes, is "to conform to the Law of the Whole, and in devout silence follow that; not questioning it, obeying it as unquestionable."[42] In stark contrast to the Nietzschean idealization of will, Carlyle asserts that "Great souls are always loyally submissive, reverent to what is over them; only small mean souls are otherwise."[43] Nowhere is the hero-worshipper called upon for anything like the total surrender of self that characterizes the hero. On the contrary, the role of hero-worshipper is entered into by exercising discretionary choice in "electing" the hero as one's leader and oneself as his follower. In both *Past and Present* and *On Heroes and Hero-Worship* Carlyle lays great emphasis on the importance to a society of selecting the leaders it will follow. Thus Carlyle, who, as we have seen, satirized political elections, nevertheless maintained that an election "is a most important social act; nay, at bottom, the one important social act."[44] The contradiction between these starkly opposite evaluations of the worth of elections is, I think, on the surface merely. The elections which Carlyle speaks of as among the most important social acts are not at all like the routinely administered ballotings by which one chooses between candidates for institutional office; indeed, as we shall see shortly, the decision to follow a hero is invariably a repudiation of the routinely offered choices. Electing a leader in Carlyle's sense is a matter of great moment and takes on some of the characteristics associated with a religious conversion, for it constitutes no less than a decision as to what one's own calling is to be; to be truly meaningful, an election must be not so much a choice *between* potential leaders as a choice *of* a leader. What is more, insofar as it is a true election it is in a very real sense an election of oneself into the role of charismatic followership as much as it is an election of the hero. Such an "election" is the beginning of action for the individual making the decision, for in casting one's lot with a hero one commits oneself to an active role in the cause the hero leads; in contrast, the political election is an end of action, for in casting a ballot one votes for a candidate to whom, if he is successful, one will delegate one's potential for action.

Carlyle's belief that the hero is called upon to submit to superior powers whereas his followers are permitted to exercise discretion in choosing or not choosing to follow him is a logical corollary of his understanding of herohood as primarily a matter of insight into the true state of social or even cosmic affairs. In this respect the distinction between the hero and the hero-worshipper exclusively depends upon the fact that the former has his insight directly, via an intuitive apprehension of reality or an explicit communication from god, whereas the follower gains insight only indirectly, from the mouth of the hero himself. Followership, therefore, is essentially a voluntaristic, noncoercive relationship to the hero, for the follower "obeys those whom he esteems better than himself, wiser, braver; and will forever obey such; and even be ready and delighted to do it." [45]

In recognizing that submission is relevant to hero-worship primarily with regard to the hero's relationship to *his* source of authority rather than with regard to the follower's relationship to the hero, Carlyle anticipated what was to become, in the writings of Max Weber, one of the most important and paradoxical aspects of the theory of charismatic power. Thus Weber notes on the one hand that the charismatic leader "does not derive his 'right' from their [his followers'] will, in the manner of an election. Rather, the reverse holds: it is the *duty* of those to whom he addresses his mission to recognize him as their charismatically qualified leader." But on the other hand it is also the case that "The genuinely charismatic ruler is responsible precisely to those whom he rules," [46] for although he invariably does not "regard . . . his quality [of charisma] as dependent on the attitudes of the masses toward him," the fact remains that "It is recognition on the part of those subject to authority which is decisive for the validity of charisma." [47] In other words, although the hero is self-appointed—that is, he sees himself as appointed by god or by necessary forces in world history—and tends to see his followers as duty-bound to acquiesce in his charismatic authority (just as he himself is duty-bound to acquiesce in the dictates of his authority source), it is nevertheless the case that the followers have no duty to the hero except insofar as they accept the validity of his charisma and acknowledge that his path is the true one for them.

Carlyle drew two conclusions from this understanding of the nature of duty in a charismatic relationship. In the first place, he maintained that hero-worship is in no way incompatible with the traditional Protestant emphasis on "private judgment." The notion that

Protestantism stands for freedom of private judgment as against the institutionally coerced judgments of Roman Catholicism is, Carlyle argues, deeply mistaken. The Catholic Church may indeed define for its votaries various forms of belief, but it can do so only because its votaries are convinced that Roman Catholicism is on the whole valid. "The sorriest sophistical Bellarmine, preaching sightless faith and passive obedience, must first, by some kind of *conviction*, have abdicated his right to be convinced. His 'private judgment' indicated that, as the advisablest step *he* could take." [48]

At first glance this argument itself seems somewhat sophistical, and we may well wonder at the validity of contending that the abdication of the right to judgment constitutes a legitimate exercise of judgment. In this connection, however, we should note that the case here is not really comparable to the seemingly analogous case, discussed by John Stuart Mill, involving the question of whether the concept of freedom entails the right to sell oneself into slavery. The difference between the two—and it is enough of a difference to render them incommensurable—is that the situation Carlyle is dealing with involves an ongoing process whereas Mill is concerned with what obviously must be a single irreversible event. The person who accepts the role of followership and thereby exercises his option to renounce his private judgment does so for as long as and insofar as he continues to be convinced of the validity of the charismatic claims of the leader.

The second conclusion Carlyle derived from his understanding of the role of submission with respect to charismatic authority led him to minimize the distinction between hero and hero-worshipper. As he saw it, both parties in the relationship submit to what they take to be the true and just mandate of god and/or history and are, through this submission, acting out of their own convictions. Unlike Nietzsche, for whom hero and hero-worshipper are diametrically opposed concepts, Carlyle argues that the difference between them is merely one of degree, for the hero is a man with enough power of vision to see the truth of the world as it stands before him, whereas the follower has power of vision sufficient only for seeing the truth when it is shown to him. It is for this reason that Carlyle was able to say that hero-worship itself is a form of heroism. "The Valet does not know a Hero when he sees him!" Carlyle told his audience at the lectures on heroes and hero-worship, echoing the point made by both Goethe and Hegel. "Alas, no: it requires a kind of *Hero* to do that . . . ," he explained, just as, in *Past and Present*, he reminded his readers that hero-worship was possible only "by being ourselves of heroic mind." [49]

There is nothing fanciful in Carlyle's notion that only a heroic mind can choose to follow a hero, for the hero and his followers are always a band of rebels, compacted together in a daring and invariably dangerous mission. The charismatic leader and his followers are inevitably a revolutionary force inasmuch as their mission is based on a sense of duty unconnected to the institutional sources which legitimate authority in the sociopolitical world. From the point of view of legitimate institutions, therefore, charismatic authority at best can stand as merely an alternative to them, but in most cases it will directly threaten them. "Charismatic domination," Weber writes, "means a rejection of all ties to any external order. . . . Hence, its attitude is revolutionary and transvalues everything; it makes a sovereign break with all traditional or rational norms. . . ." "From a substantive point of view, every charismatic authority would have to subscribe to the proposition, 'It is written . . . , but I say unto you . . .'" [50]

Because charisma is by definition a counterlegitimate force, the charismatic leader requires of his followers the courage to renounce all normal ties to society and to turn their backs on what they have been taught to see as a legitimate order. The type of "passive obedience" Ernst Cassirer accuses Carlyle of preaching can have no place in the camp of the hero.[51] It was not docility of temperament that induced "thirteen followers" to take up Muhammad's mission and go with him into the desert; [52] if those who followed Cromwell can be accused of passive obedience, then legitimate authority is in more trouble than it realizes. "I am come to set a man at variance against his father," Jesus warned his disciples as a way of reminding them that charismatic followerhood demands the courage to say no to all normal bonds of loyalty. "He that loveth father or mother more than me is not worthy of me," he declared, making clear that it is precisely passive obedience that must be renounced if one is to join in the active obedience of charismatic followership.[53]

Although critics of theories such as Carlyle's often contend that submission to a charismatic leader readily degenerates into a permanent system of subordination, in fact this danger is effectively minimized by the principled nature of Carlyle's support of charismatic leadership. Charisma is, as Weber explains, an extremely unstable political base. It tends either to collapse when faced with temporary defeats or to routinize itself into an institutional structure which is by its nature no longer charismatic. Although this latter possibility has led to the charge that Carlyle's hero theory is inherently totalitarian, such a criticism could be valid only if Carlyle's ideas about heroes were considerably less self-conscious than they are, if they had been developed as political propaganda rather than as political theory. As propaganda, a defense of the prerogatives of any particular leader on the grounds of his charismatic election indeed could be transformed readily into support of the leader even after he had used his charismatic mandate to build a system of dictatorial institutions.

As theory, however, the defense of the charismatic hero retains its integrity despite practical disappointments. It is in the nature of political theory to be self-conscious and critical, to stand aside from the pragmatic vicissitudes of politics and to measure them by its own unchanging yardstick. The hero, being human and fallible, may attempt to cash in his charisma, to erect a dictatorial apparatus, but it is precisely at this point that those who, like Carlyle, are committed on principle to nonbureaucratic and nonstatist types of leadership will turn from him as from a traitor. Moreover, it is not inconceivable that a charismatic leader himself, if he is in principle committed to maintaining the charismatic and revolutionary nature of his own rule, would resist attempts to institutionalize his leadership. Indeed, Richard H. Solomon, in his provocative study of Maoist China, suggests that the Cultural Revolution of the late 1960s sprang from just such an impulse on the part of Mao Tse-tung: "it has been Mao himself . . . ," Solomon writes, "who has resisted the trend toward reconsolidation of domestic political order out of his fears that the momentum of social change would die. The Cultural Revolution is not a manifestation of the failure of Party rule; quite the contrary, it is a result of Mao's objection to the Party's success." [54]

Perhaps Carlyle was being naive in his belief that charismatic leaders and their followers could remain true to their principles, but I can find nothing inherently unreasonable in his faith that there is no better training for resistance to the imposition of power than the combination of self-assertion and self-discipline required for membership in a band of rebel followers. And when these traits are combined with a conscious, theoretical commitment to charismatic rebellion itself, the dangers of a lapse into totalitarianism are, at the very most, no greater than they inevitably must be so long as the means of massive coercion exist.

Carlyle's call for a rebirth of the spirit of hero-worship is, we should now be able to see, a call for resistance rather than for submission. When Carlyle criticized contemporary culture on the grounds that the mass of men no longer seemed able or willing to find and follow heroes, he distinguished between two contrasting types of non-hero-worshippers. On the one hand there are the "Valets," a term taken, via Hegel or, more likely, Goethe, from the aphorism that no man is a hero to his valet and applied to all those who are constitutionally or on principle opposed to acknowledging the existence of men superior to themselves. The second type of non-hero-worshipper is the "Flunkey," the very antithesis of the Valet. Just as the Valet is the man temperamentally indisposed to perceiving heroism where it exists, so the Flunkey is a man temperamentally disposed to perceiving it where it does not exist. It is Flunkeyism, Carlyle warns, that will be the undoing of democracy in England, for the very deference which Bagehot was to celebrate a few decades later as the magical mortar that held the British sociopolitical system together meant to Carlyle that, for the most part, the *demos* of England was fatally disposed to defer to its social superiors rather than to its true betters. Never much worried that the masses, under democracy, would become self-willed and disinclined to accept the leadership of wiser men, Carlyle greatly feared that, through an excess of deference, they would submit themselves to the leadership of respectable quacks. "Seek only deceitful Speciosity, money with gilt-carriages, 'fame' with newspaper-paragraphs, whatever name it bear, you will find only deceitful Speciosity; godlike Reality will be forever far from you," he warned.[55]

Time and again, therefore, Carlyle uses the hero theory to remind his readers of the dangers of excessive willingness to defer to self-proclaimed or socially acknowledged superiors. In this sense, the first task of the man who would worship heroes is a revolutionary task—the withholding of deference from all those not worthy of it and the ejection of them from government. When the spirit of hero-worship is fully developed, Carlyle prophesies, "we shall . . . know quacks when we see them; cant, when we hear it, shall be horrible to us! We will say, with the poor Frenchman at the Bar of the Convention . . . : '*Je demande l'arrestation des coquins et des lâches.*' 'Arrestment of the knaves and dastards': ah, we know what a work that is; how long it will be before *they* are all or mostly got 'arrested':—but here is one; arrest him, in God's name; it is one fewer! We will, in all practicable ways, by word and silence, by act and refusal to act, energetically demand that arrestment,—'*je demande cette arrestation-là!* '—and by degrees infallibly attain it." [56]

Most commentators on Carlyle's hero theory have emphasized the hero-worshipper's loyalty to his leader, and in doing so they have forgotten that loyalty in this context must be preceded by a courageous act of disloyalty to the established order, which is the habitat of the "knaves and dastards" whose arrestment is the first order of business in a heroic world. In general, the literary critics who have had their innings with Carlyle have followed Freud in assuming that the relationship between a follower and a charismatic leader is modeled on and therefore stands as a continuation of normal patrilineal authority. The family, according to Freud, is the prototype of all authority relationships: "What began in relation to the father," Freud wrote, "is completed in relation to the group," for "The leader of the group is still the dreaded primal father. . . ." [57] Such an analysis of group leadership is valid only if one is aware—as Freud himself was but as literary Freudians tend not to be—that an identification of this nature is a two-edged weapon, for to whatever extent the leader of the group "is still" the primal father, he is also precisely *not* the father. To say that the charismatic leader replaces the father is to indicate some of the tensions inherent in the situation of the follower, who can perceive himself as loyal insofar as he sees the hero as the father, and can perceive himself as criminal insofar as he sees the hero as taking the place of the father. Undoubtedly, no relationship of charismatic leader and follower is totally free of this ambivalence, and there is probably no point at all in taking either of the polarized halves of it to be the essential feature of the relationship as a whole. It is simultaneously true that the charismatic figure continues "what began in relation to the father" and that, as Max Weber observed, charisma "is contrary to all patriarchal domination." [58] The charismatic hero takes on the roles of father, priest, and king, but in doing so he is a stranger in the father's place, an iconoclast in the priest's, and a regicide in the king's.

4. The Seventh Hero

"I am for permanence in all things," Carlyle wrote, knowing full well that there could be no permanence in the historical world.[59] All clothes grow old, he had recognized from the start, and require to be cast off; new clothes must be made to replace them. With each moment that passes, some bold and heroic insight ossifies itself into an institutional form, routinizes itself, and thus becomes no longer capable of generating true political action. It becomes, in Karl Mannheim's terminology, an occasion for administrative and reproductive functioning rather than for political creativity. With each moment, therefore, one hopes that a hero will arise to call upon all those who are willing to become "sansculottes"—to go with him outside of the institutional sphere, and there establish a new order, a new culottism, which is in turn fated to be overthrown by the next sansculottes.

"[I]n this Time-World of ours there is properly nothing else but revolution and mutation," Carlyle had acknowledged in his *History of the French Revolution,* and it therefore followed that the only permanence possible to man was the permanence of revolutionary change itself.[60] In his attempt to build a political system on the basis of revolutionary charisma, Carlyle had finally arrived at the only possible completion for the system of his thought. From whichever angle one approaches it, all of Carlyle's thought points to this one overriding conclusion. In terms of his lifelong search for a mode of self-realization, a way out of the enervating solipsism of the world of self-centered egoism, which would at the same time avoid the alienation or annihilation of self that resulted from simple work in the routinely present world of organized social categories, Carlyle had long known that creative action in the time-world of history was the possibility that must be explored. Yet the hero-actor must be a revolutionary because all true action is inherently revolutionary, a repudiation of the world of formula and a commitment to the creation of new modes of social interrelationship. As a political ideology which takes as its highest ideal a continuous openness to historical action, Carlyle's theory of political action is a doctrine of permanent revolution.

Moreover, revolution entails by definition the universalization of herohood, as Carlyle had shown by laying bare the way the French Revolution had abrogated the monopoly of political action formerly enjoyed by kings, courtiers, and legislators, and had moved the historical arena out onto the streets. "The most indubitable feature of a revolution," Leon Trotsky has written, in a statement which accurately reflects Carlyle's sense of the matter, "is the direct interference of the masses in historic events. In ordinary times the state, be it monarchical or democratic, elevates itself above the nation, and history is made by specialists in that line of business—kings, ministers, bureaucrats, parliamentarians, journalists. . . . The history of a revolution is for us first of all a history of the forcible entrance of the masses into the realm of rulership over their own destiny." [61]

Carlyle's hero is preeminently the man who forces his way into the realm of rulership over his own destiny, and his followers are those who make it possible for him to do so by their readiness to enter the world of creative action with him. This asymmetrical dependency in the relationship of leader and follower is at the heart of the radical meaning of Carlyle's hero theory, for the presence of a heroic disposition among those from whom the hero is to draw his followers is, as we have seen, a vital prerequisite for the hero's own career. Conversely, the heroic readiness of the masses makes the existence of the hero, as authoritative leader of others, in an important sense irrelevant. The very process which makes the hero possible, the coming into being of a mass of people prepared and willing to act resolutely on what they believe to be the true nature of things, necessarily creates a revolutionary situation in which the people will refuse to tolerate sham, quackery, and the imposition upon themselves of government by those unfit to govern.

For this reason Carlyle, who preached of the duty to find and follow a hero, never felt the personal necessity of subordinating himself to a leader, never found a contemporary hero to worship. More than a few students of Carlyle have noted this fact as a discrepancy in his teachings on hero-worship, maintaining that secretly Carlyle always had himself in mind when he spoke of heroes. Far from being a discrepancy, however, this is as it should be. *On Heroes and Hero-Worship* deals with six types of heroism, but it points inexorably toward a seventh hero—the hero as oneself. Precisely because true hero-worship is to Carlyle a form of heroism, the coming of the hero is not a matter of crucial moment to the man ready for action. "[W]e will strive and incessantly make ready, each of us, to be worthy to serve and second such a First-Lord!" Carlyle writes of the hero. "We shall then be as good as sure of his arriving; sure of many things, let him arrive or not." [62]

With his hopes centered on the formation of a world permanently open to political action—a permanently revolutionary world—Carlyle felt, as he reflected on the centuries of revolution that had commenced with the Protestant Reformation, much reason for optimism. "In all this wild revolutionary work, from Protestantism downwards, I see the blessedest result preparing itself. . . . If Hero mean *sincere man*, why may not every one of us be a Hero?" he asked in 1840. Why not, indeed, he answered three years later: " 'Hero-worship,' if you will,—yes, friends; but, first of all, by being ourselves of heroic mind. A whole world of Heroes . . . that is what we aim at!" [63]

Notes

In addition to the standard bibliographic information, the notes usually contain, in parentheses, dates of first publication of the work, translation, or edition identified immediately before the parentheses. A parenthetical date after the title of a translated work is the date of original publication in the original language; a parenthetical date after the name of a translator is the date of original publication of the translation cited. When modern reprints are used, the date of original publication of the work being cited follows the title. For example, G. M. Young, *Victorian England: Portrait of an Age* (1936), 2nd ed. (1953) (London: Oxford University Press, 1960), means that the edition used for the purpose of citation is the one published by Oxford Press in 1960, that *Victorian England* was originally published in 1936, and that the second edition first appeared in 1953. The absence of such parenthetical dates, the reader should note, does not necessarily imply that the edition cited is the first.

I. THE REJECTION OF SELF

1. Lionel Trilling, *The Opposing Self: Nine Essays in Criticism* (1955) (New York: Viking Press, 1959), p. ix.

2. Søren Kierkegaard, *The Sickness Unto Death* (1849), trans. Walter Lowrie (Garden City, N.Y.: Doubleday & Company, Anchor Books, n.d.), pp. 163 and 162. The discovery that the self could be defined by and grounded in itself, through self-consciousness, was of course Hegel's contribution to the absolutization of self described here; see *The Phenomenology of Mind* (1807), trans. J. B. Baillie (New York: Harper & Row, 1967), Part B, "Self-Consciousness."

3. The psychopathological element behind such a conflicted set of beliefs and perceptions should be relatively apparent. I refer readers interested in pursuing this further to James L. Halliday, *Mr. Carlyle, My Patient: A Psychosomatic Biography* (New York: Grune & Stratton, 1950), an interesting book despite the title. Also, see below, note 28 to Chapter II.

4. G. M. Young, *Victorian England: Portrait of an Age* (1936), 2nd ed. (1953) (London: Oxford University Press, 1960), p. 75.

5. *The Centenary Edition of the Works of Thomas Carlyle*, ed. H. D.

Traill, 30 vols. (London: Chapman and Hall, 1896–1899), 1:133. Hereafter this edition will be cited as *Works*, followed by volume and page numbers in Arabic numerals. (For convenience of reference, Carlyle's multi-volume works, such as his *History of the French Revolution*, which constitutes the second, third, and fourth volumes of the Centenary Edition, will be cited by Roman numerals referring to the volume number within the work in question. Hence: *Fr. Rev.*, I, II, and III, rather than *Works*, 2, 3, and 4.)

6. *Works*, 5:9.

7. Hannah Arendt, *The Human Condition* (1958) (Garden City, N.Y.: Doubleday & Company, 1959), p. 237.

8. Immanuel Kant, *Critique of Pure Reason* (1781), trans. F. Max Müller (1881) (Garden City, N.Y.: Doubleday & Company, 1966), p. xxxii.

9. Arendt, *The Human Condition*, p. 242.

10. Letter from James Mill to Francis Place, December 6, 1817; quoted in Elie Halévy, *The Growth of Philosophic Radicalism* (1901–1904), trans. Mary Morris (Boston: Beacon Press, 1955), p. 451.

11. David Alec Wilson, *Carlyle Till Marriage (1795–1826)* (London: Kegan Paul, Trench, Trubner & Co., 1923), p. 117.

12. *Works*, 26:158.

13. Charles Frederick Harrold, *Carlyle and German Thought, 1819–1834*, Yale University Studies in English, no. 82 (New Haven: Yale University Press, 1934).

14. *Works*, 26:13.

15. *Works*, 26:13–14; emphasis added.

16. Quoted in Harrold, *Carlyle and German Thought*, p. 68.

17. M. H. Abrams, *The Mirror and the Lamp: Romantic Theory and the Critical Tradition* (1953) (New York: W. W. Norton & Company, 1958), p. 129.

18. On this score, Carlyle stands as the very model of Hegel's "unhappy consciousness," with its continuous vacillations between the three "way[s] in which particularity is connected with unchangeableness. In one form it [consciousness] comes before itself as opposed to the unchangeable essence. . . . At another time it finds the unchangeable appearing in the form of particularity. . . . In the third case, it discovers *itself* to be this particular fact in the unchangeable." *The Phenomenology of Mind*, p. 253.

19. *Works*, 26:149.

20. *Works*, 26:150. Just as we can find passages in which Carlyle takes an absolutist position, and others in which he accepts the principles of relativism, so we can find yet others in which he seems to lean both ways simultaneously. Thus in his 1827 essay "The State of German Literature" he quotes with approval a passage in which Schiller distinguishes the personal, idiosyncratic, and "historical" elements in literature from the unconditioned, eternal, and absolute elements: "The Artist, it is true, is the son of his age; but pity for him if he is its pupil, or even its favourite! . . . The matter of his works he will take from the present, but their form he will derive from a nobler time; nay, from beyond all time, from the absolute unchanging unity of his own nature" (*Works*, 26:57). Such a passage seems to go both ways. On the one hand, it emphasizes the absolute and unchanging elements in art, at the expense of

the idiosyncratic, personal, and historical. On the other hand, it seems to locate this absolute and unchanging unity in the artist himself, and insofar as this is the case, the passage leans toward rationalistic subjectivism.

21. *Works*, 26:208.

22. *Works*, 26:210.

23. See Chapter IV.

24. Erich Auerbach, *Mimesis: The Representation of Reality in Western Literature* (1946), trans. Willard Trask (Garden City, N.Y.: Doubleday & Company, 1957), pp. 4 and 5.

25. *Ibid.*, p. 13.

26. See Hegel, *The Phenomenology of Mind*, pp. 81–82: "The truth is the whole. The whole, however, is merely the essential nature reaching its completeness through the process of its own development. Of the Absolute it must be said that it is essentially a result, that only at the end is it what it is in very truth. . . ."

27. Karl Löwith, *From Hegel to Nietzsche: The Revolution in Nineteenth-Century Thought* (1941), trans. David E. Green (Garden City, N.Y.: Doubleday & Company, 1967), p. 126.

28. *Works*, 25:84.

29. *Works*, 25:101.

30. *Works*, 26:33, 34, 36.

31. *Works*, 26:287, 288.

32. *Works*, 26:272.

33. "The importance of biography in historiography has increased extraordinarily. It was anticipated by the novel. Carlyle was, perhaps, the first to grasp its full significance. . . ." Wilhelm Dilthey, *Pattern and Meaning in History: Thoughts on History and Society*, ed. H. P. Rickman (New York: Harper & Row, 1962), p. 92.

II. THE BORDERS OF THE PUBLIC WORLD

1. Letter to Sterling, February 23, 1843, in Alexander Carlyle, ed., *New Letters of Thomas Carlyle* (New York and London: John Lane, Bodley Head, 1904), I, 282.

2. G. D. H. Cole and Raymond Postgate, *The British Common People, 1746–1946* (New York: Barnes & Noble, 1961), p. 90. (There seems to be some confusion about the title of this book, which bears the name *The British People* on its title page. It was originally published in England under the title *The Common People*.)

3. Thomas Carlyle, *Reminiscences* (1881), ed. C. E. Norton (New York: E. P. Dutton & Co., 1932), p. 31.

4. *Ibid.*

5. Cf. Henry Grey Graham, *The Social Life of Scotland in the Eighteenth Century*, 2nd ed. (London: Adam and Charles Black, 1900), vol. I, Chap. 7.

6. James Anthony Froude, *Thomas Carlyle: A History of the First Forty Years of His Life, 1795–1835* (London: Longmans, Green, and Co., 1882), I, 45. Hereafter this work, comprising the first two volumes of Froude's biography of Carlyle, will be cited as *Life*, I and II. The remaining two volumes, *Thomas Carlyle: A History of His Life in London, 1834–1881*, 2nd ed. (London: Longmans, Green, and Co., 1885), will be cited as *Life*, III and IV.

7. See, among numerous excellent treatments of this subject, Michael Walzer, *The Revolution of the Saints: A Study in the Origins of Radical Politics* (Cambridge, Mass.: Harvard University Press, 1965).

8. *Works*, 27:86 ("On History").

9. Max Weber, *The Sociology of Religion* (1922), trans. Ephraim Fischoff (Boston: Beacon Press, 1964), p. 173.

10. *Ibid.*, p. 166.

11. See, for example, his letters to Mill of May 1, 1833, and January 20, 1834, in Alexander Carlyle, ed., *Letters of Thomas Carlyle to John Stuart Mill, John Sterling and Robert Browning* (1923) (New York: Haskell House, 1970), pp. 53 and 94. In *Sartor Resartus* Carlyle speaks of Teufelsdröckh's "high Platonic Mysticism" (*Works*, 1:52).

12. *Life*, I, 330.

13. Weber, *The Sociology of Religion*, pp. 170 and 171.

14. Karl Löwith, *Meaning in History* (1949) (Chicago: University of Chicago Press, Phoenix Books, n.d.), pp. 175 and 142–143.

15. Friedrich Nietzsche, *The Will to Power* (1901), trans. Walter Kaufmann and R. J. Hollingdale (New York: Random House, 1968), p. 185.

16. Of course, Mill had been involved in politics practically from his infancy, but Carlyle seems not to have realized this. For a considerable period of time Carlyle fancied he had found in Mill a fellow "mystic" and a disciple. As Mill's active political involvement became more intense in the late twenties and early thirties, and as he became increasingly caught up in the Reform movement, Carlyle came to look upon what he imagined to be a change in Mill's priorities as a sort of betrayal of their shared world-fleeing mysticism. See Emery Neff, *Carlyle and Mill: An 'Introduction to Victorian Thought* (1924), 2nd ed., rev. (New York: Octagon Books, 1964), esp. Chap. 1.

17. *Two Notebooks of Thomas Carlyle: From 23d March 1822 to 16th May 1832*, ed. Charles Eliot Norton (New York: Grolier Club, 1898), p. 226.

18. *Ibid.*, p. 141. A year later he repeated this statement almost verbatim in his public writings; cf. *Works*, 27:86.

19. *Ibid.*, pp. 203–204; *Life*, II, 205.

20. *Life*, II, 308.

21. Letter of April 18, 1833, in *Letters to Mill, Sterling and Browning*, p. 50.

22. See *Life*, II, 48, where he describes himself, in a letter to his brother John, as living in a "solitude, which I believe is not to be equalled out of Sahara itself." Cf. *Reminiscences*, p. 58.

23. Giuseppe Mazzini, "The Genius and Tendency of the Writings of Thomas Carlyle" (1843), in *Life and Writings of Joseph Mazzini* (London: Smith, Elder, & Co., 1891), IV, 95–96.

24. Mazzini in *The Monthly Chronicle*, vol. 23, January 1840; quoted in Richard Hengist Horne, *A New Spirit of the Age* (1844) (London: Henry Frowde, Oxford University Press, 1907), p. 447.

25. John Stuart Mill, "The Spirit of the Age," in *Essays on Politics and Culture*, ed. Gertrude Himmelfarb (Garden City, N.Y.: Doubleday & Company, 1963), pp. 1 and 3; originally published in *The Examiner*, January 6-May 29, 1831.

26. *Works*, 28:19.

27. "The fever . . . must needs burn itself out, and burn out thereby the Impurities that caused it . . . ," Carlyle wrote (*Works*, 28:40). This somewhat dialectical idea was later expanded in *Sartor Resartus*, where the crucial scene depicts the casting out of the Everlasting No, the negation of the negation.

28. *Works*, 28:27 and 16. Carlyle's discussion of the internal conflict between the life principle and the death principle in man is in many ways strikingly similar to the treatment of this theme in Norman O. Brown's *Life against Death: The Psychoanalytic Meaning of History* (1959) (New York: Random House, Vintage Books, n.d.). This is hardly surprising in light of the fact that Brown's work is largely a study of the same patterns of anal pathology that tormented Carlyle acutely throughout his adult life. Indeed, despite the fact that Brown does not mention Carlyle, Part Five of his book, "Studies in Anality," is far more useful to the reader who wants to undertake a psychoanalytic study of Carlyle than are any of the studies dealing specifically with Carlyle.

29. *Works*, 28:4.

30. *Works*, 28:2. Cf. Rousseau's *Discourse on the Origin and Foundation of Inequality among Men* (i.e., the "Second Discourse," 1755): "If nature destined us to be healthy, I almost dare affirm that the state of reflection is a state contrary to nature and that the man who meditates is a depraved animal." *The First and Second Discourses*, trans. Roger D. and Judith R. Masters (New York: St. Martin's Press, 1964), p. 110.

31. *Works*, 28:3.

32. *Works*, 28:27.

33. E.g., *Works*, 1:156.

34. *Works*, 28:27.

35. Hannah Arendt, *The Human Condition* (1958) (Garden City, N.Y.: Doubleday & Company, 1959), Chap. 1.

36. Karl Mannheim, *Ideology and Utopia: An Introduction to the Sociology of Knowledge* (1929), trans. Louis Wirth and Edward Shils (New York: Harcourt, Brace & World, Harvest Books, n.d.), pp. 113–114.

37. G. W. F. Hegel, *The Phenomenology of Mind* (1807), trans. J. B. Baillie (New York: Harper & Row, 1967), p. 239.

38. *Works*, 1:157 and 28:43.

39. *Works*, 28:27.

40. Horne, *A New Spirit of the Age*, p. 449; John Sterling, "On the Writings of Thomas Carlyle," in *Essays and Tales of John Sterling, Collected and Edited with a Memoir of His Life* by Julius Charles Hare (London: John W. Parker, 1848), I, 320.

41. For a time, too, it worked the other way, making it possible for the disturbingly radical bias of his early essays to go virtually undetected among the pages of orthodox Whiggery's *Edinburgh Review*.

42. *Works*, 28:148.

43. *Works*, 28:150.

44. *Works*, 29:205–207.

45. *Works*, 10:23.

46. *Works*, 10:23–24.

47. *Fr. Rev.*, I, 20.

48. *Works*, 28:166.

49. *Works*, 29:173–174 (*Chartism*).

50. G. K. Chesterton, *William Cobbett* (London: Hodder and Stoughton, 1925), p. 23.

51. Crane Brinton, *English Political Thought in the Nineteenth Century* (1933) (New York: Harper & Row, 1962), pp. 43–60; the first sentence of Brinton's essay labels Owen a crank.

52. E.g., Sidney and Beatrice Webb, *The History of Trade Unionism*, rev. ed., extended to 1920 (London: Longmans, Green and Co., 1920), esp. pp. 154–164; Cole and Postgate, *The British Common People*, Chap. XXII; E. P. Thompson, *The Making of the English Working Class* (New York: Random House, 1966), esp. pp. 779–806.

53. In recent times this has been the fate of Paul Goodman, as he himself was well aware; see his *New Reformation: Notes of a Neolithic Conservative* (New York: Random House, 1970).

54. *The Phenomenology of Mind*, p. 85.

55. *Works*, 28:138 (rearranged) and 148.

56. *Works*, 27:57.

57. *Works*, 27:58.

58. *Works*, 27:67.

59. *Works*, 27:67.

60. *Works*, 27:79.

61. *Works*, 27:66. Later, in his *History of the French Revolution*, he will level the same criticism against the constitutionalists of the Gironde; see above, pp. 124–125.

62. Thompson, *The Making of the English Working Class*, p. 82. The connection between liberalism and growing state centralism has been observed by a number of thinkers, among them Jacob Burckhardt, who held it to be axiomatic that "The more radically the sacred right of the State . . . dies out, the more its secular rights expand." *Force and Freedom: Reflections on History* (1870–1871), ed. James Hastings Nichols (Boston: Beacon Press, 1964), p. 227.

63. Emery Neff, *Carlyle and Mill*, and *Carlyle* (New York: W. W. Norton & Company, 1932); Eric Bentley, *A Century of Hero-Worship: A Study in the Idea of Heroism in Carlyle and Nietzsche, with Notes on Wagner, Spengler, Stefan George and D. H. Lawrence* (1944), 2nd ed. (Boston: Beacon Press, 1957). See also Eric Williams, *British Historians and the West Indies* (New York: Charles Scribner's Sons, 1966), where Carlyle is labeled a "neo[sic]-fascist."

64. *Works*, 27:61.

65. Letter of March 21, 1833, in *Letters to Mill, Sterling and Browning*, p. 44.

66. *Works*, 27:70.

67. See Engels' review of *Past and Present* in the *Deutsch-Französische Jahrbücher* (1844) and Mazzini's essay on Carlyle from the same year in *Life and Writings of Joseph Mazzini*, IV, 56–109.

68. Barrington Moore, Jr., *Political Power and Social Theory: Seven Studies* (New York: Harper & Row, 1965), pp. 200–203. But see above, Chapter IX, for an analysis of the question of the authoritarianism of the hero theory.

69. *Works*, 10:254 and *History of . . . Frederick the Great*, I, 6.

70. *History of Trade Unionism*, p. 85.

71. *The Making of the English Working Class*, p. 668.

72. See especially Chap. 2, "The Machine Breakers," in Hobsbawm's

Labouring Men: Studies in the History of Labour (1964) (Garden City, N.Y.: Doubleday & Company, 1967).

73. Graham Wallas, *The Life of Francis Place* (*1771–1854*) (New York: Alfred A. Knopf, 1919), pp. 245, 316, and 250.

74. Cf. Kenneth Burke, *A Grammar of Motives* (1945) (Cleveland: World Publishing Company, 1962), p. 10.

75. *Works*, 28:25.

III. THE ANNIHILATION OF SELF

1. *Works*, 1:242.
2. Cf. *Works*, 26:211 and 23:15.
3. On May 14, 1834, Emerson wrote to Carlyle: "Can it be that this humour proceeds from a despair of finding a contemporary audience & so the Prophet feels at liberty to utter his message in droll sounds." On August 12 Carlyle answered: "You say well that I take up that attitude because I have no known public, am *alone* under the Heavens, speaking into friendly or unfriendly space; add only that I will not defend such attitude, that I call it questionable, tentative, and only the best that I in these mad times could conveniently hit upon." Joseph Slater, ed., *The Correspondence of Emerson and Carlyle* (New York: Columbia University Press, 1964), pp. 98 and 103. For an insightful critique of the style of *Sartor* from another friend of Carlyle's who was put off by the "lawless oddity" of the Clothes Philosophy, see the long letter from John Sterling to Carlyle which Carlyle reprints in his *Life of Sterling* (*Works*, 11:108–117).
4. Letter of September 24, 1833, in Alexander Carlyle, ed., *Letters of Thomas Carlyle to John Stuart Mill, John Sterling and Robert Browning* (1923) (New York: Haskell House, 1970), p. 74.
5. See Archibald MacMechan's edition of *Sartor Resartus* (Boston: Ginn & Company; London: Athenæum Press, 1897). MacMechan's voluminous notes make clear that the book is a continuous tissue of private jokes and personal allusions, as though it were written to be fully enjoyed only by its author. But then, what book isn't?
6. Lytton Strachey, *Portraits in Miniature and Other Essays* (1931) (New York: W. W. Norton & Company, 1962), pp. 182–183.
7. Letter to Sterling, June 4, 1835, in *Letters to Mill, Sterling and Browning*, p. 192.
8. *Works*, 1:24.
9. *Works*, 1:25.
10. See his letter to his mother in which he describes himself as "a kind of missionary . . . to the British heathen"; quoted in *Life*, I, 378.
11. *Works*, 27:77 ("Signs of the Times").
12. Letter of November 14, 1822; quoted in *Life*, I, 170.
13. Letter of December 1820; quoted in *Life*, I, 94.
14. *Life*, II, 443–444.
15. Quoted in Karl Löwith, *From Hegel to Nietzsche: The Revolution in Nineteenth-Century Thought* (1941), trans. David E. Green (Garden City, N.Y.: Doubleday & Company, 1967), p. 333.
16. "The Garment of God," Carlyle says, borrowing the phrase from Goethe.
17. *Works*, 1:150.

18. *Works*, 1:123.

19. Thomas Carlyle, *Reminiscences* (1881), ed. C. E. Norton (New York: E. P. Dutton & Co., 1932), p. 100.

20. Kenneth Burke, *A Grammar of Motives* (1945) (Cleveland: World Publishing Company, 1962), pp. 138 and 140.

21. *Works*, 1:117.

22. *Works*, 1:196.

23. *Works*, 1:153.

24. See above, pp. 27–29.

25. *Works*, 5:174 (*On Heroes and Hero-Worship*).

26. Edmund Burke, "Speech . . . upon the Occasion of a Petition of the Unitarian Society," May 11, 1792, in *The Works of the Right Honourable Edmund Burke*, rev. ed. (Boston: Little, Brown and Company, 1866), VII, 44.

27. Certainly I would not be the first to suggest that a modern government's toleration of free speech is often proportional to its sense that there is little danger of ideas realizing themselves as action. "If you have no doubt of your premises or your power . . . ," Justice Holmes wrote, "to allow opposition by speech seems to indicate that you think the speech impotent. . . ." *Abrams v. U.S.*, 250 U.S. 616, 630 (1919). In proportion as such a government sees the formation of this connection as probable, it increasingly will approach Burke's position.

28. Erik H. Erikson, *Childhood and Society* (1950), 2nd ed. (New York: W. W. Norton & Company, 1963), p. 279.

29. Georg Wilhelm Friedrich Hegel, *The Philosophy of History*, trans. J. Sibree (New York: Dover Publications, 1956), p. 29.

30. *Works*, 1:137.

31. Max Weber, *The Theory of Social and Economic Organization* (1925), trans. A. M. Henderson and Talcott Parsons (New York: Free Press, 1964), p. 118.

32. *Works*, 1:31.

33. *Works*, 29:184 (*Chartism*).

34. *Works*, 1:236.

35. See above, pp. 27–29.

36. Hannah Arendt, *The Human Condition* (1958) (Garden City, N.Y.: Doubleday & Company, 1959), p. 9.

37. G. W. F. Hegel, *The Phenomenology of Mind* (1807), trans. J. B. Baillie (New York: Harper & Row, 1967), pp. 238–239.

38. Arendt, *The Human Condition*, pp. 9–10.

39. *Works*, 1:119.

40. *Works*, 1:127.

41. *Works*, 1:134.

42. *Works*, 1:133 and 134.

43. See above, p. 26.

44. *Works*, 1:134–135.

45. *Works*, 1:127.

46. *Works*, 1:135.

47. *Works*, 1:103.

48. Or half-learned. "Space is a mode of our sense, so is time," he wrote in his Journal in 1830, adding, in parentheses, "This I only half understand." *Life*, II, 84.

49. *Works*, 1:43.

50. *Works*, 1:132.

51. Karl Marx, *Economic and Philosophic Manuscripts of 1844*, ed. Dirk J. Struik, trans. Martin Milligan (New York: International Publishers, 1964), p. 114.

52. Karl Marx, *Capital: A Critique of Political Economy* (1867), ed. Frederick Engels, trans. Samuel Moore and Edward Aveling (1887) (New York: International Publishers, 1967), I, 329.

53. *Works*, 1:149.

54. *Works*, 1:153.

55. *Works*, 1:153.

56. *Works*, 1:135.

IV. THE MAKING OF HISTORY

1. Hannah Arendt, *On Revolution* (New York: Viking Press, 1965), p. 45.

2. Frederick Engels, *The Origin of the Family, Private Property and the State* (1884) (New York: International Publishers, New World Paperbacks, n.d.), p. 101.

3. William Cobbett, *Cobbett's Legacy to Labourers; or, What is the Right which the Lords, Baronets, and 'Squires have to the Lands of England? In Six Letters, Addressed to the Working People of England* (London: William Cobbett, 1834), Letter 2.

4. Christopher Hill, *Puritanism and Revolution: Studies in the English Revolution of the Seventeenth Century* (1958) (New York: Schocken Books, 1964), pp. 50–122.

5. E. P. Thompson, *The Making of the English Working Class* (New York: Random House, 1966), esp. Chap. IV. In the course of the nineteenth century the connection between revolutionism and historical argument underwent a significant change which should be mentioned here. As Christopher Hill notes (*Puritanism and Revolution*, pp. 110–111), beginning around 1820 the working classes began to lose interest in Saxon history while the middle classes, with their Gothic Revival, appropriated this period as their own. By the end of the nineteenth century this transformation was complete, with Saxon lore appearing, of all places, in the proceedings of the Fabian Society. See Margaret Cole, *The Story of Fabian Socialism* (Stanford: Stanford University Press, 1961), p. 119.

6. Karl Mannheim, *Ideology and Utopia: An Introduction to the Sociology of Knowledge* (1929), trans. Louis Wirth and Edward Shils (New York: Harcourt, Brace & World, Harvest Books, n.d.), p. 210. For further discussion of this matter, see above, Chapter VIII, section 1.

7. Thomas Hobbes, *The Elements of Law: Natural & Politic* (1650), ed. Ferdinand Tönnies (Cambridge: At the University Press, 1928), p. 11.

8. Benedetto Croce, *History of Europe in the Nineteenth Century* (1931), trans. Henry Furst (New York: Harcourt, Brace & World, 1963), p. 87.

9. *Fr. Rev.*, I, 211, and *Works*, 1:196 (rearranged).

10. *Works*, 25:101.

11. *Works*, 27:89 and 88 ("On History").

12. Isaiah Berlin, *Karl Marx: His Life and Environment* (1939), 3rd ed. (New York: Oxford University Press, 1963), p. 53.

13. *Works*, 27:89.

14. *Works*, 27:89.

15. Franz Neumann, *The Democratic and the Authoritarian State: Essays in Political and Legal Theory*, ed. Herbert Marcuse (New York: Free Press, 1964), p. 122.

16. See above, Chapter V, section 1, for a detailed account of this aspect of Carlyle's *History*.

17. Georg Wilhelm Friedrich Hegel, *The Philosophy of History*, trans. J. Sibree (New York: Dover Publications, 1956), p. 10.

18. *Ibid.*, p. 19.

19. Karl Marx, *Pre-Capitalist Economic Formations* (1857–1858), trans. Jack Cohen (New York: International Publishers, 1965), p. 83.

20. See above, Chapter I, section 3, esp. pp. 12–13.

21. *Fr. Rev.*, I, 28.

22. *Reflections on the Revolution in France* (1790), in *The Works of the Right Honourable Edmund Burke*, rev. ed. (Boston: Little, Brown and Company, 1865), III, 406.

23. Niccolò Machiavelli, *The Prince* (New York: Modern Library, n.d.), pp. 4–5.

24. Harold J. Laski, *The Rise of European Liberalism: An Essay in Interpretation* (1936) (London: George Allen & Unwin, 1962), p. 31.

25. See Max Weber, *The Theory of Social and Economic Organization* (1925), trans. A. M. Henderson and Talcott Parsons (New York: Free Press, 1964), p. 185: "[T]he concept of substantive rationality," Weber warns, "is full of difficulties. It conveys only one element common to all the possible empirical situations; namely, that it is not sufficient to consider only the purely formal fact that calculations are being made on grounds of expediency by the methods which are, among those available, technically the most nearly adequate. . . . Substantive rationality cannot be measured in terms of formal calculation alone, but also involves a relation to the absolute values or to the content of the particular given ends to which it is oriented. In principle, there is an indefinite number of possible standards of value which are rational in this sense."

26. Joseph A. Schumpeter, *Capitalism, Socialism and Democracy* (1942), 3rd ed. (1950) (New York: Harper & Row, 1962), pp. 122–123.

27. Edmund Burke, "Observations on a Late Publication, intituled 'The Present State of the Nation,' " in *Works*, I, 398.

28. William James, *The Varieties of Religious Experience: A Study in Human Nature* (1902), enlarged ed. (New Hyde Park, N.Y.: University Books, 1963), p. 73.

29. *Autobiography of John Stuart Mill: Published from the Original Manuscript in the Columbia University Library* (New York: Columbia University Press, 1924), p. 150.

30. *Unto This Last*, in *The Works of John Ruskin* (Library Edition), ed. E. T. Cook and Alexander Wedderburn (London: George Allen, 1903–1912), XVII, 25–26.

31. *Fr. Rev.*, III, 248.

32. *Fr. Rev.*, III, 247.

33. Hegel, *The Philosophy of History*, p. 33.

34. *Fr. Rev.*, III, 138.

V. SINEWS AND INDIGNATION

1. *Works,* 1:236 and 27:82.

2. Letter of September 24, 1833, in Alexander Carlyle, ed., *Letters of Thomas Carlyle to John Stuart Mill, John Sterling and Robert Browning* (1923) (New York: Haskell House, 1970), pp. 70–71.

3. William Cobbett, *Rural Rides in the Southern, Western and Eastern Counties of England* . . . (1830), ed. G. D. H. and Margaret Cole (London: Peter Davies, 1930), I, 196, 228, and 162.

4. The spread of revolutionary opinions was for Pitt no mere hypothetical danger. Behind the mutinies in the British navy in 1797 he claimed to be able to see the hand of republican agitators. "The whole affair was of that colour and description which proved it to be not of a native growth, and left no hesitation in the mind of any thinking man to determine whence it was imported. . . ." To make matters worse, Pitt claimed that it was possible "to connect the discontents on board the fleet with the other species of sedition upon shore. . . ." Speech of June 2, 1797, in William Pitt, *Orations on the French War, to the Peace of Amiens* (London: J. M. Dent & Co., Everyman's Library, n.d.), pp. 233 and 232.

5. Quoted, with no source given, in Gwyn A. Williams, *Artisans and Sans-Culottes: Popular Movements in France and Britain during the French Revolution* (New York: W. W. Norton & Company, 1969), p. 106.

6. J. L. Hammond and Barbara Hammond, *The Skilled Labourer, 1760–1832* (1919) (New York: Harper & Row, 1970), p. 371.

7. *Works,* 27:82.

8. *Works,* 26:400.

9. *Works,* 26:406.

10. *Works,* 29:149–150 (*Chartism*).

11. *Life,* II, 18. Froude reports this statement as delivered privately to himself; but cf. *Works,* 5:201: "Truly, without the French Revolution, one would not know what to make of an age like this at all."

12. *Fr. Rev.,* I, 5.

13. *Fr. Rev.,* I, 8.

14. *Works,* 29:162 (*Chartism*).

15. *Fr. Rev.,* I, 12 and 13.

16. *Fr. Rev.,* I, 9.

17. *Fr. Rev.,* I, 9 and 13.

18. See Max Weber, *The Theory of Social and Economic Organization* (1925), trans. A. M. Henderson and Talcott Parsons (New York: Free Press, 1964), p. 124.

19. *Fr. Rev.,* I, 11.

20. *Fr. Rev.,* I, 21.

21. *Fr. Rev.,* I, 14.

22. Edmund Burke, *Reflections on the Revolution in France* (1790), in *The Works of the Right Honourable Edmund Burke,* rev. ed. (Boston: Little, Brown and Company, 1865), III, 406.

23. *Ibid.,* III, 279–280 and 282. We are certainly not without analogs of such thinking today; there is no shortage of commentators unwilling to see in the dissatisfactions of today's youth anything other than a sign of the fact that they have nothing to be dissatisfied about. The theory of

"revolutions of rising expectations" is the codification of such thinking and the elevation of it to the status of a historical law.

24. Both quotations are from Gaetano Salvemini, *The French Revolution, 1788–1792* (1905), trans. I. M. Rawson (New York: W. W. Norton & Company, 1962), p. 52. Salvemini's point, I should indicate, is the opposite of mine; he is trying to show that the Revolution was already in train by the 1750s.

25. J. L. Hammond and Barbara Hammond, *The Village Labourer, 1760–1832: A Study in the Government of England before the Reform Bill* (1911) (New York: Harper & Row, 1970), pp. 190–192.

26. Jules Michelet, *History of the French Revolution* (1846), ed. Gordon Wright, trans. Charles Cocks (1847) (Chicago: University of Chicago Press, 1967), p. 79.

27. *Fr. Rev.*, I, 14.

28. *Fr. Rev.*, I, 21. Cf. III, 93, where Carlyle paraphrases the indictment against Louis, not inaccurately, as follows: "Louis, who wert King, art thou not guilty to a certain extent, by act and written document, of trying to continue King?"

29. On absenteeism, see Alexis de Tocqueville, *The Old Régime and the French Revolution* (1856), trans. Stuart Gilbert (Garden City, N.Y.: Doubleday & Company, 1955), Part Two, Chap. 1. The inequality of French taxation was a watchword among economists; see Adam Smith, *An Inquiry into the Nature and Causes of the Wealth of Nations* (1776), ed. Edwin Cannan (1904) (London: Methuen & Co., 1961), II, 381–383, 433–438.

30. *Fr. Rev.*, I, 7.

31. Georges Lefebvre, *The French Revolution* (New York: Columbia University Press, 1969), vol. I, *From its Origins to 1793*, trans. Elizabeth Moss Evanson, pp. 102–115.

32. *Fr. Rev.*, I, 159.

33. *Fr. Rev.*, I, 164.

34. *Fr. Rev.*, I, 166–167.

35. *Fr. Rev.*, I, 112.

36. *Fr. Rev.*, I, 207.

37. *Fr. Rev.*, I, 200.

38. Lefebvre, *The French Revolution*, I, 115–116.

39. *Fr. Rev.*, II, 243–244.

40. P. A. Kropotkin, *The Great French Revolution, 1789–1793* (1909), trans. N. F. Dryhurst, 2 vols. (New York: Vanguard Press, 1927); see above, pp. 92–93.

41. Crane Brinton, *The Anatomy of Revolution* (1938), rev. (1952) and expanded ed. (New York: Random House, 1965), Chap. 3, sec. V.

42. *Fr. Rev.*, I, 130–131.

43. *Fr. Rev.*, II, 134–135.

44. *Fr. Rev.*, I, 234.

45. *Fr. Rev.*, III, 88.

46. *Fr. Rev.*, III, 137–138.

47. *Fr. Rev.*, III, 123.

48. *Fr. Rev.*, III, 123 and 138.

49. *Fr. Rev.*, III, 174.

50. R. B. Rose, "Eighteenth Century Price-Riots, the French Revolution and the Jacobin Maximum," *International Review of Social History*, 4, no. 3 (1959), 442.

51. Albert Mathiez, *The French Revolution* (1922), trans. Catherine Alison Phillips (New York: Grosset & Dunlap, 1964), p. 317.

52. Georges Lefebvre, *The French Revolution* (New York: Columbia University Press, 1969), vol. II, *From 1793 to 1799*, trans. John Hall Stewart and James Friguglietti, p. 50.

53. Kropotkin, *The Great French Revolution*, II, 407–408.

54. *Fr. Rev.*, II, 203.

55. *Fr. Rev.*, I, 113, 114.

56. E. J. Hobsbawm, *Primitive Rebels: Studies in Archiac Forms of Social Movement in the Nineteenth and Twentieth Centuries* (1959) (New York: W. W. Norton & Company, 1965), p. 110.

57. Williams, *Artisans and Sans-Culottes*, p. 10.

58. George Rudé, *The Crowd in History: A Study of Popular Disturbances in France and England, 1730–1848* (New York: John Wiley & Sons, 1964), pp. 35–36. The relevant selections from the *Annual Register* may be found in G. D. H. Cole and A. W. Filson, *British Working Class Movements: Selected Documents, 1789–1875* (London: Macmillan & Co., 1951), pp. 21–25.

59. Indeed, he sometimes even seems to be unaware of the political activities of the working classes in England up to the very eve of the Reform Bill; see his *Chartism*, where he speaks of the "Constitutional controversy . . . of the Working Classes, which now debates itself everywhere these fifty years, in France specifically since 1789, in England too *since 1831*. . . ." *Works*, 29:179; emphasis added.

60. Georg Wilhelm Friedrich Hegel, *The Philosophy of History*, trans. J. Sibree (New York: Dover Publications, 1956), p. 19.

61. Note made by Bentham in his own copy of his *Fragment on Government*; quoted in Mary Peter Mack, ed., *A Bentham Reader* (New York: Pegasus, 1969), p. 55.

62. Quoted in J. L. and Barbara Hammond, *The Town Labourer: The New Civilization, 1760–1832* (1917) (Garden City, N.Y.: Doubleday & Company, 1968), p. 253.

63. E. P. Thompson, *The Making of the English Working Class* (New York: Random House, 1966), pp. 65 and 67.

64. See John Stuart Mill, *Principles of Political Economy: with some of their applications to social philosophy* (1848), rev. ed. (1866) (New York: Colonial Press, 1900), II, 221–224 (Book IV, Chap. II, sec. 5).

65. *Fr. Rev.*, I, 211–212.

66. From *Confessions d'un révolutionnaire* in *Selected Writings of Pierre-Joseph Proudhon*, ed. Stewart Edwards, trans. Elizabeth Fraser (Garden City, N.Y.: Doubleday & Company, 1969), p. 156.

67. *Fr. Rev.*, II, 123.

68. *Fr. Rev.*, III, 114.

69. *Fr. Rev.*, I, 35.

70. *Fr. Rev.*, III, 223.

71. *Fr. Rev.*, III, 26.

72. This phrase is the title of Chapter V in Book III, Volume III, of Carlyle's *History*.

73. *Fr. Rev.*, III, 114.

74. *Fr. Rev.*, I, 251.

75. *Fr. Rev.*, III, 288.

76. *Fr. Rev.*, III, 142.

77. *Fr. Rev.*, III, 231.

78. *Fr. Rev.*, III, 223.

79. See A. R. Schoyen, *The Chartist Challenge: A Portrait of George Julian Harney* (London: William Heinemann, 1958), and G. D. H. Cole, *Chartist Portraits* (London: Macmillan & Co., 1941).

80. John Sterling, "On the Writings of Thomas Carlyle," in *Essays and Tales of John Sterling, Collected and Edited with a Memoir of His Life* by Julius Charles Hare (London: John W. Parker, 1848), I, 371 and 366. Although they are hostile, Sterling's comments on *The French Revolution* are recommended as a refreshing change from the common run of Carlyle scholarship, which interprets his *History* as a counterrevolutionary work and which rarely notices, as Sterling did, that Carlyle was temperamentally an incendiary.

81. *Fr. Rev.*, III, 43.

82. *Fr. Rev.*, III, 311. Carlyle is in error here; Silesia was ceded to Prussia at the end of the Silesian Wars of 1740–1742 and 1744–1745. The Seven Years War began in 1756.

83. *Fr. Rev.*, III, 47–48; for a similar argument, with respect to Cromwell, see Carlyle's *Oliver Cromwell's Letters and Speeches*, I, 408.

84. *Fr. Rev.*, III, 107.

85. *Fr. Rev.*, II, 263.

86. *Fr. Rev.*, III, 26.

87. *Fr. Rev.*, III, 311.

88. *Fr. Rev.*, III, 288.

89. *Fr. Rev.*, III, 24.

90. *Fr. Rev.*, III, 309.

91. For example, the club of English bourgeois radicals who so angered Burke when they sent their congratulatory message to the French National Assembly had denominated themselves the "Revolution Society" in honor of the principles of 1688. As Cole and Filson have noted (*British Working Class Movements*, p. 39), the Revolution Society's "Congratulatory Address to the National Assembly in France was written as from a country which had established its fundamental liberties and had no further need of revolution." Cf. Williams, *Artisans and Sans-Culottes*, p. 70.

92. *Fr. Rev.*, III, 314–315.

93. *Fr. Rev.*, III, 314.

VI. REVOLUTION AND THE STATE

1. J. L. Talmon, *The Origins of Totalitarian Democracy* (1951) (New York: W. W. Norton & Company, 1970), p. 41.

2. *Ibid.*, pp. 90 and 106.

3. Jean-Jacques Rousseau, *The First and Second Discourses*, trans. Roger D. and Judith R. Masters (New York: St. Martin's Press, 1964), pp. 158–159.

4. Jean-Jacques Rousseau, *The Social Contract* (1762), trans. Maurice Cranston (Baltimore: Penguin Books, 1968), p. 59 (Chap. 5).

5. *Ibid.*, pp. 60 and 62–63 (Chaps. 6 and 7).

6. *Ibid.*, p. 62.

7. *Ibid.*, p. 63.

8. Hannah Arendt, *The Origins of Totalitarianism* (1951), 2nd ed. (Cleveland: World Publishing Company, 1958), p. 297.

9. Kenneth Burke, *A Grammar of Motives* (1945) (Cleveland: World Publishing Company, 1962), pp. 35–38.

10. Arendt, *The Origins of Totalitarianism*, p. 302.

11. Edmund Burke, "Speech on a Motion for a Committee to Inquire into the State of the Representation of the Commons in Parliament," May 7, 1782, in *The Works of the Right Honourable Edmund Burke*, rev. ed. (Boston: Little, Brown and Company, 1866), VII, 94.

12. Woodrow Wilson, *Congressional Government: A Study in American Politics* (1885) (Cleveland: World Publishing Company, 1956), pp. 26–27.

13. Kenneth Burke, *A Grammar of Motives*, p. 362.

14. See *Leviathan*, Chap. XVIII, for a catalog of the *"Rights* and *Facultyes"* of the sovereign in a contractual state. Hobbes lists twelve such absolute rights, deriving them directly from the fact that a contract exists and considering it supererogatory to inquire into the specific nature of the contract itself. *Hobbes's Leviathan: Reprinted from the Edition of 1651* (Oxford: At the Clarendon Press, 1929), pp. 133–143.

15. Max Weber, "Politics as a Vocation" (1921), in *From Max Weber: Essays in Sociology*, ed. and trans. H. H. Gerth and C. Wright Mills (1946) (New York: Oxford University Press, 1958), p. 78.

16. R. M. MacIver, *The Modern State* (1926) (London: Oxford University Press, 1964), p. 151. The definition referred to in the text is to be found on p. 22: "The state is an association which, acting through law as promulgated by a government endowed to this end with coercive power, maintains within a community territorially demarcated the universal external conditions of social order."

17. James Mill, *An Essay on Government* (1819) (Indianapolis: Bobbs-Merrill Company, 1955), pp. 49–50.

18. Thomas Hobbes, *The Elements of Law: Natural & Politic* (1650), ed. Ferdinand Tönnies (Cambridge: At the University Press, 1928), p. 55.

19. Hobbes, *Leviathan*, p. 98 (Chap. XIII).

20. Rousseau, *Second Discourse*, p. 160.

21. *Ibid.*, pp. 160 and 159. So striking is the contrast between Rousseau and Mill on this score that Mill's argument as a whole is an uncannily accurate paraphrase of the speech Rousseau puts into the mouth of the hypothetical rich man who "invented specious reasons to lead them [the poor] to his goal."

22. Adam Smith, *An Inquiry into the Nature and Causes of the Wealth of Nations* (1776), ed. Edwin Cannan (1904) (London: Methuen & Co., 1961), I, 1–2. See above, Chapter VIII, section 2, for a further discussion of the division of labor.

23. See, for example, the subsection entitled "Relation of State and Law to Property," in Karl Marx and Friedrich Engels, *The German Ideology, Parts I & III* (1846), ed. R. Pascal (New York: International Publishers, 1963), pp. 58–63.

24. E. P. Thompson, *The Making of the English Working Class* (New York: Random House, 1966), p. 67.

25. John Ruskin, *Unto This Last*, in *The Works of John Ruskin* (Library Edition), ed. E. T. Cook and Alexander Wedderburn (London: George Allen, 1903–1912), XVII, 44.

26. Mill, *An Essay on Government*, p. 50.

27. Ralf Dahrendorf, *Essays in the Theory of Society* (Stanford: Stanford University Press, 1968), p. 226.

28. Adolf A. Berle, *Power* (New York: Harcourt, Brace & World, 1969); Karl W. Deutsch, *The Nerves of Government: Models of Political Communication and Control* (New York: Free Press, 1963), p. 124. This inability of modern political theorists to perceive power as a major category of sociopolitical functioning is nowhere more starkly apparent than in Talcott Parsons' distinction between "power" and "authority"; Parsons defines authority as "an institutionally recognized right to influence the actions of others," whereas power is the same ability to influence others "in so far as [this] ability . . . [is] not institutionally sanctioned." *Essays in Sociological Theory* (1949), rev. ed. (New York: Free Press, 1964), p. 76.

29. Franz Neumann, *The Democratic and the Authoritarian State*, ed. Herbert Marcuse (New York: Free Press, 1964), pp. 6–7.

30. C. A. Bodelson, *Studies in Mid-Victorian Imperialism* (New York: Alfred A. Knopf, 1925), p. 180. The quotation is from Bodelson's paraphrase of Froude's speech.

31. Michael Walzer, *The Revolution of the Saints: A Study in the Origins of Radical Politics* (Cambridge, Mass.: Harvard University Press, 1965), pp. 37–38.

32. Rousseau, *Second Discourse*, p. 177.

33. It is often said that National Socialist ideology in Germany is a case of a power ideology being used to justify a totalitarian regime. I refers readers interested in discovering the fallacy of this view to Fritz Stern's *The Politics of Cultural Despair: A Study in the Rise of the Germanic Ideology* (1961) (Garden City, N.Y.: Doubleday & Company, 1965). The "cultural despair" Stern writes about is precisely the perception, on the part of the ideologues he studies, of an intense incongruity between the cultural superiority of the German people and their condition of powerlessness. The will to power is then justified in terms of this cultural superiority and directly in the face of the lack of power. Clearly, power is not being used here as a self-legitimating principle.

34. *Fr. Rev.*, I, 38. The laws to which Carlyle refers are not instances of ethical or jurisprudential legality; they are laws in much the same sense as the laws of physics are laws, for the relevant sense of "law" as he uses the term is as an account of the actually operant actions and interactions of the elements of society. In this we can see, for what it is worth, an anticipation of the principles of modern relativistic sociology and cultural anthropology.

35. *Fr. Rev.*, I, 215.

36. *Fr. Rev.*, III, 138.

37. Again, cf. Rousseau's *Second Discourse* (p. 173), where Rousseau argues "that any government that . . . always worked exactly according to the ends of its institution, would have been instituted unnecessarily. . . ."

38. *Fr. Rev.*, II, 30.

39. *Fr. Rev.*, II, 211.

40. *Fr. Rev.*, II, 203.

41. *Fr. Rev.*, II, 244.

42. *Works*, 1:195.

43. *Works*, 1:199. Carlyle quoted this phrase (including the "shuddering admiration") as a description of himself in a letter to John Stuart

Mill dated March 21, 1833; see Alexander Carlyle, ed., *Letters of Thomas Carlyle to John Stuart Mill, John Sterling and Robert Browning* (1923) (New York: Haskell House, 1970), pp. 44–45.

44. *Fr. Rev.*, II, 110.
45. *Fr. Rev.*, I, 211.
46. David Caute, *The Left in Europe since 1789* (New York: McGraw-Hill Book Company, 1966), pp. 166–167.
47. *Fr. Rev.*, II, 110–111.
48. *Fr. Rev.*, II, 111.
49. *Fr. Rev.*, II, 110.

VII. THE ENGLISH REVOLUTION

1. Letter of November 25, 1839, in Alexander Carlyle, ed., *New Letters of Thomas Carlyle* (London and New York: John Lane, Bodley Head, 1904), I, 173–174. Froude reprints the same letter, *Life*, III, 172, but with the following version of the list of political parties: "Girondins, Radicals, do-nothing Aristocrats, Conservatives, and unbelieving dilettante Whigs." As Froude seems not to have noticed when he "normalized" the punctuation in this passage, Carlyle tended to identify the Philosophical Radicals of the 1830s with the Gironde and to apply his denunciations of the one to the other. Cf. his letter to John Stuart Mill, October 9, 1836: "On the whole I am sick of the Girondins. To confess a truth, I find them extremely like our present set of respectable Radical Members." Alexander Carlyle, ed., *Letters of Thomas Carlyle to John Stuart Mill, John Sterling and Robert Browning* (1923) (New York: Haskell House, 1970), p. 137.
2. Letter of December 1839, in Francis E. Mineka, ed., *The Earlier Letters of John Stuart Mill, 1812–1848* (Toronto: University of Toronto Press, 1963), II, 414.
3. Letter of December 6, 1839, in *Letters to Mill, Sterling and Browning*, pp. 171–172.
4. Letter of December 5, 1839. The passage quoted here can be found in *Life*, III, 173, but Froude does not give the date or the correspondent. The letter as a whole, *except for this passage*, can be found in *New Letters*, I, 175–176. Undoubtedly because he found them offensive, Alexander Carlyle replaced the sentences quoted here, and a few others, with ellipsis points. In any case, Carlyle's memory was faulty here; Mill hardly could have rejected the piece "two years ago," for Mill had expressed interest when Carlyle mentioned plans for such an essay, and it was Carlyle who closed the subject by announcing that he had given up "this notion of writing on the working classes." Letter of January 1838, in *Letters to Mill, Sterling and Browning*, p. 163.
5. *Works*, 29:118 and 119.
6. *Works*, 29:119.
7. *Two Notebooks of Thomas Carlyle: From 23d March 1822 to 16th May 1832*, ed. Charles Eliot Norton (New York: Grolier Club, 1898), p. 160.
8. *Works*, 29:126. Actually, Carlyle is no more—and no less—baffled on this matter than are modern economic historians, who have been engaged in a continual debate for quite a few decades now about the standard of living of British workers in the early nineteenth century. Cf. E. J. Hobsbawm, "The British Standard of Living, 1790–1850," in

Labouring Men: Studies in the History of Labour (1964) (Garden City, N.Y.: Doubleday & Company, 1967), and Sir John Harold Clapham, *An Economic History of Modern Britain*, 3 vols. (Cambridge: At the University Press, 1926–1938), for examples of the pessimistic and optimistic theses.

9. See G. K. Chesterton, *William Cobbett* (London: Hodder and Stoughton, 1925), p. 212.

10. Quotations in this and the preceding paragraph from *Works*, 29:127–128.

11. 4 and 5 William IV, cap. 76.

12. Carlyle, who did not greatly appreciate Dickens, did not have even this to say in its favor.

13. *Works*, 29:130.

14. Even Asa Briggs, who is generally sympathetic to the New Poor Law, admits this, blandly calling Chadwick's claim "misleading in that the commissioners . . . made no attempt to analyse the causes and nature of poverty. . . ." *The Making of Modern England, 1783–1867: The Age of Improvement* (1959) (New York: Harper & Row, 1965), pp. 278–279, where the quotation from Chadwick is also to be found.

15. *Works*, 29:129.

16. *Works*, 29:141.

17. Andrew Ure, *The Philosophy of Manufactures: or, An Exposition of the Scientific, Moral, and Commercial Economy of the Factory System of Great Britain*, 2nd ed., corrected (London: Charles Knight, 1835), p. 23.

18. *Works*, 29:131.

19. *Works*, 29:156.

20. *Works*, 29:187 and 190.

21. *Works*, 29:160.

22. *Miscellaneous Works of Lord Macaulay*, edited by his sister Lady Trevelyan (New York: Harper & Brothers, 1880), V, 263.

23. *Works*, 20:29 (*Latter-Day Pamphlets*).

24. *Works*, 29:121.

25. *Autobiography of John Stuart Mill: Published from the Original Manuscript in the Columbia University Library* (New York: Columbia University Press, 1924), p. 137; *Works*, 29:191.

26. *Works*, 29:192.

27. *Works*, 1:156.

28. *Works*, 1:129.

29. *Works*, 1:156.

30. *Works*, 29:153.

31. *Fr. Rev.*, III, 2.

32. *Works*, 29:152.

33. *Works*, 29:137.

34. John D. Rosenberg, *The Darkening Glass: A Portrait of Ruskin's Genius* (New York: Columbia University Press, 1961), p. 141.

35. Barrington Moore, Jr., *Social Origins of Dictatorship and Democracy: Lord and Peasant in the Making of the Modern World* (Boston: Beacon Press, 1967), p. 16.

36. P. Kropotkin, *Memoirs of a Revolutionist* (1899) (New York: Grove Press, 1970), p. 290.

37. *Ibid.*

38. The quotation is from a letter to his mother, January 2, 1827; quoted in *Life*, I, 378.

39. This consideration explains Carlyle's unremitting denunciations of the various attempts by the upper classes to act out of a moral sense of responsibility to those with whom they did not share any bonds of obligation; such philanthropism at best could do no more than cover up the true state of affairs.

40. *Works*, 29:118.

41. Letter to John Stuart Mill, December 6, 1839, in *Letters to Mill, Sterling and Browning*, p. 172.

42. See above, pp. 41ff.

43. The quotation is taken from a letter to his wife, September 4, 1831; quoted in *Life*, II, 190.

VIII. WEALTH AND POWER

1. See Grace J. Calder, *The Writing of "Past and Present": A Study of Carlyle's Manuscripts* (New Haven: Yale University Press, 1949).

2. Quoted in *ibid.*, p. 9.

3. *Life*, III, 223.

4. Letter to Emerson, August 29, 1842, in Joseph Slater, ed., *The Correspondence of Emerson and Carlyle* (New York: Columbia University Press, 1964), p. 328. In *Past and Present* the connection between the seventeenth and the nineteenth centuries is expressed in terms of an equation of Chartism and Cromwellism: "On the whole, a Parliament working with a lie in its mouth, will have to take itself away.... At all hours of the day and night, some Chartism is advancing, some armed Cromwell is advancing, to apprise such Parliament: 'Ye are no Parliament. In the name of God,—go!' " *Works*, 10:254.

5. *Life*, III, 282.

6. See above, p. 21.

7. Letter to John Sterling, February 23, 1843, in Alexander Carlyle, ed., *New Letters of Thomas Carlyle* (New York and London: John Lane, Bodley Head, 1904), I, 282.

8. Emery Neff, *Carlyle and Mill: An Introduction to Victorian Thought* (1924), 2nd ed., rev. (New York: Octagon Books, 1964), p. 37.

9. Quoted in Emery Neff, *Carlyle* (New York: W. W. Norton & Company, 1932), p. 206.

10. Friedrich Engels, "Die Lage Englands" (1844), in *Deutsch-Französische Jahrbücher* (Darmstadt: Wissenschaftliche Buchgesellschaft, 1967), p. 152; my trans.

11. See Eric Bentley, *A Century of Hero-Worship: A Study in the Idea of Heroism in Carlyle and Nietzsche* (1944), 2nd ed. (Boston: Beacon Press, 1957); and Ernst Cassirer, *The Myth of the State* (New Haven: Yale University Press, 1946).

12. See above, Chapter IV, section 1.

13. Karl Marx, *The Civil War in France* (1870–1871) (New York: International Publishers, 1968), p. 59.

14. Georges Sorel, *Reflections on Violence* (1906), trans. T. E. Hulme and J. Roth (New York: Collier Books, 1961), p. 50.

15. One should think that this point is so obvious that it need not be

made. A survey of the literature on Carlyle, however, convinces me otherwise.

16. Bentley, *A Century of Hero-Worship*, p. 61.

17. *Works*, 10:269.

18. G. K. Chesterton, *William Cobbett* (London: Hodder and Stoughton, 1925), p. 23.

19. Adam Smith, *An Inquiry into the Nature and Causes of the Wealth of Nations* (1776), ed. Edwin Cannan (1904) (London: Methuen & Co., 1961), I, 17 and 19.

20. Emile Durkheim, *The Division of Labor in Society* (1893), trans. George Simpson (1933) (New York: Free Press, 1964), p. 234.

21. *Works*, 10:146.

22. Karl Marx, *Capital: A Critique of Political Economy* (1867), ed. Frederick Engels, trans. Samuel Moore and Edward Aveling (1887) (New York: International Publishers, 1967), I, 356.

23. *Works*, 10:195.

24. *Works*, 10:280.

25. *Works*, 10:281–282.

26. *Works*, 10:147.

27. Cf. *Capital*, I, 194, where Marx argues that in the industrialist's purchase of the worker's labor power "the laws that regulate the exchange of commodities have been in no way violated. Equivalent has been exchanged for equivalent."

28. *Works*, 10:219; cf. p. 212: "Liberty, I am told, is a divine thing. Liberty when it becomes the 'Liberty to die by starvation' is not so divine!"

29. *Works*, 10:213.

30. See above, Chapter III, section 2.

31. *Works*, 1:133.

32. See *Works*, 5:173, where the condition of modern man is described in precisely the terminology used in *Sartor* to describe Carlyle-Teufelsdröckh's spiritual condition.

33. *Works*, 10:219.

34. *Works*, 10:274.

35. *Works*, 10:3.

36. See Thorstein Veblen, *The Theory of Business Enterprise* (1904) (New York: New American Library, n.d.), p. 78: "[T]he interest of the managers of a modern corporation need not coincide with the permanent interest of the corporation as a going concern; neither does it coincide with the interest which the community at large has in the efficient management of the concern as an industrial enterprise." See also his *Absentee Ownership and Business Enterprise in Recent Times: The Case of America* (1923) (Boston: Beacon Press, 1967), *passim*.

37. *Works*, 10:171.

38. *Works*, 10:176.

39. William Cobbett, *Cobbett's Legacy to Labourers; or, What is the Right which the Lords, Baronets, and 'Squires have to the Lands of England? In Six Letters, Addressed to the Working People of England* (London: William Cobbett, 1834), p. 140.

40. *Works*, 10:165.

41. *Works*, 10:140.

42. E.g., *Works*, 10:208.

43. *Works*, 10:178.

44. *Works*, 30:45.

45. *Works*, 10:173.

46. *Works*, 10:162.

47. Karl Marx and Friedrich Engels, *The German Ideology, Parts I & III* (1846), ed. R. Pascal (New York: International Publishers, 1963), p. 91.

48. *Works*, 10:207.

49. *Works*, 10:170.

50. *Works*, 10:182–184.

51. *Works*, 10:169.

52. *Works*, 1:89.

53. *Works*, 10:141.

54. Veblen, *Absentee Ownership*, p. 78.

55. Veblen's term.

56. Veblen, *Absentee Ownership*, p. 79.

57. Cf. *Works*, 30:35, where Carlyle addresses his Captain of Industry in the following terms: "The glory of a workman, still more of a master-workman, That he does his work well, ought to be his most precious possession; like 'the honour of a soldier,' dearer to him than life. That is the ideal of the matter:—lying, alas, how far from us at present! But if you yourself *demoralise* your soldier, and teach him continually to invoke the Evil Genius and to *dis*honour himself,—what do you expect your big Army will grow to?—"

58. I should note in passing that, once the division of labor between industrial personnel and business personnel was fully accomplished, Carlyle's mistake has reappeared in the works of a number of thinkers who have taken this division as a confirmation of Carlyle's faith that these two aspects of industrial enterprise are separable. Veblen, of course, is one, but see also James Burnham, *The Managerial Revolution: What is Happening in the World* (New York: John Day Company, 1941); and John Kenneth Galbraith, *The New Industrial State* (Boston: Houghton Mifflin Company, 1967).

59. Both quotations from Christopher Hill, *Puritanism and Revolution: Studies in the English Revolution of the Seventeenth Century* (1958) (New York: Schocken Books, 1964), pp. 210 and 220.

60. Smith, *Wealth of Nations*, I, 437–438.

61. I am again using the terminology of Max Weber here. Weber trichotomizes human activity into three realms: the social, which is concerned with relationships of status; the political, which is concerned with relationships of power; and the economic, which is concerned with relationships of wealth. See *The Theory of Social and Economic Organization* (1925), trans. A. M. Henderson and Talcott Parsons (New York: Free Press, 1964).

62. Dickens too deals with the notion that to be recognized as wealthy is to be wealthy. The Lammles in *Our Mutual Friend* are a case in point. But Dickens is more naive than Trollope in his treatment of this theme, for he seems to have dismissed it as a delusion of opportunists where Trollope recognized it as a significant fact of modern social and economic life.

63. See above, pp. 116ff.

64. Ferdinand Tönnies, *Community & Society (Gemeinschaft und Gesellschaft)* (1887), trans. and ed. Charles P. Loomis (New York: Harper & Row, 1963), p. 76.

65. *Works*, 10:293.

66. *Works*, 1:184.

67. *Works*, 10:67.

68. Talcott Parsons, *Essays in Sociological Theory* (1949), rev. ed. (New York: Free Press, 1964), pp. 61–62; see also p. 234.

69. *Works*, 10:146.

70. See Jean-Jacques Rousseau, "First Discourse" (1750), in *The First and Second Discourses*, trans. Roger D. and Judith R. Masters (New York: St. Martin's Press, 1964), p. 52: "Let our politicians . . . learn for once that with money one has everything, except morals and citizens."

71. See *Works*, 10:185 and 257.

IX. A WHOLE WORLD OF HEROES

1. *Works*, 1:200; letter to Mill, February 24, 1841, in Alexander Carlyle, ed., *Letters of Thomas Carlyle to John Stuart Mill, John Sterling and Robert Browning* (1923) (New York: Haskell House, 1970), p. 174.

2. *Works*, 27:79; see above, p. 38.

3. *Works*, 29:159 (*Chartism*).

4. Quoted in Graham Wallas, *The Life of Francis Place (1771–1854)* (New York: Alfred A. Knopf, 1919), pp. 192 and 155.

5. *Autobiography of John Stuart Mill: Published from the Original Manuscript in the Columbia University Library* (New York: Columbia University Press, 1924), p. 74.

6. Elie Halévy, *The Growth of Philosophic Radicalism* (1901–1904), trans. Mary Morris (Boston: Beacon Press, 1955), p. 429.

7. *The Works of Jeremy Bentham*, ed. John Bowring (1838–1843) (New York: Russell & Russell, 1962), X, 82. The quotation is taken from an autobiographical fragment included by Bowring in his *Memoirs of Bentham*.

8. John Stuart Mill, *Utilitarianism*, 2nd ed. (London: Longman, Green, Longman, Roberts, and Green, 1864), p. 12. "What Utilitarianism Is," originally published in 1861, was reprinted as Chap. 2 of *Utilitarianism* two years later. For a fine critique of Mill and his relation to radical democracy, see Alexander Herzen's essay, "John Stuart Mill and His Book on Liberty," in *My Past and Thoughts: The Memoirs of Alexander Herzen* (1855), trans. Constance Garnett, ed. Dwight Macdonald (New York: Alfred A. Knopf, 1973), pp. 458–467.

9. See Sidney and Beatrice Webb, *Industrial Democracy*, 2nd ed. (London: Longmans, Green and Co., 1920), Chaps. 1 and 2. We should note that, even with respect to trade union government, the workers soon became aware of the inefficiency of this ideal form of democracy, and before long the "Iron Law of Oligarchy" began to make itself felt in the form of an evolution toward a representational system involving paid professional and quasi-professional unionists.

10. Walter Bagehot, *The English Constitution* (1867), in *The Works and Life of Walter Bagehot*, ed. Mrs. Russell Barrington (London: Longmans, Green, and Co., 1915), vol. V, esp. Chaps. 2 and 3; see p. 350: "The mass of the English people are politically contented as well as politically deferential."

11. See the section entitled "Conservatism and Class" in Samuel H. Beer, *British Politics in the Collectivist Age* (New York: Random House, 1969), pp. 251–255.

12. William Lovett, *Life and Struggles of William Lovett In his Pursuit of Bread, Knowledge & Freedom, with some short Account of the different Associations he belonged to & of the Opinions he entertained* (1876) (London: MacGibbon & Kee, 1967), p. 75.

13. *Works*, 10:219 (*Past and Present*).

14. See above, Chapter VII, section 3.

15. See Emery Neff, *Carlyle* (New York: W. W. Norton & Company, 1932), and *Carlyle and Mill: An Introduction to Victorian Thought* (1924), 2nd ed., rev. (New York: Octagon Books, 1964); Ernst Cassirer, *The Myth of the State* (New Haven: Yale University Press, 1946); Eric Bentley, *A Century of Hero-Worship: A Study in the Idea of Heroism in Carlyle and Nietzsche* (1944), 2nd ed. (Boston: Beacon Press, 1957).

16. Edmund Burke, "Speech to the Electors of Bristol," November 3, 1774, in *The Works of the Right Honourable Edmund Burke*, rev. ed. (Boston: Little, Brown and Company, 1865), II, 96.

17. One example of this idea that a member of Parliament need not represent the specific interests of his constituents can be found in Cobbett's speech at the Manchester hustings in 1831, in the course of which he explained that it was not necessary for the greatest industrial city in England to be represented by a man with the industrial interest at heart, and that a farmer such as himself would do quite as well; see *Cobbett's Manchester Lectures, in support of his Fourteen Reform Propositions* (London: William Cobbett, 1832), pp. 21–22. Matthew Arnold's analysis of the Barbarians, Philistines, and Populace in *Culture and Anarchy* judges each class on the basis of its competency to act as the final arbiter on legislation. Mill's defense of plural voting also assumes that a legislature should be designed so as to maximize the impact of wisdom rather than to accurately reflect the proportional strengths of the various interests within the society. So far as I am aware, the idea that a parliament is a forum rather than an arena is one of the few universal assumptions of Victorian political thought. We might note in passing that this pretty notion, which may seem hopelessly naive to many modern Americans, is less fanciful with respect to the British legislature than it would be with respect to American political institutions, in part because of the British habit of returning members who commonly are not representative of the regional constituencies for which they stand. "It does not often happen," Sir Ivor Jennings observes, ". . . that Muddleton is represented by a Muddletonian." This fact itself speaks volumes for the persistence of English faith in the forum model. Ivor Jennings, *The British Constitution* (1941), 5th ed. (Cambridge: At the University Press, 1966), p. 16.

18. Walter Bagehot, *Physics and Politics* (1869), in *The Works and Life of Walter Bagehot*, VIII, 125.

19. *Works*, 20:233 (*Latter-Day Pamphlets*).

20. *Works*, 5:1.

21. Sidney Hook, *The Hero in History: A Study in Limitation and Possibility* (1943) (Boston: Beacon Press, 1955), pp. 15–16 and 59.

22. Albert Mathiez, *The French Revolution* (1922), trans. Catherine Alison Phillips (New York: Grosset & Dunlap, 1964), p. 16.

23. *Fr. Rev.*, I, II; see above, pp. 81–82.

24. *Fr. Rev.*, II, 180–181.

25. *Fr. Rev.*, II, 154.

26. *Fr. Rev.*, II, 296.

27. *Works*, 5:56–57.

28. Georg Friedrich Wilhelm Hegel, *The Philosophy of History*, trans. J. Sibree (New York: Dover Publications, 1956), p. 30.

29. *Works*, 5:45, 67, 54, 84, 103, 123, and 148.

30. *Fr. Rev.*, I, 125, and *Works*, 5:191.

31. *Fr. Rev.*, III, 47 and 23; II, 19.

32. E.g., *Fr. Rev.*, II, 53; III, 8.

33. *Works*, 5:135.

34. Hegel, *The Philosophy of History*, p. 30.

35. *Works*, 5:226.

36. *Works*, 5:122; again, cf. Hegel, *The Philosophy of History*, p. 31: "They are *great* men, because they willed and accomplished something great; not a mere fancy, a mere intention, but that which met the case and fell in with the needs of the age."

37. *Works*, 5:134.

38. *Works*, 5:21.

39. *Works*, 5:216; on "Valets," see note 49 below.

40. *Works*, 27:86 ("On History").

41. Friedrich Nietzsche, *The Will to Power* (1901), trans. Walter Kaufmann and R. J. Hollingdale (New York: Random House, 1968), p. 79.

42. *Works*, 5:56.

43. *Works*, 5:179.

44. *Works*, 10:75; cf. 5:196–197.

45. *Works*, 10:241–242.

46. Max Weber, "The Sociology of Charismatic Authority," in *From Max Weber: Essays in Sociology*, trans. and ed. H. H. Gerth and C. Wright Mills (1946) (New York: Oxford University Press, 1958), pp. 246–247 and 249.

47. Max Weber, *The Theory of Social and Economic Organization* (1925), trans. A. M. Henderson and Talcott Parsons (New York: Free Press, 1964), pp. 359–360.

48. *Works*, 5:124. For an excellent discussion of the obligations owed a revolutionary movement and its leaders by the followers, see Michael Walzer, *Obligations: Essays on Disobedience, War, and Citizenship* (Cambridge, Mass.: Harvard University Press, 1970), Chap. 8, "The Obligation to Live for the State."

49. *Works*, 5:184 and 10:35; see Hegel, *The Philosophy of History*, p. 32: "'No man is a hero to his *valet-de-chambre*,' is a well-known proverb; I have added—and Goethe repeated it ten years later—'but not because the former is no hero, but because the latter is a valet.'"

50. *From Max Weber*, p. 250; *Theory of Social and Economic Organization*, p. 361.

51. See Cassirer, *The Myth of the State*, p. 193: "But notwithstanding all his spiritualism he [Carlyle] becomes, in matters of politics, one of the most resolute advocates of passive obedience. . . . True spontaneity is reserved to the few elect. As to the others, the mass of the reprobates, they have to submit under the will of these elect, the born rulers."

52. See *Works*, 5:58.

53. Matthew 10:35, 37.

54. Richard H. Solomon, *Mao's Revolution and the Chinese Political Culture* (Berkeley: University of California Press, 1971), p. 509.

55. *Works*, 10:83.

56. *Works*, 10:35–36.

57. *The Standard Edition of the Complete Psychological Works of Sigmund Freud*, ed. James Strachey (London: Hogarth Press and the Institute of Psycho-Analysis, 1953–1966), XXI, 133 (*Civilization and Its Discontents*, 1930), and XVIII, 127 (*Group Psychology and the Analysis of the Ego*, 1921).

58. *From Max Weber*, p. 248.

59. *Works*, 10:280.

60. *Fr. Rev.*, I, 211.

61. Leon Trotsky, *The Russian Revolution: The Overthrow of Tzarism and The Triumph of the Soviets*, ed. F. W. Dupee, trans. Max Eastman (1932) (Garden City, N.Y.: Doubleday & Company, 1959), pp. ix–x.

62. *Works*, 10:260.

63. *Works*, 5:127 and 10:35.

Index

Abrams, M. H., 8
Action: labor, work, and, 27-28, 57-58;
modern conceptions of, 53-54; relation to thought and feeling, 52-53,
127, 137. *See also* Carlyle, Thomas,
action in
Advertising, 164-165
Alison, Dr. William, 159
Arendt, Hannah, 6, 63, 109, 115, 123; on
labor, work, and action, 27-28, 57-58, 177; on "rights of man," 112-113
Argenson, marquis d', 83
Aristotle, 68-69
Arkwright, Richard, 56
Arnold, Matthew, 5, 136, 186; quoted,
25
Auerbach, Erich, 11

Bagehot, Walter, 183, 186, 187, 199
Bailly, Jean-Sylvain, 90
Bentham, Jeremy, 37, 38, 54, 74; as
democrat, 179, 181; on freedom,
96; on legislatures, 186; as statist, 38-39
Benthamism, 38-39; as ideology of feelings, 52-53. *See also* Political Economy; Westminster Radicalism
Bentley, Eric, 39, 151-152, 186
Bergson, Henri, 67
Berlin, Isaiah, 66
Blake, William, 73, 75, 76
Breteuil, baron de, 87
Brienne, Loménie de, 93
Brinton, Crane, 35, 88
Broglie, duc de, 87
Burke, Edmund, 39, 64-65, 73, 77-78,
84, 98, 103, 125, 182, 186; on British constitution, 113-114; on causes
of French Revolution, 69, 82-83; on
connection between thought and action, 53-54; organic theory in, 125-126
Burke, Kenneth, 44, 50, 113, 114-115

Cabarrús (or Cabarus), Thérésa, 107
Calvin, John, 121-122
Calvinism, relation to political involvement, 18-20
Carlyle, James, 17-18. *See also* Carlyle,
Thomas, relation to father
Carlyle, Jane Welsh, 147
Carlyle, Margaret, *see* Carlyle, Thomas,
relation to mother
Carlyle, Thomas: action in, 20-21, 23,
27-29, 35, 44, 52-62, 138-139, 143,
177-178, 201; activism, 35-36, 44, 138-139, 143; on advertising, 164-165;
on "Annihilation of Self," 29, 34,
61-62, 158, 201; on aristocracy, 80-81, 161-162; authoritarianism in, 41,
175; on "Captains of Industry," 160,
163-164, 165-166; on "Cash Nexus,"
142, 171-175; on Chartist movement,
93, 130-132; "Clothes Philosophy,"
45, 49, 68, 99; conception of class
relations, 100-101; conception of history, 12-14, 26, 66, 68-70, 75-76, 187;
conception of "satanic-divine," 47,
101; conception of society, 55-56,
124, 172-173; on "Condition-of-England Question," 131-132; conservatism of, 148-149, 161-162; "conversion," 59-60; on Corn Laws, 160-161;
cosmic perspective in, 23, 32-33; on
Cromwell, 41, 146-147, 192-193
  on democracy: 135-136, 137, 178-188, 199; antidemocratic position, 179,
184-187; democracy as inadequate
substitute for action, 187-188; parlia-

Carlyle, Thomas (*continued*)
mentary democracy, 184-187; democracy as protest movement, 178-179
   as dialectician, 8-9, 26, 166; distinction between business and industry, 159-160, 164-166; on division of labor, 154-157; fascism of, 121; on free-market system, 157-159
   on French Revolution: attitude toward Reign of Terror, 102-106; bourgeois and popular phases, 88-91, 92-93; causes of, 81-84; early attitude toward, 77-79; incomplete nature of, 105-106; organic nature of, 125-127; role of philosophes in, 82-85, 90; role of sansculottes in, 92-93, 99-102
   "Gospel of Work," 28-29, 60-62, 158
   hero theory: 120, 175, 176, 188-203; ambivalence of, 200; compared to Nietzschean theory, 193-194, 196; criticism of, 189-190; hero as charismatic leader, 195-196, 200; hero as delegate of his followers, 193, 202; hero as rebel, 197-200, 201-202; hero-worship and action, 194, 201; historical limits of hero, 191-192; revolutionary implications of, 194, 197-203; role of submission in, 194-196; totalitarian implications of, 198; universalization of herohood, 201-203
   on "Ideopraxis," 54-56; on industrial capitalism, 156, 164-166; as intellectual, 35-36; intellectual isolation of, 144-145; medievalism in, 148-152; on "Morrison's Pill," 31-32; mysticism in, 19-20, 55; nihilism in, 23, 29; on "Organisation of Labour," 156-157, 163; on Political Economy, 152-168, 173-174; political quietism of, 16-22, 29-34; on power, 80-81, 120-121, 174-175; on power and its relation to government, 101-102; on private property, 160-162; psychopathology of, 175, 205, 209; on rational and irrational in history, 75-76; on "reform of the heart," 139-140, 142-143, 167, 172; relation to Benthamism, 37-39; relation to conservatism, 39-40; relation to contractualist political theory, 55; relation to father, 3, 50; relation to Hegel, 12; relation to mother, 48, 50; relation to radical movements, 40-43; relation to rationalist thought, 5-7, 43-44, 55; relation to St. Simonianism, 156, 163-164; relation to working class, 143-144; religion, 2, 4-7, 18-20, 47-51

   on revolution: 56; as class warfare, 104; as a creative force, 127; dangers of, 167-168; definition of, 97-99, 105-106; organic nature of, 125-127; on permanent revolution, 126-127, 201-202; on revolutionary government, 99-102, 105-106; sense of impending revolution, 139, 143, 148, 167, 174
   suicidal impulses, 52, 58-59, 62; technique as historian, 67, 76
   Works: "Biography," 14; "Burns," 13; "Characteristics," 14, 15, 23, 26-27, 43-44; *Chartism*, 40, 80 (quoted), 128-145; "Corn-Law Rhymes," 15, 30, 33, 35-36; *Frederick the Great*, 41 (quoted); "Goethe," 4-7, 10; "Goethe's Helena," 9; *On Heroes and Hero-Worship*, 146, 176, 188-193, 194, 203; "On History," 14; *History of the French Revolution*, 32-33, 40, 67-70, 75-76, 79-107, 108, 124, 125-127, 146, 185, 201; *Life of Schiller*, 12, 66; *Past and Present*, 15, 31-32, 34, 40, 76, 146-175, 176, 178, 194, 196; "Richter," 7-8; *Sartor Resartus*, 3, 4, 5, 19, 28-29, 45-62, 68, 77, 99, 107, 126, 127, 138, 158, 172, 176; "Shooting Niagara: And After?" 162, 166; "Signs of the Times," 14, 15, 23-24, 36-39, 43, 77, 78, 106, 142, 178; "The State of German Literature," 13; "Voltaire," 78-79; *Wilhelm Meister* (translation), 45
Cassirer, Ernst, 186, 197
Caute, David, 127
Chadwick, Edwin, 133
Chartism: and democracy, 183; history of, 129-130
Chesterton, G. K., 33, 152
Clarendon, Lord, 168
Cobbett, William, 17, 33, 34, 52, 64, 78, 132, 152, 160-161, 163, 186
Coke, Edward, 186
Cole, G. D. H., 16
Coleridge, Samuel Taylor, 39, 73
Constitutionalism, 113-115; constitution as self-legitimating principle, 114-115. See also Social contract theory
Cooper, Thomas, 149
Corday, Charlotte, 91
Corn Laws, 30, 160-161
Courrier, Paul-Louis, 163
Croce, Benedetto, 65
Cromwell, Oliver, 41, 146-147, 192-193, 197

Dahrendorf, Ralf, 120, 178
Danton, Georges-Jacques, 83, 192
Democracy, 178-188; and action, 184,

187; participatory and delegational forms, 182-183; and social equality, 180-182
Descartes, René, 5-6, 8, 27
Desmoulins, Camille, 87
Dickens, Charles, 18, 31-32, 73, 133; on "reform of the heart," 141-142; on wealth and status, 170
Diderot, Denis, 8
Dilthey, Wilhelm, 14
Disraeli, Benjamin, 182
Division of labor, 153-156
Durkheim, Emile, 154, 171

Eliot, T. S., 53
Elliott, Ebenezer, 30, 78
Emerson, Ralph Waldo, 46, 147; on radicalism of *Past and Present*, 148-149
Engels, Friedrich, 63-64, 151; on Carlyle's radicalism, 40; on *Past and Present*, 149
Erikson, Erik H., 54

Feuerbach, Ludwig, 49
Foulon, Joseph-François, 87
Fourier, François-Marie, 141
French Revolution: and constitutionalism, 89-90, 99, 124-125; bourgeois phase, 86-88; causes of, 79-86; Committee of Public Safety in, 102, 105, 106; effect on historical thinking, 63; fall of Bastille, 87; formation of National Assembly, 86; Girondins in, 86, 88, 90-91, 124-125, 127; Jacobins in, 89-92, 125-127; popular phase, 92-93; Reign of Terror, 102-106; relation of philosophes to, 82-84, 90; relation to English politics, 77-78; role of mob in, 93; sansculottes in, 88-90, 97-102. *See also* Carlyle, Thomas, on French Revolution
Freud, Sigmund, 75, 200
Froude, James Anthony, 79, 106, 121, 186

Gast, John, 42
Goethe, Johann Wolfgang von, 4, 7, 10, 45, 53, 62, 196, 199
Goodman, Paul, 54
Government: and the market, 118-119; and power, 120-123; classless, 136-137. *See also* Social contract theory

Halévy, Elie, 181
Hammond, J. L. and Barbara, 78, 84
Harney, George Julian, 103
Harrold, Charles Frederick, 7
Hartley, David, 6
Hegel, Georg Wilhelm Friedrich, 10, 27, 144; action in, 35; on alienation, 58; conception of history, 11-12, 65-68; dialectic in, 26; free and servile labor distinguished, 28, 58, 60, 61; on heroes and valets, 196, 199; on role of masses in history, 95; on World-historical men, 54, 191-192
Heisenberg, Werner, 6
Heroes, *see* Carlyle, Thomas, hero theory
Hill, Christopher, 64
History: Hegelian conception of, 11-12, 65-68; historical causation, 65-70; as linear process, 70-71; Machiavellian conception of, 70-71; philosophy of, 70-76; relation to modern thought, 11-14; and revolutionary thought, 63-65, 150-151; and the self, 10-14; as sum of individual actions, 188
Hobbes, Thomas, 55, 64, 70, 109, 115, 154; on relation of private property and state, 117
Hobsbawm, E. J., 42, 94
Hook, Sidney, 189
Horne, Richard Hengist, on Carlyle's nihilism, 29
Hume, David, 8

James, William, 73-74
Joyce, James, 57

Kahn, Herman, 70
Kant, Immanuel, 6, 8, 60
Kierkegaard, Søren, 2
Knox, John, 191
Kropotkin, Peter, 88, 92-93, 140, 151

Labor: differentiated from work and action, 27-28, 57-58; division of, 153-156; "Organisation of," 156-157, 163
Lafayette, marquis de, 88, 89
Laissez-faire: and the poor laws, 133-135; relation to democracy, 188. *See also* Carlyle, Thomas, on Political Economy; Political Economy
Laski, Harold J., 72
Lefebvre, Georges, 86-87
Legitimacy (political): absolutization of, 111-112; distinction between abstract and historical rights, 64, 112-113; of French ancien régime, 81-82, 85; relation to force, 115-122. *See also* Power; Social contract theory
Liancourt, duc de, 87
Liberalism: ahistorical nature of, 150; conception of freedom, 95-96; conception of state, 115-116, 122-123; on role of force in politics, 116-118, 120, 122. *See also* Social contract theory

Lloyd, David, 168-169
Locke, John, 37, 55, 70, 109
Lockhart, John, 128-129
London Corresponding Society, 18, 41
London Working Men's Association, 183
Louis XV, 80, 85
Louis XVI, 69, 82, 86, 87, 190-191
Lovett, William, 42, 130, 137, 183
Löwith, Karl, 11, 20
Luddism, 42
Luther, Martin, 191, 192-193

Macaulay, Thomas Babington, 136
Machiavelli, Niccolò, 109; theory of historical causation, 70-72
MacIver, R. M., 115
Malthus, Thomas Robert, 132, 134
Mannheim, Karl: action in, 27-28, 177, 201; on revolutionary use of history, 64
Mao Tse-tung, 198
Marat, Jean-Paul, 91, 103, 105, 106, 192
Marcuse, Herbert, 137
Marx, Karl: on action, 27; on alienation, 158; conception of class relations, 101, 163; conception of history, 68, 71; critique of Political Economy, 153, 155, 166-167; critique of "utopianism," 141; on division of labor, 155-156; on economic determinism, 170-171; on free-market system, 157-158; on industrial capitalism, 156; on parliamentary democracy, 137; relation to British economists, 118; on use of historical models, 150; on work, 60-61; and Young Hegelians, 144
Mathiez, Albert, 92, 190
Mazzini, Giuseppe: on Carlyle's nihilism, 22-23, 29; on Carlyle's radicalism, 40
Michelet, Jules, 84
Medievalism, political implications of, 149-152
Mill, James: and rationalism, 6-7; Essay on Government, 116-120, 170
Mill, John Stuart, 20, 21, 40, 46, 73, 77, 97, 136, 137, 145, 176, 186, 196; and Carlyle's Chartism, 128-129; critique of Benthamism, 74, 181-182; on democracy, 180-182; elitism of, 181-182; "The Spirit of the Age," 24-25
Mirabeau, comte de, 87, 191-192
Mitchell, Robert, 6
Mobs: in eighteenth-century England, 94-95, 97; in French Revolution, 93
Moore, Barrington, Jr., 41, 140
Morris, William, 34, 73, 141, 149, 164

Mosca, Gaetano, 137
Muhammad, 191, 197
Mysticism, 19-20

Nationalism, and historical relativism, 12-13
Necker, Jacques, 87, 93
Neff, Emery, 39, 148, 186
Neumann, Franz, 67, 120
Newman, John Henry, 73
New Poor Law, 31, 132-134
Newton, Isaac, 6
Nietzsche, Friedrich, 20, 193-194, 196

O'Brien, James Bronterre, 103, 136
O'Connor, Feargus, 30, 130, 182
Organic theory: Carlyle's revolutionary use of, 123-127
Orléans, duc d', 86
Orwell, George, 95
Overproduction, 159-160
Owen, Robert, 34, 35, 110, 141, 151

Paine, Thomas, 79
Parsons, Talcott, 173
Pater, Walter, 57
Philosophes, and French Revolution, 82-84, 90
Philosophical Radicals, 38-40. See also Bentham, Jeremy; Benthamism; Liberalism; and Westminster Radicalism
Pitt, William, 78
Place, Francis, 42, 43, 180, 182
Plato, 110, 150
Political Economy, 38; atomism of, 155, 173; Carlyle's critique of, 152-168, 173-174; economic determinism in, 170-171; free-market system in, 157-158; on poverty as a natural phenomenon, 134, 137; on wealth and power, 119-120
Popular radical movements, 41-42
Postgate, Raymond, 16
Poverty: application of laissez-faire to, 133-134; in England, 132-135, 159
Power: and wealth, 119; liberal denial of, 116, 120; relation of power theory of the state to totalitarianism, 120-123; relation to government, 101-102; relation to legitimacy, 115-122; relation to wealth and status, 170-171, 174-175; revolutionary implications of power theory, 122-123
Price, Richard, 77
Priestley, Joseph, 77-78
Property, private: basic to Political Economy, 153; Carlyle on, 160-162; industrial, 162-164; landed, 160-162; James Mill on, 116-120; Rousseau

on, 117; Smith on, 118; in social contract theory, 116-117
Proudhon, Pierre-Joseph, 99, 151
Pugin, Augustus Welby, 152

Rationalism: antirationalist reaction, 73-75; formal and substantive rationality distinguished, 72-73; and maximization, 73; and religion, 5
Relativism: in Carlyle's early essays, 10; and history, 10-11; and religion, 5
Religion, see Carlyle, Thomas, religion
Revolution: and charismatic relationships, 197; as class warfare, 104; as creative force, 127; defined by Carlyle, 97-99; from above, 140-141; and history, 63-65, 150-151; permanent, 126-127, 201-202; relation of action to, 56, 201
Ricardo, David, 30, 157
Richter, Jean Paul, 7, 8, 12
Robespierre, Maximilien de, 83, 92, 97, 109-110, 192
Roland, Jean-Marie, 92
Romanticism: and history, 71; as ideology of thought, 52-53
Rosenberg, John D., 140
Rousseau, Jean-Jacques, 79, 83, 109; critique of property theory, 117; on power and legitimacy, 122; on social contract, 110-112
Rudé, George, 94
Ruskin, John, 31, 34, 73, 119, 136, 149, 151, 156, 164; on Political Economy, 74-75; on "reform of the heart," 140-141

Saint-Just, Louis Antoine Léon de, 103
Saint-Simon, Claude-Henri, 141, 156, 163-164
Schumpeter, Joseph A., 73
Scotland, political situation in Carlyle's youth, 16-18
Scott, Walter, 10
Self: alienation of, 158; conceptions of, 1-2; and history, 10; work as annihilation of, 61-62. See also Carlyle, Thomas, on "Annihilation of Self"
Shakespeare, William, 191
Shaw, George Bernard, 31, 73
Shelley, Percy Bysshe, 8, 33
Sieyès, Abbé, 86
Sinclair, Upton, 83
Smith, Adam, 119, 171; on division of labor, 153-154; on origins of society, 118; on wealth, power, and status, 169-170
Social contract theory: constitutional and organic states, 113-115; and private property, 116-117; relation to totalitarianism, 109-115
Society: Carlyle's conception of, 55-56; relation to political and economic realms, 171-173
Solomon, Richard H., 198
Sorel, Georges, 151
Spinoza, Benedict, 49
State: absolutization of, 113-115; as monopoly of force, 115
Sterling, John, 15, 128, 148; on Carlyle's French Revolution, 103; on Carlyle's nihilism, 29
Strachey, Lytton, 46

Talmon, J. L., 112, 115, 123; on totalitarian implications of contract theory, 109-110
Tennyson, Alfred, 5
Thackeray, William Makepeace, 168, 170
Thompson, E. P., 38, 42, 64, 96, 119
Tocqueville, Alexis de, 98, 181
Tönnies, Ferdinand, 171
Totalitarianism: and hero theory, 197-198; and overlegitimation of the state, 115; and power theory, 120-122; and social contract, 109
Trades union movement, 34, 42, 182
Trilling, Lionel, 1
Trollope, Anthony, 170-171
Trotsky, Leon, 201

Ure, Andrew, 134
Utopianism, 150-151

Veblen, Thorstein, 119, 159-160, 165-166, 171
Vico, Giovanni Battista, 67
Voltaire, 56, 79, 83

Walzer, Michael, 121-122
Wealth: and power, 170-171, 174-175; and status, 168-171
Webb, Sidney and Beatrice, 42, 182
Weber, Max, 81; on charismatic leadership, 195, 197, 200; conception of society, 55-56; definition of the state, 115-116; distinction between formal and substantive rationality, 73, 75, 76, 171; on inner-worldly asceticism, 18-19
Westminster Radicalism, 54; on democracy, 179-182
Williams, Gwyn A., 94
Wilson, Woodrow, 114

Yeats, William Butler, 73
Young, G. M., 5